Organizational Resilience

Managing the Risks of Disruptive Events — A Practitioner's Guide

Organizational Resilience

Managing the Risks of Disruptive Events — A Practitioner's Guide

James J. Leflar
Marc H. Siegel

CRC Press
Taylor & Francis Group
Boca Raton   London   New York

CRC Press is an imprint of the
Taylor & Francis Group, an **informa** business

CRC Press
Taylor & Francis Group
6000 Broken Sound Parkway NW, Suite 300
Boca Raton, FL 33487-2742

© 2013 by Taylor & Francis Group, LLC
CRC Press is an imprint of Taylor & Francis Group, an Informa business

No claim to original U.S. Government works

Printed on acid-free paper
Version Date: 20130123

International Standard Book Number-13: 978-1-4398-4137-2 (Hardback)

This book contains information obtained from authentic and highly regarded sources. Reasonable efforts have been made to publish reliable data and information, but the author and publisher cannot assume responsibility for the validity of all materials or the consequences of their use. The authors and publishers have attempted to trace the copyright holders of all material reproduced in this publication and apologize to copyright holders if permission to publish in this form has not been obtained. If any copyright material has not been acknowledged please write and let us know so we may rectify in any future reprint.

Except as permitted under U.S. Copyright Law, no part of this book may be reprinted, reproduced, transmitted, or utilized in any form by any electronic, mechanical, or other means, now known or hereafter invented, including photocopying, microfilming, and recording, or in any information storage or retrieval system, without written permission from the publishers.

For permission to photocopy or use material electronically from this work, please access www.copyright.com (http://www.copyright.com/) or contact the Copyright Clearance Center, Inc. (CCC), 222 Rosewood Drive, Danvers, MA 01923, 978-750-8400. CCC is a not-for-profit organization that provides licenses and registration for a variety of users. For organizations that have been granted a photocopy license by the CCC, a separate system of payment has been arranged.

Trademark Notice: Product or corporate names may be trademarks or registered trademarks, and are used only for identification and explanation without intent to infringe.

Library of Congress Cataloging-in-Publication Data

Leflar, James J.
  Organizational resilience : managing the risks of disruptive events : a practitioner's guide / James J. Leflar and Marc H. Siegel.
    pages cm
  Includes bibliographical references and index.
  ISBN 978-1-4398-4137-2 (alk. paper)
    1. Organizational effectiveness. 2. Risk management. 3. Risk assessment. I. Siegel, Marc H. II. Title.

  HD58.9.L44 2013
  658.15'5--dc23   2012050066

Visit the Taylor & Francis Web site at
http://www.taylorandfrancis.com

and the CRC Press Web site at
http://www.crcpress.com

To my parents, Ann and James Leflar; my brother, Sam Leflar; and my niece, Rachel Pollock—gone, but never forgotten. And, to my sister, Ann, and my great nephew, Jack Pollock.

Jim Leflar

To my wife, Linda Zangwill, and my daughters, Dahlia, Maya, and Emma Siegel. And to my parents, Bernard and Irene Siegel.

Marc Siegel

CONTENTS

ACKNOWLEDGMENTS

When I started this project, several colleagues told me that it would be a labor of love; they were correct. I have always taken the approach that education is never ending and that opportunities to better myself are a fundamental aspect of being a professional. The material and value of this book are the product of years of experience, education, and interaction with my peers—I owe everything to their patience, guidance, and friendship. The very essence of this book is that one person is not capable of producing the level of synergy necessary to address the risk issues facing organizations. To my colleagues and friends who have helped me along the way, thank you.

Many years ago, I worked with the following Business Continuity Professionals and I gained a more robust understanding of BCP/DR through my interaction with them. To Mark Kern, John Sweeney, John Nones, and Steve Guss, thank you for bringing your business continuity "A" game each day. Through many "lessons learned," I saw what worked, and more importantly, what didn't work in a complex and changing environment.

Thank you to Jim Gallagher and Joan Burrell for being friends.

I would like to thank my friends for tolerating my excuses for neglecting them during the time I have spent on this project. Tony, I was responsible for the genesis of the Rhino joke. They say public confession is good for the soul, but I'm not convinced of that; I think that I just owe you the truth as your trusted ally. However, Rick played his part as the enabler and, in truth, no one objected; as I remember things, there was quite a bit of laughter. I hope that makes you feel better, Tony.

Several people deserve special attention because they have patiently assisted me in the actual development of this work. When I started on the path of developing this project, I sought suggestions from several colleagues and experienced authors on the best way to present the proposal. Richard Wright, James Lukaszewski, and Scott Watson helped get me started and I sincerely thank them for their guidance and friendship.

I was fortunate enough to work with Dr. Marc Siegel on the development of the ANSI/ASIS SPC.1-2009 Standard and I have called upon him many times during this project for assistance, eventually hooking him into helping write the manuscript. He has always come through and given generously of his knowledge, time, and resources. I really owe an enormous debt to Marc and appreciate his invaluable assistance. His suggestions on improvements to this manuscript were insightful and helped elevate the final product in both clarity and accuracy. I do not think it is an exaggeration to say that this project would not have happened without his assistance.

Fortune smiled again and provided me with an opportunity to interact with Grant Lecky and Johan Du Plooy, with the result of some valuable information and feedback on this work. Johan provided his insights on actually implementing the ANSI/ASIS SPC.1-2009 standard in South Africa, along with his comments of the work herein. His contribution cannot be overstated.

Finally, a huge thanks to Mark Listewnik, Amber Donley, and Jay Margolis, my editors, for tolerating all my questions, concerns, suggestions, and their willingness to take a chance on me; it has certainly been an exciting trip.

I look forward to further adventures with all of these highly knowledgeable, thoughtful, kind, and professional friends.

Jim Leflar

I would like to thank Jim for giving me the opportunity to contribute to this work. I appreciate his patience in dealing with my frenetic travel schedule, especially not trying to phone me, which for me is almost always at some strange hour.

I would like to acknowledge the contributions that Susan Melnicove, Sue Carioti, and Aivelis Opicka have made to our profession. Without them there would be no ANSI/ASIS standards. They are truly the engine that drives the ASIS International standards program.

Special thanks go to Maya Siegel for her critiquing and editing the manuscript and not making too many jokes about me being English-challenged.

I would also like to thank my family, Linda Zangwill, Dahlia, Maya, and Emma Siegel, for their patience and understanding during the course of writing this book. I'm sure it had nothing to do with me telling them that they would be in the movie.

I hope this book inspires risk, security, crisis, and continuity managers to realize that in reality they are actually business managers helping to manage risk, security, crises, and continuity.

Marc Siegel

INTRODUCTION

SUPPORTING THE BUSINESS MISSION

Making assumptions is always a dangerous undertaking, but we shall take the gamble and assume that you are reading this book because you are either in a position to implement the information contained herein, or you are preparing for the possibility. In either case, this book shall provide valuable information that will allow you to succeed in moving an organization toward becoming more resilient through the use of organizational resilience management. Yes, the movement toward resiliency is a process and not a simple implementation of a policy or procedure. The analogy of a trip corresponding to implementing organizational resilience is appropriate and valuable. During a trip, you experience new ways of living, and learn to appreciate these new perspectives. You learn the value of doing things differently, and at looking at the world through a slightly different set of parameters. This is what happens when you begin to travel down the roadway of organizational resilience management; it is not a straight line, but a winding path requiring patience and tolerance. There is a good deal of learning that will have to take place during the trip and that is why it is necessary to have patience and tolerate the learning process. Old beliefs and habits will have to be modified into something new. That is part of the fun and adventure of taking this trip.

Organizational resilience is a goal to achieve and organizational resilience management is the way to achieve that goal. One of the real values of organizational resilience management (ORM) is that in developing and implementing this approach, there are further benefits in addition to the obvious intended result of implementation. Personnel learn to work together, they learn to appreciate and understand the concerns of other managers, and they gain experience by moving through the process of putting all the pieces together for a more resilient organization. Also, there is a shared experience derived from the participants going through the process of working on ORM that has real benefits in mitigating issues from becoming more serious. People learn to address issues in a more urgent fashion while minimizing negative consequences.

It is our sincere intent to provide a valuable and much-needed presentation that enables practitioners to achieve the desired goals of effective organizational resilience through cost-effective methods. Building a resilient organization is a cross-disciplinary and cross-functional endeavor; therefore, "practitioners" may come from a variety of disciplines, all of which contribute to helping the organization achieve its objectives.

The primary goal of this book is to provide readers with an understanding of organizational resilience and how to manage risk through the use of the ANSI/ASIS SPC.1-2009 Standard. We shall endeavor to provide a concise, clearly understandable approach to successfully addressing the various challenges and techniques necessary to plan, prepare, and implement organizational resilience management in your organization. The reader will gain valuable insight into cutting through the complexities and identifying the key issues and techniques for successful implementation of organizational resilience management. The ANSI/ASIS SPC.1-2009 Standard is applicable to public, private, and not-for-profit organizations. This book focuses on organizational resilience management being an integral component of the overall business management of an organization. Organizational resilience needs to be seen within the context of protecting and creating value for the organization. Although the public sector has a mission and culture different from the private sector, many of the concepts and suggestions contained within this book can be used within the public arena. However, it is necessary to understand that benefits to the organization do not always translate equally from private to public.

INTRODUCTION TO THE ANSI/ASIS.SPC.1

A critical resource and the foundation for this book is the American National Standards Institute, Inc. (ANSI) approved ASIS International Standard on *Organizational Resilience: Security, Preparedness, and Continuity Management Systems—Requirements with Guidance for Use* (ANSI/ASIS SPC.1-2009). The standard is International Organization for Standardization (ISO) compatible with all management system standards to allow for seamless integration with ISO standards and to promote international relevance. The ANSI/ASIS SPC.1-2009 has been adopted by other countries (e.g., the Netherlands and Denmark) and served as the basis for the ISO 28002:2010 standard for resilience in organizations and their supply chains. In June of 2010, the U.S. Department of Homeland Security Public Sector–Preparedness Program (PS-Prep Program) approved ANSI/ASIS SPC.1-2009 for adoption as a national preparedness standard for private sector organizations, but adherence to the

PS-Prep Program is not necessary for use of the ANSI/ASIS SPC.1-2009 Standard and is not discussed in any detail in this book. The PS-Prep Program may be of value to some organizations and should be reviewed in more detail if a certification program is desirable for your organization. The PS-Prep Program is still in its infancy and the business value of the certification process has yet to be demonstrated. Remember, the goal of using any standard should be to enhance performance. The objective is to continually improve an organization's resilience and not to simply have a certification plaque hang on the wall of the main lobby of the corporate headquarters. Certifications are valuable if the reason and meaning for those certifications benefit the organization; we're looking for substance and not flash.

As the only ANSI-approved standard on organizational resilience management, it was a logical decision to use *Organizational Resilience: Security, Preparedness, and Continuity Management Systems—Requirements with Guidance for Use* (ANSI/ASIS SPC.1-2009) as the foundation for this book. It is reasonable to claim that this standard has been in development for many years in accordance with the development and evolution of planning for potentially disruptive events. Many disciplines address aspects of anticipating, assessing, preventing, protecting, mitigating, responding, recovering, and adapting to potential, undesirable, and disruptive events. Organizational resilience management is the result of many years of experiential knowledge and testing, culminating in a holistic systems approach that effectively blends the various risk issues necessary for achieving organizational resilience.

WHAT ARE STANDARDS?

Standards impact our daily lives even if we don't notice them. We take for granted that our ATM card will work in bank machines around the world, that electronic components will be compatible in different devices, and chemical warning symbols can be understood regardless of your language. It is common to hear the term "standards" used in official and common language discussions, but there may be some confusion over the real meaning of the word. Standards are consensus-based specifications that define materials, methods, processes, services, or practices. A standard is not a regulation, rule, or law, but rather an agreed upon model that is used as a measure against which an outcome may be evaluated.

Standards help assure a defined, measurable, and consistent level of performance. They serve as tools to demonstrate a consistent and acceptable level of quality, performance, and reliability. Management system standards, such as the ANSI/ASIS SPC.1-2009, specify a management process for what the organization does to manage its processes, services, or activities. It is like an Italian recipe; it tells you "what" you need to do, but lets you determine the "how" to fit your taste. A management system standard is not a checklist; it is a management framework viewed from the perspective that all the parts make up the whole. So, understanding the relationships and interactions between the elements of a management system is key to successful implementation.

ABOUT THE AUTHORS

James J. Leflar, Jr. (MA, CPP, CBCP, MBCI) is the security administrator at Johns Hopkins Bloomberg School of Public Health with responsibility for crisis management, business continuity, and security administration. He was an active member of the technical committees and working groups of the ANSI/ASIS SPC. 1-2009 and ANSI/ASIS SPC. 4-2012 standards. He continues to be active in OR standards development and is an active member of the ISO, U.S. Technical Advisory Group (TAG) 223 for Societal Security, Working Group 4—Preparedness and Continuity. Currently, Leflar is an active member of the ASIS International Crisis Management and Business Continuity Council as well as a member of the Advisory Board and Editorial Board for the Disaster Resource Guide.

Marc Siegel, PhD, is the commissioner heading the ASIS International Global Standards Initiative developing international and national risk management, resilience, security, and supply chain standards as well as providing training on their implementation. He is a RABQSA (Registrar Accreditation Board [RAB] Quality Society of Australasia [QSA]) international certified business improvement lead auditor as well as a certified trainer and skills assessor. As an adjunct professor in the College of Business Administration and the Master's Program in Homeland Security at San Diego State University, Dr. Siegel pioneered the concept of applying a systems approach to security and resilience management for organizations and their supply chains. His work includes providing training and guidance on the implementation of risk, resilience, and security management systems as well as risk management in regions of conflict and weakened governance for the protection of assets and human rights. Dr. Siegel chaired the technical committee and working group for the ANSI/ASIS SPC.1: 2009.

1

Managing Risk to Optimize Performance

ORGANIZATIONAL RESILIENCE AND BUSINESS MANAGEMENT

Building a resilient organization is part of any good business management strategy. In order to thrive and survive, organizations need to adapt to an ever-changing environment. To be agile and resilient in order to achieve the organization's objectives, the organization needs to leverage all the disciplines that contribute to managing risk. For organizations to cost-effectively manage risk, they must develop balanced strategies to adaptively, proactively, and reactively address maximizing opportunities and minimizing the likelihood and consequences of potential, undesirable, and disruptive events.

Organizational resilience is a business management strategy that abandons the old approach of managing risk in siloed disciplines, but instead uses a multidisciplinary systems' approach to increase the adaptive capacity of the organization. The ANSI/ASIS SPC.1-2009 was the first standards initiative to buck the trend of what seems to be an endless stream of discipline specific standards being generated by ISO (International Organization of Standards). The ANSI/ASIS SPC.1-2009 views managing the risks of potential, undesirable, and disruptive events within the context of a single business management strategy as envisioned in the ISO 31000 risk management standard.

WHY MANAGE RISK?: THE BUSINESS CASE

An organization is primarily concerned with accomplishing operational goals that are aligned with and intended to achieve the strategic business goals. Examples of these goals are making a profit for a corporation or providing a service for nonprofit organizations. Typically, organizations have departments that are designed to protect the interests of the organization, e.g., security aims to protect against likely threats, and business continuity addresses the outcomes due to unacceptable business interruptions. The problem with these separate or silo approaches is that the separate department goals may be redundant and are not an efficient use of the limited resources available to achieve business goals. Department goals and practices must be aligned with the operational and strategic goals of the organization; otherwise, there is no legitimate reason for the goal. Having multiple departments working to achieve the same or similar risk-oriented goals is wasteful and counterproductive to those strategic goals. The convergence of these similar but disparate operations is best viewed as coming together through the thread of risk and resilience management. Risk management provides the underpinnings to allow security, crisis management, business continuity management, etc. to achieve consistent and thoroughly aligned strategies. The ability to assess and treat risk within the context of the organization's goals is the most efficient way to effectively consider risk.

Exhibit 1.1 is a partial list of typical risk sources and risk consequences. The risk source is something that has the possibility of creating uncertainty in the organization, preventing the organization from achieving its objectives, and may result in consequences to the organization. For instance, a thunderstorm may have consequences or it may simply go by without incident. The storm is the source of the risk and the loss of power is the consequence.

While it is important to adhere to the below mentioned principles, it also is important to have the obvious support and commitment from senior management to facilitate the development of the culture of risk management. (Note: the phrase "the management" is normally used in ISO standards language to reference the uppermost level of organizational management; top management and senior management are used interchangeably within this book.) This commitment is achieved through management policies, the assignment of resources to ensure continued operation of the risk effort, and the alignment of risk objectives with business objectives. It is absolutely essential to develop a culture that has risk management as one of the primary tenets.

List of Risks: Partial, not Comprehensive		
Category	Risk Source	Risk Consequence
Natural	Earthquake	Loss of Electricity Building Structural Damage Roadways Blocked – Damaged Fire
	Hurricane	Loss of Electricity Roadways Blocked: Flooding Water Damage to Building
	Lightning Strike	Loss of Electricity Computers Won't Operate Building Services Unavailable
	Snow Storm	Roadways Blocked Employees Can't Get to Work No Deliveries of Products or Supplies
	Thunderstorm	Loss of Electricity Roadways Blocked: Flooding Water Damage to Building
Man-Made	Electrical Equipment Failure	Loss of Electricity Building Technology Unavailable No Deliveries of Products or Supplies
	Labor Strike	Workers Strike – Work Flow Interruption No Deliveries of Products or Supplies Bad Publicity for Company
	Computer Virus	Computers Won't Operate Properly Services Unavailable to Customers Bad Publicity for Company
	Crime: Assault	Injury Increased Fear of Another Incident Negative Publicity – Reputation
	Hazardous Materials Incident	Fire Chemical Exposure Biological Exposure Radiological Exposure
	Accident – Personnel	Personnel Injured – Slip/Fall Lawsuit Negative Publicity – Reputation
	Accident – Vehicle	Property Damage Death – Injury Inability to Conduct Business

Exhibit 1.1   Risk sources and consequences table.

3

ISO 31000

All organizations face a certain amount of uncertainty and risk. In order to assure sustainability of operations and maintain resilience, competitiveness, and performance, organizations must have a system to manage their risks. The challenge is to determine how much risk and uncertainty is acceptable, and how to cost-effectively manage risk while meeting the organization's strategic and operational objectives. Given the finite resources of organizations, it is imperative to have business-friendly tools to address any array of threats, hazards, and uncertainties they may face. The ISO 31000:2009(E)—*Risk Management: Principles and Guidelines* standard is such a tool.

Risk management requires a thorough plan based on a comprehensive foundation to establish an enterprise-wide approach to understanding the organizational risks. The ISO 31000 provides guidance on the principles, framework, and process of risk management. It provides a generic perspective to managing risk that establishes a structure for organizations to integrate all of their risk management programs into a single framework. The document accurately reflects the current thinking that different disciplines of risk management should be considered in a comprehensive approach rather than "siloing" risks into separate approaches. This is the business sensible view of risk management, particularly important in these times of economic hardship and limited resources.

For organizations to cost-effectively manage risk, they should use the ISO 31000 in conjunction with the ANSI/ASIS.SPC.1 to develop balanced strategies to adaptively, proactively, and reactively address minimization of both the likelihood and consequences of potential, undesirable, and disruptive events, while also exploiting opportunities for improvement. The two standards will help an organization build a strategy for managing risk that is tailored to its business objectives that is also in sync with its overall goals and mission. It will provide the capacity for the organization to adapt to a complex and changing environment.

PRINCIPLES OF RISK MANAGEMENT

Any discussion of the ISO 31000 needs to begin with the definition of risk in the standard. Risk is "effect of uncertainty on objectives." According to the standard, "… an effect is a deviation from the expected"; therefore, risk can have either positive or negative outcomes. What seems like a simple definition is actually a profound statement on risk management. Risk management is about achieving an organization's objectives. It is not event focused, but rather objectives focused. This means that risk managers are practicing their trade in a dynamic environment. There is a need for constant communication and consultation with stakeholders (the makers and owners of risk), constant monitoring of the environment, and situational awareness. In the ISO 31000 world, risk management becomes an integration of the preemptive strategies and discipline. With built-in feedback loops in every step of the risk management process, organizations learn and evolve based on input from their environment and context of operation. Obviously, because the risk management is practiced by humans (our apologies to other species), risk management is about adapting the organization as well as adapting the environment in which the organization operates.

Conformance with ISO 31000 depends on the adherence to the fundamental principles that risk management (ISO 31000:2009(E), pp. 7–8.):

- Not only creates, but also protects organizational value
- Is an integral component to all processes
- Is intricately intertwined with decision making
- Inherently focuses on the types and nature of the uncertainty facing the organization
- Is systematically designed to ensure reliable and consistent results
- Is structured and timely so that any information obtained is current and should lead to increased efficiencies within the organization
- Is conducted through the use of the best available multisourced information
- Is based on specific organizational needs; is part of the cultural fabric of the organization
- Involves all stakeholders and decision makers
- Is highly flexible, iterative, and change based
- Results in the organization benefiting from continual improvement

While it is important to adhere to the aforementioned principles, it is important as well to have the obvious support and commitment from top management and decision makers to facilitate the development of the culture of risk management. This commitment is achieved through management policies, the assignment of resources to ensure continued operation of the risk effort, and the alignment of risk objectives with business objectives. It is absolutely essential to develop a culture that has risk management as one of its primary tenets.

The principles of risk management establish the logic and justification for an organization to implement risk management. ISO 31000 establishes the desirability of following these principles when developing and implementing risk management within an organization. The principles are not necessarily specific to the risk management world; they, in fact, are sound business management principles applicable to all organizations and to any discussion on the implementation of an initiative. Any organizational initiative requiring the expenditure of resources must create value for the organization; otherwise, there is no justification for the initiative. A consistent theme throughout this book will be the alignment of any strategy, program, or standard with the organization. Everything that is done on behalf of the organization must be of value to the organization and achieve or lend in the achievement of the business goals. These principles are also inherent underpinnings of organizational resilience management, which is completely logical given the reliance SPC.1-2009 has on sound business and risk management principles.

ESTABLISHING A FRAMEWORK

In order to establish the risk management framework for an organization, it is necessary to understand the organization from both an internal and external perspective. This requires an appreciation of both the internal and external context in which the organization exists (ISO 31000:2009(E), p. 10). All organizations have an internal and external environment; the internal environment contains the activities, culture, and personnel (everything and everyone) within the organization. The external environment contains but is not limited to supply chain partners, supply vendors, clients, consumers, constituents, contractors, service technicians, transportation systems, regulators, the legal system, and governments. Before any attempt is made to develop the framework, it is necessary to understand the organization. Identifying all relevant stakeholders is essential for a successful consultative process. Developing the framework will become much easier and more valuable to the later risk management development activities.

Key to any risk management process is establishing the risk criteria. The risk criteria provide the terms of reference upon which risk will be evaluated and prioritized. Risk criteria are a function of the internal and external context, legal and regulatory obligations, and organizational objectives. Sounds easy? It's not. Trying to ascertain an organization's level of risk acceptance and tolerance will be one of the most difficult tasks you will face in developing a risk management strategy. Risk criteria need to be defined with the intimate input of senior management in order to reflect the organization's value chain, objectives, resources, mission, and culture. Because risk management is supporting the achievement of the organization's objectives, and a tool to protect and create value, you must have a clear idea how you are going to calibrate the tool before using it; defining risk criteria provides the necessary calibration. Like any sensitive tool, recalibration is sometimes necessary. You should revisit the assumptions you make in defining the risk criteria when you are conducting the risk assessment.

The framework for the risk management process proposed in the ISO 31000 looks very similar to the Plan-Do-Check-Act model from the Total Quality Management approach to business management. The proposed framework is not specific to any one type of organizational design, but rather general in nature and allows the organization to create the necessary framework to properly function within the respective organization. The first step to establish the organizational mandate and commitment to support risk management within the organization. Obviously, without buy-in from management and decision makers within the organization, a risk management program cannot succeed. Buy-in is more than just a pat on the head; it involves a commitment to integrate risk management into all the organizational processes. This means senior management needs to be involved in creating a risk management policy and providing adequate resources. While this may appear to be a simple issue, it is not simple, and not all organizations will appreciate the need or value of risk management. Practitioners often hear senior leaders claim that they already have a risk management program (insurance) and anything more is unnecessary. While insurance is an option to treat a risk and is actually the transfer of risk from the organization to an insurance company, it is not a risk management program. Leadership must acknowledge and embrace risk management if it is going to succeed at a given organization. For risk management to be successful, it must become part of the organizational culture and this absolutely requires support and commitment from leadership in the form of a risk management policy. Without mandate and commitment, the risk management policy will not succeed.

Once a mandate and commitment is obtained, the organization can begin designing the framework for managing risk. This step sets the tone, context, and infrastructure needed to support risk management.

7

As discussed above, understanding the organization and its internal and external context provides the foundation on which you will build the house. The policy will establish the importance of risk management within the organization and, therefore, must be in alignment with the business goals, risk objectives, planned implementation strategy, and the organizational culture (ISO 31000:2009(E), p. 9). This alignment shall engender the active involvement of employees—risk management shall become part of their jobs: the risk makers and takers are the risk owners. To gain the involvement of the employees, risk must become an inherent responsibility of each person. Therefore, risk management is woven into the fabric of each position while they are performing their jobs. Furthermore, the organization's culture should be one of risk management and each risk strategy must be aligned with the business goals of the organization (ISO 31000:2009(E), p. 9).

Designing an organizational framework for managing risk must be tailored to fit the organization. Appropriate resources, including human resources, support a framework. The organization needs to identify competent people who will be responsible and accountable for managing risk. Identifying appropriate roles and responsibilities will build upon the information gathered during the policy and contextual understanding development phase, which then provides the basis for the organizational structure for risk management. Stakeholders involved in risk management should receive the necessary responsibilities and authority through specified duties in their respective job descriptions to promote success. Identification and procurement of the necessary organizational, human, training, monetary, physical, and informational resources are needed to support the framework. Risk management needs resources to fuel the process. Risk management also needs to become part of all the organization's practices and processes to run smoothly. Good communications, consultation, and monitoring are essential to supporting a dynamic framework. Good risk management practice is based on good information flow. The organization needs to establish the necessary communications protocols and mechanism capable of providing timely information to internal and external stakeholders in both normal and abnormal operating conditions. Remember that risk management is supporting the business management of the organization; therefore, information flow, control, and integrity all need to be considered when developing communication and reporting mechanisms.

The reason for designing a framework is to provide the infrastructure needed to implement the changes. Having defined the context of the organization, the organization is now ready to apply the policy and risk management processes throughout the enterprise. When defining the timing and strategy for implementing the framework to manage risk, it is important to remember that the key reason for doing risk management is to support the organization in its quest to achieve its objectives—to create and capture value. Therefore, when building the implementation approach and setting the goals of the risk management process, the practitioner needs to align the outcomes with the organization's objectives, needs, and resources.

Monitoring and performance evaluation will let the organization know if its planning and implementation strategy is working. Situational awareness and ongoing monitoring of changes in the context and environment enable the organization to determine if the risk management approach is relevant in the nonsteady state environment that is the reality for most organizations. Risk management performance is measured in terms of the risk management supporting organizational performance. Identifying deviations from the plan and changing internal and external context should be seen as a learning experience and should pave the way for the organization to adapt its plans for risk management, and even change its business management approach to meet new challenges.

Dynamic organizations adapt, grow, and mature. Continual improvement is the underlying assumption of the risk management framework. Adversity and deviations from the risk management plan should be seen as opportunities for improvement and a means for strengthening the organization. The review of the framework should look at the adequacy of the framework, the need for making both minor and major adjustments, and, most of all, opportunities for improvement.

THE RISK MANAGEMENT PROCESS

Through the use of the framework and knowledge of the organization, it is necessary to establish a process to truly understand the risks associated with an organization. Exhibit 1.2 illustrates the process described in the ISO 31000 as it applies to the ANSI/ASIS.SPC.1.

Because the risk management process is used with the ANSI/ASIS. SPC.1, it will be discussed in more detail in Chapter 6.

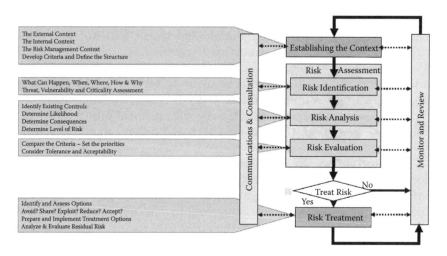

Exhibit 1.2   Risk management process diagram.

2

Managing the Risks of Disruptive Events

WHAT IS ORGANIZATIONAL RESILIENCE MANAGEMENT?

Organizational resilience (OR) is the goal that we are trying to achieve—making the organization more resilient and agile to risk-related issues. Organizational resilience management (ORM) is a risk-based management system applicable to all organizations: public, private, and governmental (ANSI/ASIS SPC.1-2009, p. vii). Organizational resilience management is how we are going to achieve organizational resilience.

Organizational resilience management is a cross-disciplinary, cross-functional approach to help an organization achieve its objectives. Change is inherent to any organization's operations; the environment in which an organization operates is in a constant state of flux. Therefore, to thrive and survive, organizations must be agile and adapt to internal and external changes in context. Ideally, organizations can anticipate changes and pre-emptively adapt. At other times, organizations need to learn from their experiences and adapt based on lessons learned. Some adaptations may be minor, while others may require significant adaptation of the organization's nature, character, purpose, or structure, even to the point of an organization reinventing itself.

Through the application of ORM principles identified in ANSI/ASIS SPC.1-2009, the managers of an organization have an excellent opportunity to develop a more resilient, risk management-oriented organization in tune with the uncertainties and risks inherent to that organization. It is important to remember that ANSI/ASIS SPC.1-2009 does not attempt to deprive the organization of the qualities that make it special, but rather it provides the guidance necessary to reap the benefits of the ORM approach to achieving resilience.

The ISO Guide 73:2009—Risk management: Vocabulary defines resilience as "the adaptive capacity of an organization in a complex and changing environment." This is the same definition used in the ANSI/ASIS SPC.1-2009. In essence, resilience is the ability of an organization to change and adapt in order to handle challenges and/or issues. The better an organization manages to reorient itself to handle change and potential, and also undesirable and disruptive events, the more resilient the organization. Organizational resilience is not one activity or discipline; it is a state of being or condition as to the ability and capacity of the organization to anticipate, prepare, execute, and evolve. OR is not a reactive process, but rather a combination of various proactive activities through the careful implementation of organizational resilience management principles. It is absolutely crucial to understand that this resilience does not happen by mistake or chance. For an organization to become resilient, it takes planning and preparation; it takes a conscious effort to become resilient. Some readers may conclude that business continuity or crisis management are synonymous with OR. Both of these preparedness disciplines have goals that result in OR, but they are not the same thing. Business continuity focuses on planning and preparing for situations that would create unacceptable business process interruptions. "Crisis management identifies potential impacts that threaten an organization and provides a framework for building resilience, with the capability for an effective response that safeguards the interests of its key stakeholders, reputation, brand, and value-creating activities as well as effectively restoring operational capabilities" (ANSI/ASIS SPC.1-2009, pp. 45–46). While both business continuity and crisis management strive to achieve a more resilient organization, they are not synonymous with ORM; they are pieces of the patchwork quilt that is ORM, a means to address risk and, therefore, aid in achieving resilience. Organizational resilience management is not a single discipline, but rather a blended consideration of the risks facing an organization. It is both a forward-looking and backward-looking approach to managing risk to achieve an organization's objectives. It is about maximizing opportunities and minimizing likelihood and consequences by removing the silos and finding the appropriate balance of adaptive, proactive, and reactive strategies.

Organizational resilience is a multidisciplinary systems approach to enhance an organization's adaptive capacity to enable it to manage and exploit risk to achieve its objectives. It is a collaborative process. The risk stakeholders within the organization (security, business continuity planning, asset management, human resources, business leaders, etc.) are the major stakeholders that must work together to develop the strategy and plans to achieve organizational resilience, but any strategy that is developed must be aligned with the business. Organizational resilience management is a management framework for action planning and decision making needed to anticipate, prevent (if possible), and prepare for and respond to changes in the environment and to events. It enhances an organization's capacity to prevent, manage, and survive undesirable events. It provides decision-making tools for organizations to take all appropriate actions to help ensure the organization's continued viability by anticipating, assessing, learning, and changing. Resilience is achieved through the contribution of a wide range of disciplines emphasizing the organization's capacity to adapt to potential adversity to minimize the likelihood of an event and use adversity for change and improvement. Organizational resilience management increases an organization's ability to achieve its objectives in the face of uncertainty and adversity as well as during nonroutine times. Organizational resilience complements quality, environmental, and occupational health and safety management, which ensures quality outcomes in routine and consistent operating environments.

The management systems approach of the ANSI/ASIS SPC.1-2009 encourages organizations to analyze organizational and stakeholder requirements and define processes that contribute to success. The ANSI/ASIS SPC.1-2009 Standard has conformance requirements that are designed to foster an understanding of the interrelatedness of the organizational business units, the viewing of functional requirements to achieve business unit viability and success, and the understanding of the myriad business unit perspectives of risk. The Standard attempts to generate increased understanding of the processes internal and external to the organization from a risk perspective. This also is always from an organizational business needs perspective. Through achieving this understanding and the implementation of the conformance requirements, an organization has greatly increased its chance of achieving OR.

Simply following the OR Standard does not guarantee success. The organization must accept the concept of breaking down the established barriers for protecting individual managerial kingdoms (functional silos)

Exhibit 2.1 Organizational resilience challenge diagram.

and actively seeking joint approaches to addressing risk through the realization that organizations are comprised of interrelated, interdependent operations. Exhibit 2.1 is an example of the organizational resilience challenges facing a university, but with slight modifications (changes in stakeholders to reflect those of a particular organization) could be an example of any organization. The diagram shows various stakeholders or attitudes coming into play, focusing on their respective issues, but without the benefit of a unified position or an understanding of other stakeholder positions. Some of the challenges are actually attitudes that must change before any serious improvement in OR can be realized. The old adage: "We've never had any trouble before," is a serious failing that is all too common. Most experienced risk management and preparedness professionals have probably heard this during their careers. While it is prudent and appropriate to carefully consider the risk and the likelihood of occurrence, it is not appropriate for managers to hide from the real possibility of an incident affecting the organization. Preparing for the unexpected, unacceptable, and ill-timed emergency is the duty of every manager. There are constant changes in the operating environment and threats facing an organization and the resulting risks, which may never have happened at an organization before, should be considered as potential issues.

RELATIONSHIP BETWEEN THE ISO31000 AND ANSI/ASIS.SPC.1

The ISO31000 was a major breakthrough in the world of risk management. The Standard provides clearly described principles, a framework, and a process for risk management. It shifts the view of risk from bad things that go thump in the night (a focus on events) to uncertainties in achieving an organization's objectives. By moving from event-focused to objectives-focused, the organization moves from reactive mode to proactive mode. Risk management becomes about creating and capturing value rather than just protecting value. Risk management is about foresight and strategic planning.

The perspective that risk management is a consultative and collaborative process means all risk owners are risk managers. Risk management is an inclusive process, top-down and bottom-up. The ISO31000 also emphasizes that managing risk is cross-disciplinary and cross-functional throughout the entire enterprise.

The ANSI/ASIS.SPC.1 follows the thinking of the ISO31000. Organizational resilience is not about "bouncing back" or just protecting the organization; it emphasizes that organizational resilience is about protecting, creating, and capturing value before, during, and after an event. The ANSI/ASIS.SPC.1 takes the same cross-disciplinary and cross-functional approach as the ISO31000 and views the need to leverage all the risk-focused disciplines to build a single business management strategy for addressing risks related to potential, undesirable, and disruptive events.

The ANSI/ASIS.SPC.1 builds on the ISO31000 by highlighting the notion that being resilient depends on the organization's capacity to adapt. To maximize opportunities and minimize likelihood and consequences, organizations must be ready to be agile in changing conditions and adapt before, during, and after an event to either prevent the event from occurring or learning from the event to realign itself, or even reinvent itself, in order to fit its new environment. Organizational resilience is truly about an organization's capacity to adapt to a complex and changing environment.

RESILIENCE FROM A FUNCTIONAL
AND OPERATIONAL PERSPECTIVE

Although organizations, small and large, share similar concerns surrounding the management of risks and the protection of the business, the difference is often in the level of complexity within the business organization to address that concern. Addressing risk is an expectation that clients, shareholders, business partners, regulators, and employees have of any organization, regardless of size. At first glance, it might seem that smaller businesses are at a disadvantage to implement an organizational resilience management system; however, the converse may be true. Smaller businesses may have one person handling multiple responsibilities, while major corporations have numerous departments dedicated to providing the necessary protective measures. Therefore, smaller businesses might not have divisional and discipline silos. It seems obvious that an organization must address risk, but recent financial industry revelations have shown that not all risk is identified or, worse, it is simply ignored. Eliminating the silos and assessing risk from a multidisciplinary perspective will help an organization better prioritize resources to protect itself from anticipated and unexpected events. By focusing on the achievement of objectives, organizations are better positioned to adapt to changes, if not by anticipating and adapting before the fact, at least learning from events to adapt and strengthen and grow the organization. Seen from this perspective, organizations can effectively manage uncertainty and capture or realize any opportunity.

One of the challenges involving risk is that many organizations are established on a functional basis. Each business unit is separate from the others and often reporting to different leaders without the benefit of any consistent, unified management structure focusing the resources toward risk management. For instance, safety, risk management, financial operations, security management, business continuity management, information technology disaster recovery, information and network security, corporate communications, corporate counsel, and crisis management are a few of the leading disciplines involved in protecting a business. It is common to think of the above disciplines as independent "professions" because they are marketed that way as courses of study in college and professional organizations with assorted certifications indicating specialized training and achievements. All of that is fine and valuable, but it creates the expectation that risks and threats against an organization fall into categories addressed by certain disciplines within the business. For instance, certain criminal issues, such as theft of information and proprietary secrets, may fall into the physical and/or information security realms, while crisis management and/or business continuity management might consider the consequences of the theft. Considering the business needs to manage the integrity of its information, rather than each discipline separately, a more reasonable approach is to "blend" the preventative measures, preparations, and response so that more than one department is involved in the resolution. This avoids duplication of efforts and provides a comprehensive strategy to prevent the loss of an asset. An incident often affects multiple stakeholders; therefore, having those stakeholders work together before an incident occurs allows for a more dynamic and, hopefully, preemptive approach to the issue. Complex issues require more complex approaches to achieving a resolution. For instance, when a disgruntled employee is investigated concerning allegations of harassment, it is necessary to include multiple "risk" stakeholders to determine the full measure of risk. Viewing the issue as a simple human resources problem that is resolved by firing the person fails to acknowledge the risks due to retaliation to both personnel and property assets of the organization. It is necessary to include at least human resources, physical security, data security, the department manager of the employee, and any other appropriate stakeholders (e.g., mental health professionals) that your organization may have that will help develop a full picture of the risk. In addition, the team needs to understand a key precept of organizational resilience—an incident avoided or prevented does not become a crisis. While preemptive adaptation may avoid a problem from materializing, nevertheless, the organization should always assess how it can further adapt and evolve in order to avoid similar threats of adversity in the future.

It is quite true that many risk issues require the talents of specialists to effectively understand and address, but this separation of duties is also part of the problem. All too often, risk management operations are organized as completely discrete business operations with separate goals and perspectives. This "silo" approach to operations is detrimental to effective comprehensive risk management efforts. Organizational resilience management is a systematic, enterprise-wide approach that fosters the inclusion of different risk management-oriented disciplines as noted above, thus, creating a synergy not realized with disparate approaches. ORM does not seek to replace or eliminate any department or discipline within an organization, but rather seeks to include all disciplines to gain a more effective and efficient risk resolution operation. This inclusive risk-based approach allows for preparedness at the earliest stages, thereby preventing an issue from becoming a more serious concern. For example, an organization's main data center should have a number of risk managers as stakeholders. All stakeholders work together to address the various concerns, such as data security and maintenance of servers (Information Technology), electrical and HVAC (Facilities Management), physical security (Corporate Security), space planning (Corporate Real Estate/Facilities), compliance (Risk Management), etc., and a variety of third-party vendors performing other duties. All of these stakeholders have a vested interest in developing an integrated approach to managing the risk of the data center instead of independent approaches.

The actual organizational structure also may lead to the aforementioned silo effect more often than any philosophical approach to addressing duties. If departmental managers report to different senior managers, the issue may be as simple as disparate perspectives: competing priorities (and budgets), lack of a perceived problem, or organizational politics. The functional divisions in Exhibit 2.2 are examples of possible "silo" causing situations, and Exhibit 2.3 is an example of how to avoid those silos. This example may not be feasible in some organizations because this level of change almost always only happens from the senior-most leadership. Gaining a senior-level sponsor is not only helpful; it is critical if this sort of change is being considered.

Exhibit 2.2 is an example of an organization with a more "silo" type of approaching risk issues. Each division consists of a number of departments

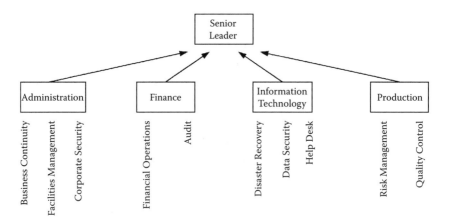

Exhibit 2.2   Silo structured example of organization.

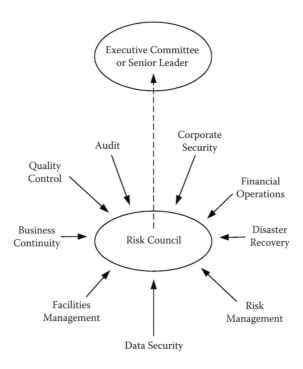

Exhibit 2.3 Risk Council structured example of organization.

that address certain areas of risk. While this example is certainly not exhaustive, it does provide a possible structural design that may lead to a less effective approach to addressing risk. Please keep in mind that this organizational structure is common and may be adjusted to improve how risks are managed. It is not the intent of this book to bring about massive change in an organization by completely redesigning departments and reporting alignments. The intent is to build awareness and understanding of how small changes may see considerable results. Exhibit 2.3 reflects a small change in the form of the Risk Council that is comprised of the various stakeholders. This Council would have the ability to report a single, comprehensive message to the senior leader concerning risk issues. It may appear that the Risk Council is just another level of bureaucracy between the lower level departments and senior management, but that is not the intent. The Risk Council would consist of any and all appropriate stakeholders and to include some representation from senior management. Effective Risk Councils have the ability to focus all risk issues, plans, and responses so that a single message with a holistic, organization-wide perspective is presented to senior management. This approach is more likely to garner positive results because of the comprehensive, unified vision of the Council instead of separate departmental concerns trying to jockey for position on a busy agenda. Yes, this sounds very easy to achieve, but it takes time and effort from all involved. It also requires trust between the members which may take time to develop.

The first step in getting beyond the siloing mentality is to understand that effective organizations build a single *business* management system as an expandable framework and add all the subdisciplines to support the business. Individuals from different disciplines who think in terms of "now we've got our own management system standard" are missing a key point. You do not invest the time and resources to build stand-alone discipline specific management systems. The objective is to support the business objectives; the disciplines are tools to support the overall business management strategy.

ORM is predicated on a holistic, systems perspective of the organization; all levels, all departments must be part of the effort to build a resilient organization, but complete involvement of all departments is not necessary at the beginning of the project. In fact, it is possible that the involvement of the business units will depend on the level of ability to participate. Involvement in this project is based on the needs of the organization and the respective ability of each business unit to effectively participate. (Further discussion of this issue will be detailed in Chapter 9, Maturity Model.) It also depends on organizational priorities and their risk profile. With given risks identified, some organizations might emphasize likelihood management and start by focusing the effort in their security and asset protection departments. Some risks lend themselves to more of a consequence management perspective, therefore, starting with more of crisis and business continuity management focuses. In either case, the organization should always look for opportunities in adversity and build its approach as a framework to integrate all perspectives as the company matures. The OR Standard provides a good explanation of how a "systems and process" approach is applicable to this discussion:

> The management systems approach encourages organizations to analyze organizational and stakeholder requirements and define processes that contribute to success. A management system can provide the framework for continual improvement to increase the probability of enhancing security, preparedness, response, continuity, and resilience. It provides confidence to the organization and its customers that the organization is

able to provide a safe and secure environment, which fulfills organizational and stakeholder requirements.

This *Standard* adopts a *process approach* for establishing, implementing, operating, monitoring, reviewing, maintaining, and improving an organization's organizational resilience (OR) management system. An organization needs to identify and manage many activities in order to function effectively. Any activity using resources and managed in order to enable the transformation of inputs into outputs can be considered to be a process. Often the output from one process directly forms the input to the next process (ANSI/ASIS SPC.1-2009, p. vii).

The ANSI/ASIS.SPC.1 uses a combination of process and systems approach. The easiest way to understand this is to look at the human body. We want to better understand how a person functions, survives, and thrives. To understand how a person works, we not only need to have an idea of how the elements that make up the body work (heart, lungs, brain, nervous system, etc.), but we also need to understand how all the elements work together because the human can only exist if all the elements are working together. To say a person is healthy is not to say that all the organs are healthy, but rather all the organs and their functional interrelationships are healthy. Likewise, the systems approach to viewing an organization is important to fully understand how the various departments/groups are independent and cross-functionally related. For instance, the IT department may be the conduit for the organization, pumping information to all the departments. An example of a particular department is finance. These financial operations allow the business to function in a competitive market. At the same time, the IT department is sustaining the security and human resources departments. While it is important to understand the workings of all these departments to run a business, the business is only healthy if all the departments are working together to achieve the objectives of the organization. One of the primary purposes of the IT department is to provide a functioning computer network with applications that allows the finance department to perform internal and external financial operations. These financial operations allow the business to function in a competitive market. Because IT also provides the same network to other groups within the company, and, perhaps, other departments use the same applications to perform their respective functions, it is obvious that IT touches each department within the organization. The above simplistic example shows how one department benefits from another and allows a department to have a purpose (without a clear purpose, the department would not exist). When viewing your particular company, you are likely to find much more complex relationships than the above example—all departments benefiting from and assisting other departments. The more complex the interdependencies in your organization, the greater the importance of developing an enterprise-wide perspective when considering what is necessary for preparedness planning; as you perform the Criticality Assessment (CA), this will become much more understandable and obvious. See Chapter 6 and Exhibit 6.2 for more details.

The systems approach to preparedness is highly desirable because it brings logic and understanding to how things work in the organization as well as how to manage risk. Using the above example of IT, it is obvious that the IT infrastructure (voice and data) in a modern, technologically advanced organization is a central cog of the business and it is critical that this infrastructure is protected from unacceptable interruptions. Using the systems approach, we have seen how departments are interrelated, therefore, any efforts to address ORM also require the involvement of multiple stakeholders. Stakeholders must be shown the value of their participation and the benefit of working together. For an organization to become resilient, all members of the organization must be involved; remember, it is all about risk and the regular staff are the ones dealing with risk issues every day. In essence, we are describing a culture of risk management. The focus is on adapting to a complex and changing environment ideally to prevent events from materializing, and, if they do, responding, recovering, learning, and strengthening. This will not be a quick or necessarily easy accomplishment. For all members of an organization to really become involved in the risk management functions as described in ORM, it will require education, effective communication, and the inclusion of ORM principles into the values of the organization.

BENEFITS OF RESILIENCE MANAGEMENT

The primary benefit of resilience management is the optimization of resources as organizations eliminate silos and work collaboratively to maximize opportunities and minimize the likelihood and consequences of risks to support the organization's objectives. ORM creates a risk management culture throughout the organization where all individuals are empowered to take appropriate actions to identify opportunities to protect and create value for the organization. The capacity for resilience is found in an organization's culture, attitudes, and values. In creating appropriate competence, culture, attitudes, and values, an organization builds its capacity to anticipate an event, to resist it by adapting, and to recover by focusing on strengthening and growing the organization. By creating a dynamic culture of adaptation and innovation, the organization creates the agility to address an ever-changing environment by adapting itself, and, when possible, its environment.

There are three types of timeframes an organization needs to consider to be resilient:

1. Ensuring the outcomes of routine and consistent operating environments (typically quality, occupational health and safety, and environmental management)
2. Issues involving the long-term performance of the organization (typically, sustainability, social responsibility, and source reduction management)
3. Risks related to achievement of objectives in uncertain, adverse, and nonroutine times (typically security, crisis, and continuity management).

To identify opportunities to drive adaptation and innovation, a cross-disciplinary perspective covering the three timeframes is essential. This also will avoid duplication and save money. For example, plastics injection molding companies often have hazard waste disposal problems. Is this an environmental, security, procurement, public relations, or process problem? Likely it is a shared problem. Viewing the problem from a siloed approach may result in competing solutions and duplicate expenditures. However, a collaborative, cross-disciplinary approach will look at the life cycle of the process and all related functions leading to a solution that addresses the root cause—waste generation. Changing procurement practices or chemical substitutions may result in significant savings to the organization and solve its environmental, security, procurement, public relations, and process problems.

Resilience capacity is strongest in an organization that:

- Eliminates silos to create cross-functional, cross-disciplinary collaboration
- Views uncertainty and adversity as an opportunity to adapt, innovate, and strengthen the organization
- Anticipates, learns, and adapts change and adversity to prevent an event from materializing, mitigates the consequences should it occur, and learns from an incident to adapt and strengthen itself to avoid potential recurrences and to exploit opportunities

- Emphasizes preemptive measures (prevention) and adaptability as its top priority
- Identifies, anticipates, and assesses emerging challenges and threats to the achievement of objectives
- Understands its value chain
- Monitors, learns from, and adapts to change (preferably before an event)
- Understands the impact of threats on its operations and lives of people working on its behalf as well as its supply chain and external stakeholders
- Maps its relationships, interdependencies, and dependencies with stakeholders and critical infrastructure to develop and maintain supportive relationships
- Assures the competence and willingness of persons working on behalf of the organization to support the organization to achieve objectives to prevent, respond to, and recover from adversity
- Prevents, responds to, and recovers from events as a collaborative organizational team
- Adapts to potential and actual events with the agility to strengthen the organization and assure integrity of functions
- Articulates clear organizational objectives and establishes a proactive plan to prevent, respond to, and recover from an adverse event
- Leads with clear direction while enabling devolved problem solving

BUILDING A RISK AND RESILIENCE MANAGEMENT CULTURE

Developing a culture within the organization that recognizes the significant value of weaving risk management into the daily affairs of all organizational members is extremely important. Many risk operations have awareness programs that attempt to educate employees on pertinent issues through routine alerts, messages, and similar forms of communication. These awareness programs are valuable, but consider the influence of using the ORM project to blend risk management into the daily lives of the employees, in addition to the aforementioned awareness programs. Instead of having people think that the responsibilities associated with typical risk management fall exclusively into the domain of the risk management department, an organization would have an entire workforce dedicated to accepting and seeking out opportunities to improve the resilience of the organization. Yes, it is possible to implement and succeed at this effort if the right people support the initiative. Senior management, including the chief executive and all the midlevel and subordinate managers and supervisors, must understand and promote the concept that membership within the organization requires active involvement in risk management. The challenge is to instill the sense of obligation, as described earlier, as a moral imperative, to acknowledge that risk management is something that each group member must accept as a requirement of group membership. This is a policy decision that must be made at the top of the organization for success.

The development of this culture of risk management may be more difficult in some organizations because of the previously established norms within an organization. Some people may have developed bad habits from ineffective managers. This can be corrected with time and effort, but the real issue involves the basic policies coming from senior management. People need to see the value of their actions and that certain behaviors are not only acceptable, they are expected, rewarded, and praised by those in power. When an employee identifies and reports (follows through on) a risk that needs to be addressed, it is necessary to immediately acknowledge the importance of that behavior so that others will see the value. The average employee has the greatest opportunity to both witness a risk issue and influence a positive outcome in addressing that risk, which is why it is so important to develop and support the culture of risk management. Managers are expected to recognize and support risk management initiative, but the average employee is not always expected to go beyond the immediate duties of his or her job. Risk managers usually are not process managers or engineers. Engaging the process owners into the risk management process will more likely provide results that support the value-generating aspects of the business.

To affect this level of change within an organization, it is necessary to build new pieces into the fabric of the organization: update job descriptions to reflect the importance of risk management, include employees from all levels of the organization in efforts to address resilience, acknowledge organization-wide accomplishments or significant efforts to address risk, and perhaps have reward incentives to show a greater level of involvement or accomplishment. Think back to the discussion of the maturity model and the various phases or stages of ORM accomplishment. Simple names recognizing organizational accomplishment are a great way to build a sense of involvement and unity.

Organizations are faced with risk issues in every aspect of their existence. There is positive and negative risk in each process and activity from the simplest to the most complex. Each department within an organization is likely to have established plans and practices to address risk matters. The plans are critical components to increasing the resilience of an organization in conjunction with ANSI/ASIS SPC.1-2009. These plans are "where the rubber meets the road" and are in constant use by the members of those departments. As discussed earlier in this book, left to their individual, myopic, and uncoordinated approaches, it is very possible that a strong "silo" structure will develop within an organization. This silo approach is not deliberately malicious, but the result creates the antithesis of the desired holistic approach to viewing risk. Silos force people to look into their own areas and perceived responsibilities and not from an organization-wide perspective. The implementation of ORM will create an opportunity for these departments to work from a unified approach to risk issues. It is appropriate and, perhaps, helpful to view the ORM efforts as strategic and the department-level plans and procedures as tactical. ORM is the coordinating, high-level risk perspective that brings all of the tactical department-level plans, practices, and general efforts to perform their respective functions, into a consistent synergistic approach of resiliency within the organization. The necessary procedures to address and resolve situations are contained in the department (stakeholder) plans and are critical to the organization's ability to prevent, prepare, and respond to a situation. The stakeholder plans, when in conformance with the ORM Standard, are necessary to ensure the proper preparation and response to disruptive events and the resiliency of the organization. Each department has critical processes and activities that are necessary for the successful completion of a mission-critical goal. Ensuring that these activities are addressed from an ORM perspective contributes to the goal of organizational resiliency. ORM helps move the organization to that goal in a more organized and consistent fashion.

A visual depiction of the foundations that permit the establishment of organizational resilience is provided in Exhibit 2.4.

During the development of plans and procedures, it is not uncommon for senior managers to avoid making clear policy decisions in favor of having staff work out the procedural details concerning the response ORM efforts. This is a common mistake on the part of the senior managers because they fail to understand the relationship between policies

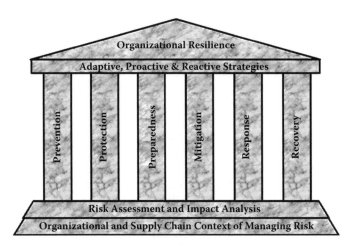

Exhibit 2.4   Organizational resilience relationships.

and procedures. It is necessary, and extremely important, to link a procedure to a policy in order to justify the procedure and give it a clear
connection to the organizational values that are the underpinnings of
the organization's culture. Practitioners that have written procedural
manuals or emergency security or response plans understand the need
to have procedures follow the policy decisions. Process and procedural
issues are extremely difficult to establish without the policies to establish
the high level framework. (See Exhibit 2.4 for an example of this relationship.) Senior managers like to have procedures in place, but want to be
able to consider policy issues at the time of the critical decision. This is a
serious failing on the part of these managers and reflects a fundamental
misunderstanding of what is needed to make important decisions during
an emergency when an event may materialize. High-level policy issues
should not be subject to an emergency. The basic values of the organization should not change; however, the prepared procedures may have to be
modified to provide the desired result of organizational resilience. After
an event, though it is always advisable for an organization to learn from
the event and strengthen itself through adaptation.

Because organizational values are the essential underpinnings of
the organizational culture, they should not be subject to change during
a crisis. This is sometimes a difficult concept for managers to embrace
because they may want something that will be quick and easy to implement. They generally try to solve a problem with a direct intervention

allowing personnel to move to the next issue. Some senior managers want to make the actual policy decision at the time of the emergency. They fail to understand that the policies reflect the values that drive the culture of the organization and these policies need to be established, and understood, prior to an emergency so that the plans and procedures may be in place to ensure concurrence with the organizational culture. For instance, if the organization states that it values human life and safety as its top priority, there is a clear policy decision to safeguard humans. For example, from that policy decision, it is necessary to have the procedures that are used in anticipation and response to extreme weather conditions clearly state that people should avoid unnecessary travel because of the dangerous conditions. It may take a good deal of effort to educate the senior managers on the importance of developing procedures after firm policy decisions have been made. Unfortunately, some managers will never change and the procedures will have to be developed without a clear policy; that is an organizational reality that must be faced occasionally. If this is the case, before you embark on developing the procedures, you should establish basic policy assumptions to frame your procedural objectives.

As the project team reviews the risk-oriented response or resilience management plans, it may be necessary to modify the plans to ensure a truly effective, cohesive relationship with the other department plans. This review and revision process should really happen through periodic evaluations and be a normal course of business to emphasize that ORM is simply a part of good business management. All plans must be reviewed on a regular basis to ensure currency and completeness. Plans are only as useful as the framework of relationship and interaction established around the plans. Plans are not the goal, just a tool like a stapler or computer; the process to achieve the plan is much more valuable.

It is common for emergency preparedness professionals to see tangible products like the development of procedures, contact lists, analyses, plans, and policy documents as the primary goals. While there is certainly value to having these things in place, it misses the point behind the key element of success, understanding that these are just tools to assure the viability and sustainability of the business. Furthermore, it is important to consider the intangible goals that really make the difference in preparedness. There also are intangible results, such as relationship building, understanding how and why things work, and understanding one's responsibilities both to the organization and the irreplaceable value of the process or shared experiences of building ORM. These are the long-term values within a resilient organization. The results of the aforementioned intangible products allow for a more effective response to managing changes facing the organization. Situational changes before or during an emergency event often require an alteration to an established plan in favor of a more effective response, but a cohesive team with shared experiences and a robust understanding of the bigger picture will be able to adjust to any changes. Planning for a worst case scenario is an acceptance that things will change during an emergency. When the worst case situation does not happen, the plan may be adjusted for the less serious incident. This change in the plan is accomplished with a greater degree of efficiency through a well-trained cadre of professionals with the necessary ability to understand the need to adapt to the situation.

While it is not the intent of this book to discuss in any detail the actual plans or procedures that are used before, during, or after an event, it is important to briefly discuss the use of a plan during an event. Organizational resilience management is discipline neutral when viewing risk and the management thereof. ORM facilitates the integration of multiple disciplines related to collaboratively manage risks to the organization. While ORM may be discipline neutral, the reality of organizations is that they consist of people working within functions that are described according to disciplines (e.g., Legal, Production, Security, Facilities Management, etc.). A key concept in ORM is that, in spite of being organized in functional departments for operations, it is important to recognize that risk is not departmental, but rather organizational. Risks being addressed must be viewed within the context of uncertainty in the achieving of organizational objectives, not simply departmental objectives. Therefore, plans used within departments to achieve stated goals need to be aligned to achieve organizational goals and while the risks may affect specific issues within a department, in reality, the risks affect the organization. The interdisciplinary approach of ORM needs to stay focused to building and enhancing the adaptive capacity of the organization in an ever-changing environment to achieve the organization's objectives.

The value of a given plan is based on the purpose and use of that plan. Two quotes that should be kept in mind when developing a plan:

It's not the plan that is important, it's the planning.

Dr. Graeme Edwards

and,

A common mistake people make when trying to design something fool-proof is to underestimate the ingenuity of complete fools.

Douglas Adams
Author of The Hitchhiker's Guide to the Galaxy

For the plan to have value, it is important to ensure that the contents of the plan facilitate positive results during the use of the plan. When a plan is activated, it has to be able to accomplish the stated purpose. Regardless of the actual structure of the plan or components of the plan, it is important to understand what is needed from a plan perspective. Always keep in mind that events will not follow your script, so the planning process should be a learning and awareness exercise that recognizes inherent uncertainty. Each person writing a plan will stress different aspects of it in accordance with the issues of the plan and those issues that are important to the organization. Because plans differ from one another, it is not possible to provide a listing of every itemized topic for every plan. The following are suggested typical topic sections to include within a plan. The exact topics and order are likely to change in accordance with the requirements of a particular organization. Also, the sections detailing these topics do not need to be long or excessively detailed. It is important to ensure that they are functional and provide the necessary information to allow for a complete understanding of the topic. Suggested typical topical sections to include within a plan:

- Purpose and scope of the procedure
- Assets to be protected and activities to be maintained
- Objectives and measures of success
- Situations/conditions in which each procedure will be implemented
- Implementation steps and the frequency with which the procedure is carried out
- Governance, roles, responsibilities, and authorities
- Communication requirements and procedures
- Internal and external interdependencies and interactions
- Resources needed (human, physical, information, and financial)
- Competency and training requirements
- Information flow and documentation processes
- Stand-down procedures
- Work instructions

The above list is not exhaustive and is only provided to give the reader some ideas to consider when beginning the process of determining the type and structure of a plan. A crisis management plan is not the same as a business continuity plan even though each is aimed at protecting the continuation of the business. It is expected that the professionals in each group will be able to design and develop a plan. The value of ORM is that each plan should be reviewed from the perspective of unity, cohesiveness, and effectiveness as noted in the ANSI/ASIS SPC.1-2009. The structure of the plan is dependent upon the needs of the organization and the acceptability of the approach within the operational confines of the company. For instance, Incident Command System is an excellent way to manage a situation, but not all organizations (the senior leaders, mainly) are willing to allow ICS to operate within the decision-making process of the organization. These are the types of issues that must be clarified before a plan is designed and implemented.

The human element of risk is a declaration of how personnel really make the difference in addressing risk issues. People certainly want to be safe and secure in their homes and work environments, but the necessary follow through is sometimes a problem. Having perfect plans and procedures in place mean nothing if the people fail to implement or follow them. One consistent element in this book is the claim that a culture of risk management must be established within the organization, and that really means within the personnel. People must understand the value of addressing risk, the need for working together and in conjunction with established protocols, and the positive outcome that is possible from a unified and standardized approach to managing risk. One aspect of ORM that is highly desirable is the essential change of culture within the organization to foster organizational resilience expectations and capabilities. Changing culture is extremely difficult and time consuming. With respect to ORM, we are asking the personnel at the organization to change their behavior, their perspectives toward their jobs, the organization, and their place within that organization. This certainly can be done, but will require careful crafting, persuasion, and reinforcement to convince the personnel that their efforts are both valued by management and have clear results that are understandable.

As mentioned earlier, breaking down the silos of department centric efforts to handle problems (risks) requires the personnel within those departments to view other personnel and departments as part of the solution and not as bystanders. This is an education issue that may take quite some time to really institute, especially in decentralized organizations. The more an organization is decentralized, the more difficult it is likely to be to break down the silos; since the current norm is for the staff to resolve things in a decentralized approach and not necessarily as an integrated operation involving other groups. In essence, people are used to doing things the way they have always done them, and we are suggesting that they change the old ways and implement something that very well may go against the grain of the organization. A typical university is a good example of a decentralized operation that is extremely difficult to change. Staff and faculty report to leadership via different channels of management, which may be viewed as silos, and a possible difficulty in an organization becoming more resilient. Faculty may say they are too busy to be bothered with another "administration" attempt to distract them, and staff may say that they need the participation of faculty to properly address an issue. Include any union activities and the silos become more distinct.

As difficult as the human element may be, it is crucial to the success of increasing OR within an organization. It will take senior management involvement to send the right message, time for that message to really work itself into the minds of the personnel, and then for change to begin. Changing an organization's culture is difficult, but, if the existing culture is "risk dysfunctional," then a change must be made if the goal of OR is to be achieved. Slow, steady, positive accomplishments connected with this project will bring about the impetus for long-term cultural change.

When implementing any standard, it is important for people to *want* to participate rather than feel they *have* to participate. People like to have positive reinforcement. The implementation strategy should encourage people's participation by focusing on performance improvement and recognition of improvements. The pace of implementation should be set so success breeds success. If senior management gives the impression that all they are interested in is certification, they run the risk of sending a message that the framed piece of paper is the goal. People will respond better if they know they feel they have a stake in making their lives and jobs more secure through continual improvement.

3

Management Systems Approach

WHAT IS THE MANAGEMENT SYSTEMS APPROACH?

To better understand what the ANSI/ASIS SPC.1-2009 Standard is about and why it is advisable to conform to the information contained therein, it is necessary to understand the management systems approach. A management system is a structured method of ensuring that procedures are aligned with policies and objectives for managing the organizational processes that are associated with the achievement of the organizational objectives. The organization establishes the policies, procedures, and objectives necessary to achieve the creation of a product (physical or intellectual) or service, and through the interrelated processes or activities of the organization, directs the achievement of those objectives. The expectation of continual improvement of the processes and practices is inherent in the management systems approach. The achievement of the organizational goals requires resources that are necessary for the system to function in addition to the resources that are needed to produce products and services. These resources must be viewed as part of the system. Successful organizations create value through the products and services they produce. The ORMS is a tool to support value creation and protect the activities and functions of the organization involved in this value proposition. The management systems approach has, as an underlying principle, the understanding that an organization has many parts and that they are all interrelated through process functionality and through the requirement for resources in the achievement of an objective. Modern organizations are more interrelated than ever before due to the complex development of products, the reliance on advanced technology, and the nature of international economics.

The management of the processes and the achievement of the organizational goals require the management of risk. Because risk may have both positive and negative outcomes, it is important to identify these risks and determine what, if anything should be done to ensure that the assessment and treatment of that risk is in line with the desires of the organization. ANSI/ASIS SPC.1-2009 uses a management systems approach to address risk with the intent to ensure the successful achievement of the organizational goals through risk management. Using the ANSI/ASIS SPC.1-2009 Standard ensures that the management systems approach will provide the organization with an opportunity to successfully address risk issues and provide confidence to organizational members, partners, stakeholders, and customers that the organization is capable of achieving the stated goals in a changing environment. The management system provides a sound basis for decision making to help the organization adapt, proactively and reactively, to drive sustainability and innovation. The feedback loops designed into a management system provide a structured approach for organizations to learn from adversity and make necessary changes to themselves and their environment.

A mortgage company is a good example of a complex organization relying on the processes of different departments to achieve the goal of a certain amount of profit. A mortgage application is obtained through either an online transaction or through a traditional field office. The loan is reviewed against the borrower's income and perceived ability to repay the loan, and is either rejected or approved. Once the loan paperwork is completed, it goes through a review process by different offices to ensure completeness and information verification; the information the customer provided must be checked to verify accuracy. The loan transaction documentation is stored electronically for future reference as well as in hard copy, which must be sent to a long-term storage facility. While this example is abbreviated, it illustrates the interrelated processes associated with the customers, the advertisers, the telemarketers, the field agents, the audit reviewers, the shippers, and many others. The activities of these stakeholders rely on the successful conclusion of a process that allows another process to begin; one process becomes the resource for another process. The successful completion of the aforementioned processes results in the achievement of the stated organizational goal of realizing a certain profit. A failure to address risk in any of these processes may result in the failure of the organization to achieve the goal. Routine and continual improvement must be part of the organizational philosophy because processes do not remain static. Change must be accounted for and integrated into the risk assessment.

TOTAL QUALITY MANAGEMENT AND THE PDCA MODEL

The ORM Standard uses the Plan-Do-Check-Act (PDCA) model (Exhibit 3.1) to formulate a conceptual understanding of the processes involved and clearly shows the input, process, and output of the process approach (ANSI/ASIS SPC.1-2009, viii). This model is designed to continually improve a process-oriented relationship through the analysis of the different entities or groups involved, with special attention given to how they are related. An understanding of this relationship will result in more informed decisions when trying to prepare for events. This model is used throughout the process of the ANSI/ASIS SPC.1-2009, both as an overall framework and as a useful tool for structuring the procedures for the individual elements.

Exhibit 3.2 is an explanation of the components of the Plan-Do-Check-Act model and clearly demonstrates the fundamental approach of establishing the management system, implementing the system, reviewing or auditing the system, and making necessary corrections to ensure conformance with the planned system.

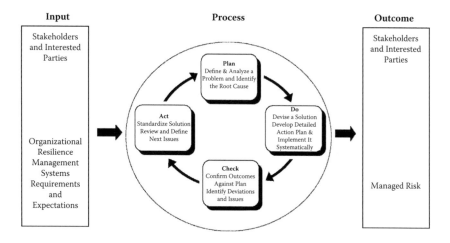

Exhibit 3.1   ANSI/ASIS SPC.1-2009 Plan-Do-Check-Act model.

Plan (establish the management system)	Establish management system policy, objectives, processes, and procedures relevant to managing risk and improving security, incident preparedness, response, continuity, and recovery and to deliver results in accordance with an organization's overall policies and objectives.
Do (implement and operate the management system)	Implement and operate the management system policy, controls, processes, and procedures.
Check (monitor and review the management system)	Assess and measure process performance against management system policy, objectives, and practical experience and report the results to management for review.
Act (maintain and improve the management system)	Take corrective and preventive actions, based on the results of the internal management system audit and management review, to achieve continual improvement of the management system.

Exhibit 3.2   ANSI/ASIS SPC.1-2009 Plan-Do-Check-Act explanatory table.

While the Plan-Do-Check-Act model is the practical, iterative approach to establishing the ORM system, the ORM system flow diagram is the essential process for implementing ANSI/ASIS SPC.1-2009. Exhibit 3.3 shows the continual motion of the process with the major activities noted below (ANSI/ASIS SPC.1-2009, p. 4) in accordance with the respective components of the Standard.

- Start: Your Organization: Plan
- Policy: Plan
- Planning:
- Implementation and Operation: Do
- Checking and Corrective Action: Check
- Management Review: Act

An important consideration to remember is that this is an iterative approach and not a terminal process. This flow diagram presents the expectation of continual review and improvement throughout the life of the effort. The actual implementation of the Standard will likely take a good deal of time because the average organization is complex.

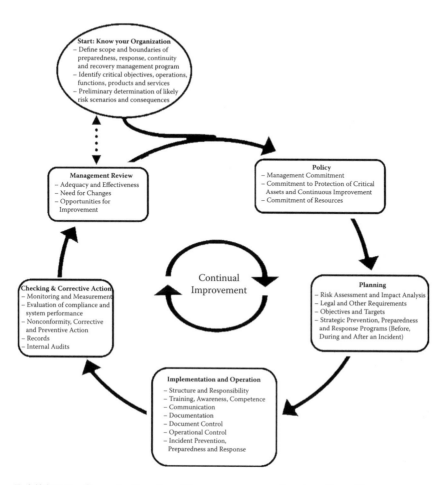

Exhibit 3.3   Organizational resilience management system flow diagram.

The greater the complexity, the longer the project will take to encompass the entire organization. However, the implementation project is really just the beginning of the long-term program. It is necessary to develop this project into a program with regular review and maintenance built into the plan. Perhaps this analogy will help illustrate the expectation of ORM. The project is only the beginning of the effort, the initial force to roll a large boulder forward. The effort will take the involvement of many people, working in unison to move the rock in the same direction, each contributing to a unified effort. Once the boulder is moving and there is momentum building, it becomes easier but still requires effort from all. The project eventually must become a program to gain the full value and benefit from the resources invested in the project.

COMMON ELEMENTS OF MANAGEMENT SYSTEM STANDARDS

All management system standards have six basic common elements:

1. Policy
2. Planning
3. Implementation and operation
4. Performance assessment
5. Improvement
6. Management review

The policy provides the framework for setting objectives and targets. It demonstrates top management's commitment to fulfill the requirements of the management system standard and to establish an overall sense of purpose, direction, and principles for action.

Planning within a management system involves identifying the context of the organization and its activities, the needs of stakeholders, risk issues, and developing a strategic approach to addressing identified issues. Planning involves identifying the needs and requirements that the organization needs to address and issues it needs to control, including meeting its legal and other requirements. Where the policy sets the framework for setting objectives and targets of the management system, the process of setting the context. Furthermore, conducting a risk assessment sets the foundation for the management system. Based on the output from the risk assessment, the organization can set clear objectives and targets, prioritizing issues to be addressed. When risk issues are prioritized, the organization can determine its risk treatment strategy and establish timeframes, resources (human, infrastructure, and financial), and roles, responsibilities, authorities, and their interrelationships which are needed to address risk issues.

Implementation and operation is where strategic goals are translated into tactical action. Operational control measures (plans and procedures) are developed and put into practice to control activities defined as risk issues and objectives. Procedures for identifying and the efficient use of resources (human, physical, financial, and infrastructure) needed to meet objectives are established. This includes the competence of individuals working on behalf of the organization. Communications arrangements for both within the organization and to/from external sources are set up. Arrangements for those who supply and contract their services to the organization that have an impact on the organization's performance are formalized. A system of management of documents and documentation to support the management system is created.

Performance assessment involves the mechanisms the organization establishes to assess its performance on an ongoing basis. This includes a process for analyzing and addressing nonconformities by determining the existence of nonconformities and the manner in which they will be addressed. System audits provide a thorough evaluation of the system elements and their efficacy.

Improvement establishes the mechanisms for eliminating the causes of detected nonconformities both in the management system and the operational processes. This includes mechanisms for eliminating the causes of detected and potential nonconformities. Inherent in this process is the concept of adapting and strengthening the management system and the operational processes based on lessons learned in the performance assessment (including reviewing the risk assessment).

Management review of the management system seeks to identify and define opportunities for improvement. Management identifies and implements improvements and new directions necessary to achieve the organization's objectives. This is done by determining its current performance, evaluating continuing suitability, adequacy, and effectiveness.

BUILDING A MANAGEMENT SYSTEM AS A FRAMEWORK

Effective organizations do not build several disparate management systems; rather they build a management system as a framework with the inherent flexibility to add disciplines of focus. There is a curious phenomenon among some disciplines where there is a feeling that "we need our own management system." This view is counterproductive. Given that management systems all contain common elements, they lend themselves to integration. Organizations should strive to eliminate silos and integrate different management system standards into a single framework. Organizations that integrate the disciplines as envisioned in the ISO 31000 and the Organizational Resilience (OR) standard will eliminate the duplication of efforts and will address risks in a more holistic and cost-effective fashion. There is a myth that the "ISO" brand indicates quality for the product or deep thought and broad involvement of all stakeholders. ISO and certification bodies have a vested interest in the proliferation of discipline-specific management system standards. This does not mean businesses need to follow this folly.

SUPPORTING A CULTURE OF CONTINUAL IMPROVEMENT

The underlying premise of Total Quality Management (TQM) and the PDCA model is to assure reliability and repeatability of processes needed to drive continual improvement. This works by promoting the awareness and commitment of all individuals involved in the management process, with teaming replacing hierarchy. The structured nature of the management approach helps establish a clear mission and clear objectives. The systems approach leverages disciplines and expertise to promote the achievement of objectives. This will lead to a sense of ownership with empowerment replacing fear. By setting clear objectives that serves as the basis for action planning, the organization practices management by measurement. The focus on learning and training drives the continual improvement cycle. The inclusive process supports the culture of continual improvement.

RECOGNITION VERSUS CERTIFICATION

Recognition or certification is a business decision based on the return on investment. Management system standards are tools for performance improvement; they are not an end in themselves. Security, crisis, and continuity management support the achievement of the organization's objectives, not the reverse. A business may find a business case for certification, but the rationale for investing the effort in implementing a management systems standard should not be a certificate on the wall; it should always be improved performance and the achievement of organizational objectives that drive the effort. If there is a clear business case, the certification is gravy.

Recognition programs help provide a stepped approach to implementation that helps exploit the human psyche's tendency to respond well to positive reinforcement. Success breeds success. Recognizing and rewarding people in a recognition program as they reach goals in implementing a management system helps them feel their efforts were worthwhile and spurs them on to even greater achievement.

4

Getting Started

DEFINING AN ORGANIZATION'S GOALS

The first question to ask is: "What am I trying to achieve?" It sounds trivial, but try to answer this question for your organization. Before you start, you need to know the overarching objectives of your organization, and then you can start thinking about identifying the uncertainties in achieving those objectives. Risks do not float around in space waiting to be treated. Risks are all about the uncertainty in achieving the objectives of your organization. Therefore, risks are unique to your unique set of objectives. Understand your organization's objectives and you have taken your first steps. Now you can start your journey to create and protect value in your organization.

It may seem unnecessary to have a discussion on values when the goal of this book is to provide guidance on the implementation of organizational resilience management (ORM), but the benefit of a discussion involving values is at the heart of risk management. The implementation of risk management practices within an organization involves decisions or a series of negotiations concerning the possible survival of the business. These negotiations are between competing issues; cost versus benefit, one goal versus another goal, and one professional opinion versus another, all of which may require funding or resources and, therefore, the basis for the aforementioned negotiation. It is not unusual for senior managers to weigh the cost of risk management against the benefit or perceived benefit of risk management proposals. Managers may decide to exploit, minimize, transfer, avoid, or accept the risk in an effort to adequately address the matter. There is nothing wrong with accepting risk if the likelihood of an event is extremely low, if the cost of resolution is prohibitively high, or if accepting the risk presents an opportunity. It does not make any sense to implement a practice if the expense bankrupts the business. However, if the reason for not implementing the correct choice is based on senior management's desire to make more money at the expense of the business, then the decision is not ethical and should be rejected as contrary to the values of the organization, i.e., assuming the organization is based on ethical grounds. There are many isssues that come into play when managers are deciding on accepting recommendations. Managers accept projects that are well designed, focused on achievable goals, and well organized; essentially, those projects that follow standard project management practices are more acceptable. The manager may not be against the project addressing the risk, but is against sponsoring a project that is not properly planned and appears likely to fail. No one wants to back a losing horse. Ensure that your project is a thoroughbred and not a mule. Doubting the project or the people on the team is not the same thing as overlooking a necessary risk treatment.

The values of the organization determine the culture of the organization. The employees learn what is important and perform in accordance with the basic values of the organization. For the organization to realize the true worth of organizational resilience management, it is necessary to inculcate the principles of ORM into the fundamental values of the organization. An organization that acknowledges and understands the nature of the interdependencies of its business operations and units, business interests, supply chain partners, cargo transport capabilities, and others, will be in a better position to address complex risk issues. Understanding the need to protect the organization from risks and understanding the complexity of organizational interdependencies are goals the project manager will face in implementing ORM. The fundamental driving element of ORM is the desire to address organizational risk. It is an acknowledgement of the need to accept the requirements associated with the values of the organization. Survival of the organization is supported and made manifest through the underpinnings of the values associated with the organization, such as trust, honor, and fidelity. As identified earlier, the values of the organization are the very fabric of the organizational culture. Some values are very obvious and experienced everyday while others are sub rosa, but are just as important as the others.

IDENTIFYING STAKEHOLDERS

As we move through this discussion of risk management, it will become evident that internal stakeholders share the same desire to prepare for the possibility of challenges or issues that have the potential to adversely affect the organization. Because each organization is somewhat different, it is advisable to move through the process of performing an assessment of the organization. For effective ORM implementation, it is necessary to evaluate the organization and identify the internal stakeholders that must be engaged to successfully achieve the organization's objectives. Failure to perform this simple task shall result in a poorly implemented and ill received product. It is not uncommon to initially conclude that the traditional "risk managers" noted above are the only stakeholders, but that is a serious mistake and will result in a less effective approach. Properly implemented ORM is an organization-wide endeavor in alignment with the far-reaching business strategy. Because this endeavor involves the entire organization, it follows that all persons who participate in, or can be affected by, the decision-making processes are relevant stakeholders in ORM, including management and personnel from all departments of the organization. Managers that were not consulted on the initial planning and development effort may view it as encroachment upon their turf. It is critical to have the stakeholders actively involved in the development of the ORM strategy. Because ORM involves the entire organization, it is important to have as many managers as possible "buy in" on this approach to increase the probability of effectiveness. Obviously, it will not be possible to include all personnel or even all managers on the project team, but it is important to include them in such a way as to show their involvement is both needed and respected. An initial briefing, either as a document, a multimedia Web cast, or if you have the luxury of gathering all the managers in one place, or an in-person presentation are good ways to generate interest and involvement. Marketing, or public relations activities surrounding the project, is an important part of the ORM effort. Generating, maintaining, and confirming the participation of the organizational personnel quite literally may mean the difference between success and failure. Educating, generating interest, avoiding misunderstandings, and maintaining the positive attitude toward the value of the project is a key component to success—easier said than done.

The example of typical stakeholders indicated in Exhibit 4.1 is not necessarily comprehensive, and because each organization is different, the stakeholders are likely to be at least slightly different. The preparations for

Typical Stakeholders	Typical Areas of Risk Concern
Physical Security	Access Control, Investigations, Asset Protection, Personnel Security
Human Resources	Personnel Issues, Labor/Union Relations
Information Security	Asset Protection, Network Security, Information Security
Business Continuity	Planning of Organizational Business Process Continuity
Disaster Recovery	Recovery of Physical Assets—Often Applied to IT Assets
Health Safety	Ergonomics, Workplace Safety
Legal	Legal Matters Pertaining to the Organization, Labor/Union Relations
Finance	Financial Operations and Protection of Financial Interests of Organization
Facility Management	Maintenance, Housekeeping, Space Planning
Risk Management	Insurance, Traditional Risk Management
Real Estate Management	Real Estate Properties, Lease Administration, Space Planning
Communications	Internal and External Communications
Organizational Managers	Achieving Organizational Goals—Performance of Personnel
Organizational Staff	Achieving Team/Group Goals—Personal Performance

Exhibit 4.1 Typical stakeholders in organizations.

the implementation of ORM involve the identification of the stakeholders at the organization in question. Exhibit 4.1 may be helpful in that effort. It is advisable to have others review the list and offer suggestions for a more comprehensive list. Allowing people to become involved and making useful contributions to the project is a great way to build consensus and "buy-in." It is better to include more stakeholders than less; excluding people may be viewed as an insult to those excluded.

Identifying external stakeholders also is key to developing a robust ORM approach. External stakeholders can both profoundly affect decisions about resilience and risk management as well as be affected by the decision-making process. External stakeholders are not always as easy to identify as internal ones. Use a systematic approach to identify all external interested parties that can introduce uncertainty to the organization's activities and who the organization will interact with when dealing with risk. Obviously, supply chain partners are key external stakeholders, as are emergency responders, regulators, community and interest groups, financial institutions, and the media.

BUILDING CONSENSUS AND GETTING BUY-IN

ORM is a top-down, bottom-up approach. Everyone needs to work in concert to achieve the outcomes the organization is seeking and to understand that they are a team seeking to achieve the organization's overarching objectives. The key to getting buy-in from all relevant stakeholders is for top management to be engaged and clearly communicate to stakeholders the importance of ORM. For success, there needs to be a mandate and commitment from the top of the organization. If stakeholders understand the reasons for ORM and the potential benefits of the program as well as see the commitment of senior management to the endeavor, they will be more likely to actively support the initiative. ORM is no exception to good generic project management practices. A well-planned project will have leadership and commitment from the top, adequate resources, and engagement of stakeholders, and, of course, have a good game plan that people feel part of.

It is easy to say that the workers must follow orders because leadership issued a mandate requiring a certain action or level of performance. However, people will do as they please and, if their behavior is to be changed, it must be done in conjunction with a reasoned approach. Yes, there are certain people that are simply contrarian and they will resist any suggestion to change, but most workers are willing to make an effort if they understand why it is important; they need to see the value. It is one of the basic assumptions of this book that the key to achieving meaningful OR is to gain the support of the people in the organization through a continued educational effort connected to ORM. In essence, it is desirable to view this connection between education, culture, and establishing personal responsibility as establishing a moral imperative. The people in the organization must have a personal sense of responsibility for risk management. Because all the departments are interrelated within the organization, it is important for people within the organization to understand that their actions and inactions have implications. Each person can make a difference by becoming an active member of the organization's risk team. This is similar to the perspective that has been generated concerning sustainability or "green" initiatives (recycling, saving electricity, etc.) within organizations. It is so important that everyone must help achieve the goal of building organizational resilience.

The structure of the project team is an organizational issue and should be based on what works at a given organization. The members of the project team must build a cohesive group that is working toward

47

acknowledged goals. The people participating in the project will probably require focused training to gain the requisite understanding of ANSI/ASIS SPC.1-2009, how to perform the Gap Analysis, and how to complete the risk assessment to contribute to the project.

The project team is likely to face the challenge of gaining acceptance and willing involvement of participants. The project team will not be able to complete the project without the assistance of the members of the organization. This is not an item for debate, but an absolute that must be recognized early in the project. Achieving OR is based on building ORM within the organization and the members of the organization are the ones that actually know the processes, do the work, and interact with practices and activities that involve risk. These people are the best first line of defense against negative outcomes of risk as well as identifying opportunities to exploit risk for positive outcomes. Gaining their support and willing participation will be one of the greatest achievements of the project because their involvement and interest will have a long-reaching influence beyond their particular involvement in the project. It is at this early stage you will be able to begin to build the desired culture of risk management within the organization.

The members of the organization, when viewed as an aggregate, actually constitute the organization and are the ones that achieve the goals necessary to create success; in essence, the people, through their actions and involvement, are the organization. The personnel working throughout the organization are the most knowledgeable and the most involved with respect to routine functions, processes, and risks. While the leaders manage and provide the resources needed to accomplish desired goals, the subordinate staff actually knows in detail how things happen within the organization. They are the most involved in every aspect of the business. Any desired change within the organization requires the involvement of the members in planning and implementation. Gaining the support of the people throughout the company, division, or department is necessary for achieving success in any OR effort.

It is advisable to develop a strategy to gain the assistance of the organizational members that involves an earnest request for help, a good explanation as to the actual value of participation in the OR effort, and reasonable incentives for assistance. Developing the desired support will require active and committed involvement by members of the organization. The commitment of those involved is critical to maintaining the energy necessary for the continued momentum of the OR effort. Never forget, ORM is about people, not pieces of paper or certifications, therefore, a successful approach is calibrated to the culture of the organization and its people, with ongoing feedback loops to reinforce the value to them of their involvement. Along with the discussion and explanation of the implementation project, it will be important that all personnel understand the reasons for the project, the benefits of going through the efforts of the project to the organization, and the personal benefits that each person may expect to realize. The continued success and operation of the organization is something that personnel should understand as a personal benefit. Because the goal of OR is to increase the resilience of the organization through managing risk, it is important to connect the monetary success of the organization to the monetary success of the individual. However, it is extremely important to ensure that the strategy of the project involves more than just providing money as a reward. Money only generates a desired interest to a certain point, but it is a great way to show the appreciation of management. Building friendly rivalry between the various subunits of the organization is a great way to create routine involvement of the personnel in the risk activities. The competition for achievement allows for the recognition of the "winners," and demonstrates the value of making the effort toward success, but ensures the continued commitment of personnel in ORM. Award certificates are a great way to indicate success, commitment, and the sincere appreciation of the senior managers. However, this really needs to be sincere commitment on the part of the senior managers to truly be effective. Subordinates will know if there is any insincerity on the part of the senior managers.

Building the involvement of all personnel into the culture of the organization is both highly beneficial and necessary to effective risk management. This effort will take time to become part of the culture and values of the organization. Real, sustained cultural change is never fast.

INITIATING THE PROJECT

It is advisable to decide in the beginning between a comprehensive and an incremental approach for the project. A comprehensive approach should be obvious from the name: a complete implementation of the standard involving all elements and requirements for the entire organization. This approach is likely to be very complex, resource intensive, and time consuming. It may be quite a long time before you see the light at the end of the tunnel. The time needed to produce results may become a practical concern, akin to sinking money into an endless well; projects are usually expected to produce results in the near-term. People will need to see demonstrable results to keep the effort going. The advantage of a comprehensive approach is that you have an opportunity to review everything involved in the project at one time and develop a comprehensive plan showing the interdependencies and various issues of the plan. While a comprehensive approach may appear to provide a great degree of control over all the issues and provide an opportunity to plan everything out from the beginning through the end of the project, the real world simply does not operate this way. It is rare that you will be able to have the necessary resources to develop and achieve the goals of the project—it is too large and too complex an effort. A typical organization will not be able to invest the time, money, and staff hours to effectively implement a project attempting to achieve all of the aforementioned requirements as will be discussed later in Exhibits 4.4 through 4.9.

The incremental approach is the more typical method for implementing this sort of project. It is possible to create a project plan that sectionalizes the requirements into phases, thereby allowing for a more manageable means of achieving the project goals. The incremental approach will provide the project team with the ability to carefully move through the listed ANSI/ASIS SPC.1-2009 requirements as individual projects (each requirement is a project or a phase of a project) or small collections of requirements formed into projects. This provides a great deal of control and economy in the implementation of a complex, organization intensive project. In accordance with the incremental design, the project could be limited to a particular business unit, division, product line, or facility/campus. The incremental approach to project management is normally the easiest and most manageable in a complex organization. While this incremental approach certainly is acceptable and quite common, it is suggested that a maturity model be applied to the organization to establish a better understanding of where the various risk interests are on a continuum. A maturity model is an assessment tool that allows for the establishment of a benchmark of the organization's resilience (ANSI/ASIS.SPC.4-2012, p. ix). Through the use of a maturity model, the project team shall clearly understand where the organization stands with respect to resilience, what needs to be done to increase the level of resilience, and a means of developing a more realistic project plan to implement ORM. The maturity model can be used to compare the ANSI/ASIS SPC.1-2009 Standard against the currently implemented preparedness-oriented measures (e.g., security plans and procedures, life-safety preparations, Business Continuity Planning/ Disaster preparations, etc.) within the organization.

The maturity model allows for the selection of smaller, more achievable goals that result in the completion of the selected goals. With each completed goal, a part of the larger puzzle is put together and provides for the demonstrated value of each successful goal. The result is that senior managers are able to see that the planned project is a success and see the value of that success. Success fosters the opportunity for continued success. The relationship between cost and benefit of a project is basically what results in more approved projects. It is recommended that an organization select the maturity model to implement ORM. Selecting an incremental approach should not be viewed as settling for less; rather, it is a valuable and wise decision. Achieving ORM is not something that is done quickly. Because many organizations have limited resources, an incremental strategy to implementation allows for a more cost-effective and smooth path to reach full implementation, which includes constant reminders of the value of ORM. Another good reason for incrementally implementing ORM is that conditions are likely to change as the various pieces of the puzzle are successfully achieved. This approach allows for a more meaningful and effective reaction to those changes. Acknowledgement of as many issues as possible is advisable, but planned in such a way to maximize efficiency and value. Remember, the implementation of OR in an organization may require, and likely for the average organization, a change of the culture. This change should be expected and planned for so that it may be shown as a successful, key aspect of the process—real, positive change can't happen without cultural change.

DETERMINING YOUR LEVEL
OF MATURITY: GAPS ANALYSIS

A necessary part of the implementation of ORM is a gap analysis of where your organization is at and what you need to do to reach your goals. A typical organization will have many risk-oriented preparations in place (e.g., security plans, business continuity plans, disaster recovery plans, crisis management plans, etc.). Implementing ORM does not mean discarding existing plans and preparations. You will be able to take advantage of prior work efforts, and where necessary, make improvements (including eliminating silos to increase efficiency). Before you panic, look at the main elements of the standard—the pieces of the puzzle. Most organizations will have many of the pieces. The main task will be to understand how the pieces fit together to see the entire picture.

Using the requirements of the ANSI/ASIS SPC.1-2009 Standard, it is possible to develop a simple assessment matrix to determine what elements of the standard the organization already has in place and what needs to be improved to be in conformance with the standard. An example would be Exhibit 4.2.

For each of the elements and requirements of the standard, an evaluation is made to determine if the element and requirements exist, what is the evidence and documentation supporting their existence, and are they in conformance with the standard's requirements. This approach will give a good estimate as to where the organization is with regard to conformance to the standard and how much effort is needed to become fully conformant. This is essentially an audit form, which can be used for assessing the conformance to the standard at any level of maturity.

Criteria	Evidence	Documentation	Findings (Conformance or Opportunity for Improvement)				Conclusions
			Non = 0	Partial = 1	Full = 2	Opportunity for Improvement	
4.X. Clause in Standard "Element"							
Requirement ("shall" statement)							
Requirement ("shall" statement)							
Requirement ("shall" statement)							
Requirement ("shall" statement)							

Exhibit 4.2 Conformance assessment matrix.

To develop a plan of action for improving the ORM in the organization, the matrix in Exhibit 4.3 is very helpful in identifying the actions needed as well as the stakeholders and resources needed to improve ORM.

This analysis is conducted in conjunction with the risk assessment and impact analysis to gain a more complete understanding of the organization. The ISO 31000 provides a process for conducting the risk assessment. The keys to conducting a good gap analysis risk assessment are understanding the context of the organization, identifying potential sources of risk (particularly threats), understanding criticalities (critical activities and the impact of an event on them), and identifying existing risk treatment measures and their vulnerabilities. The actual ordering of these assessment processes is dependent upon the organization. Obviously, it makes sense to conduct the planning of the assessments prior to conducting actual assessments, but the ordering of analyses is a decision based on the resources of a given organization. The important thing is to do all the analyses and understand the interplays between the treatment, criticality, and vulnerability analyses. The gap analysis may also precede or follow the other assessments as dictated by the circumstances of the organization. For example, conducting the gap analysis in conjunction with a business management SWOT analysis (strengths, weaknesses, opportunities, and threats) is an effective approach. The gap analysis is likely to discover critical information pertaining to existing documents and practices and influence decisions concerning immediate risk treatment efforts. Also, the gap analysis is not a single, discrete event, but rather an ongoing process can be done more than once, as more information becomes available. Remember, our discussion is centered on a process, and the very nature of a process is that there is movement between elements; in this case, we are looking at a cycle of events that can be repeated as often as necessary.

Simplicity is highly desirable when viewing an organization because it tends to make things clear for everyone involved in the project. It is very important to show an accurate picture of the organization. Hiding "bad" news does not help the project and it will become evident when the documentation is required for review.

Element for Review	Current Status of Conformance	Relevant Stakeholders	Associated Risks	Risk Owner	Existing Risk Treatments Method	Actions Needed	Resources Needed	Time-frame	Conclusions (Priority)
Clause in Standard "Element"									
Subclause in Standard "Sub-Element"									
Subclause in Standard "Sub-Element									

Exhibit 4.3 Conformance assessment matrix: Improvements.

TAILORING IMPLEMENTATION TO REALITY

The earlier sections discussed the importance and desirability of an incremental approach to the project plan, along with the necessity of performing an analysis of current (existing) documentation against the requirements contained within ANSI/ASIS SPC.1-2009. With the knowledge gathered from the gap analysis, the project team is able to more effectively determine what needs to be done to achieve conformance with the Standard. This information will allow the organizational leaders to identify and decide on the most important risks to address. In essence, the team has established its priorities with respect to the risks facing the organization and the areas of preparation that need attention to ensure a proper protective organizational stance. Thus far, we have identified the requirements indicated in ANSI/ASIS SPC.1-2009 along with the various issues surrounding ORM implementation, but have yet to actually discuss the implementation requirements. The requirements for implementation, to follow the requirements for conformance with the ANSI/ASIS SPC.1-2009 Standard, are based on several considerations that are dependent on the specific organization and the desired level attainment with the maturity model. A significant point to remember about ANSI/ASIS SPC.1-2009 involves the ability of the user to determine how to implement the requirements. The Standard indicates the topical items (elements) that are necessary for conformance, but leaves the implementation method and details to the organization. This is extremely important because each organization is different and, to a certain extent, unique. Each organization may have a different way to implement the requirements.

Each implementation requirement indicated below clearly identifies the necessary action for each relevant section element from ANSI/ASIS SPC.1-2009. These implementation requirements should be followed in accordance with the established plan for the organization. Every organization is unique; therefore, every implementation of the requirements of the standard is a tailor-made approach. The only "best approach" is the one that drives cultural change in your organization and that makes the best use of available resources. Decisions on the approach to implementation and the pace should be based on making participants feel they are part of the team which is creating value for the organization, and making their jobs more efficient and safe. Based on the implementation requirements indicated in Exhibits 4.4 to 4.9, you should be able to make the determination in accordance with your organization's needs.

Primary Requirements for Standard	Subordinate Requirement Items	Section #	Requirement Items 4.1
Know Your Organization	Define scope and boundaries for preparedness, response, continuity and recovery management program	4.1.1	• The scope of the ORM project under discussion—entire organization or a part thereof, along with developing a perspective of continual improvement. Determine what is necessary for ORM based on the mission, goals, obligations and responsibilities of the organization.
	Identify critical objectives, operations, functions, products and services	4.1.1	• Consider critical objectives, operations, functions, products and services
	Preliminary determination of likely risk scenarios and consequences	4.1.1	• Determine risk scenarios based both on potential internal and external events that could adversely affect the critical operations and functions of the organization within the context of their potential impact.

Source: ANSI/ASIS SPC.1-2009, page 5

Exhibit 4.4 ANSI/ASIS SPC.1-2009 Standard implementation requirements.

Primary Requirements for Standard	Subordinate Requirement Items	Section #	Requirement Items 4.2
Policy		4.2.1	• Is appropriate to the nature and scale of potential threats, hazards, risks, and impacts (consequences) to the organization's activities, functions, products, and services (including stakeholders and the environment).
			• Includes a commitment to employee and community life safety as the first priority.
			• Includes a commitment to continual improvement.
			• Includes a commitment to enhanced organizational sustainability and resilience.
			• Includes a commitment to risk prevention, reduction, and mitigation.
			• Includes a commitment to comply with applicable legal requirements and with other requirements to which the organization subscribes.
			• Provides a framework for setting and reviewing OR management objectives and targets.
			• Is documented, implemented, and maintained.
			• Makes reference to limitations and exclusions.
			• Determines and documents the risk tolerance in relation to the scope of the management system.

Exhibit 4.5 ANSI/ASIS SPC.1-2009 Standard implementation requirements. (continued)

57

Primary Requirements for Standard	Subordinate Requirement Items	Section #	Requirement Items 4.2
			• Is communicated to all appropriate persons working for or on behalf of the organization.
			• Is available to relevant stakeholders.
			• Includes a designated policy ownership and/or responsible point of contact.
			• Is reviewed at planned intervals and when significant changes occur.
			• Is signed by top management and a documented review of the policy relevancy is conducted annually.
	Management commitment	4.2.2	• Establishing an OR management system policy;
			• Ensuring that OR management system objectives and plans are established;
			• Establishing roles, responsibilities, and competencies for OR management;
			• Appointing one or more persons to be responsible for the OR management system with the appropriate authority and competencies to be accountable for the implementation and maintenance of the management system;

Exhibit 4.5 (continued) ANSI/ASIS SPC.1-2009 Standard implementation requirements. (continued)

Primary Requirements for Standard	Subordinate Requirement Items	Section #	Requirement Items 4.2
			• Communicating to the organization the importance of meeting OR management objectives and conforming to OR management system policy, its responsibilities under the law, and the need for continual improvement;
			• Providing sufficient resources to establish, implement, operate, monitor, review, maintain, and improve the OR management system;
			• Deciding the criteria for accepting risks and the acceptable levels of risk;
			• Ensuring that internal OR management system audits are conducted;
			• Conducting management reviews of the OR management system; and
			• Demonstrates its commitment to continual improvement.
	Commitment to protection of critical assets and continuous improvement	4.2.2	• Identify critical assets and develop strategy to provide appropriate protection and continual improvement to protective measures.
	Commitment of resources	4.2.2	• Established management commitment to provide appropriate resources to achieve stated goals.

Source: ANSI/ASIS SPC.1-2009, page 6-7

Exhibit 4.5 (continued) ANSI/ASIS SPC.1-2009 Standard implementation requirements.

Primary Requirements for Standard	Subordinate Requirement Items	Section #	Requirement Items 4.3
Planning		4.3	• The organization shall define the scope consistent with protecting and preserving the integrity of the organization and its relationships with stakeholders, including interactions with key suppliers, outsourcing partners, and other stakeholders (for example, the organization's supply chain partners and suppliers, customers, stockholders, the community in which it operates, etc.).
	Risk Assessment and impact analysis	4.3.1	• To systematically conduct asset identification and valuation to identify the organization's critical activities, functions, services, products, partnerships, supply chains, stakeholder relationships, and the potential impact related to a disruptive incident based on risk scenarios; • To identify intentional, unintentional, and naturally-caused hazards and threats that have a potential for direct or indirect impact on the organization's operations, functions, and human, intangible, and physical assets; the environment; and its stakeholders;

Exhibit 4.6 ANSI/ASIS SPC.1-2009 Standard implementation requirements. (continued)

60

Primary Requirements for Standard	Subordinate Requirement Items	Section #	Requirement Items 4.3
			• To systematically analyze risk, vulnerability, criticality, and impacts (consequences);
			• To systematically analyze and prioritize risk controls and treatments and their related costs;
			• To determine those risks that have a significant impact on activities, functions, services, products, stakeholder relationships, and the environment (i.e., significant risks and impacts).
		4.3.1	• Document and keep this information up to date and confidential, as is appropriate;
			• Re-evaluate risk and impacts within the context of changes within the organization or made to the organization's operating environment, procedures, functions, services, partnerships, and supply chains;
			• Establish recovery time objectives and priorities;
			• Evaluate the direct and indirect benefits and costs of options to reduce risk and enhance sustainability and resilience; and,

Exhibit 4.6 (continued)   ANSI/ASIS SPC.1-2009 Standard implementation requirements. (continued)

Primary Requirements for Standard	Subordinate Requirement Items	Section #	Requirement Items 4.3
			• Ensure that the significant risks and impacts are taken into account in establishing, implementing, and operating its OR management system.
	Legal and other requirements	4.3.2	• To identify legal, regulatory, and other requirements to which the organization subscribes related to the organization's hazards, threats, and risks that are related to its facilities, activities, functions, products, services, supply chain, the environment, and stakeholders. • To determine how these requirements apply to its hazards, threats, risks and their potential impacts.
	Objectives and targets	4.3.3	• The objectives and targets shall be measurable qualitatively and/or quantitatively, and consistent with the OR management policy, including the commitments to: • Risk prevention, reduction, and mitigation; • Resilience enhancement; • Financial, operational and business continuity requirements (including continuity of the workforce);

Exhibit 4.6 (continued)   ANSI/ASIS SPC.1-2009 Standard implementation requirements. (continued)

Primary Requirements for Standard	Subordinate Requirement Items	Section #	Requirement Items 4.3
			• Compliance with legal and other requirements; and • Continual improvement.
	Strategic prevention, preparedness and response programs (before, during and after and incident)	4.3.3	• The organization shall establish and maintain one or more strategic program(s) for achieving its objectives and targets. The program(s) shall include: • Designation of responsibility and resources for achieving objectives and targets at relevant functions and levels of the organization; • Consideration of its activities, functions, regulatory or legal requirements, contractual obligations, stakeholders' needs, mutual aid agreements, and environment; and • The means and time frame by which they are to be achieved. • The organization shall establish and maintain one or more strategic program(s) for: • Prevention and deterrence—Avoid, eliminate, deter, or prevent the likelihood of a disruptive incident and its consequences, including removal of human or physical assets at risk.

Exhibit 4.6 (continued) ANSI/ASIS SPC.1-2009 Standard implementation requirements. (continued)

63

Primary Requirements for Standard	Subordinate Requirement Items	Section #	Requirement Items 4.3
			• Mitigation—Minimize the impact of a disruptive incident.
			• Emergency response—The initial response to a disruptive incident involving the protection of people and property from immediate harm. An initial reaction by management may form part of the organization's first response.
			• Continuity—Processes, controls, and resources are made available to ensure that the organization continues to meet its critical operational objectives.
			• Recovery—Processes, resources, and capabilities of the organization are re-established to meet ongoing operational requirements within the time period specified in the objectives.

Source: ANSI/ASIS SPC.1-2009, page 7-9

Exhibit 4.6 (continued) ANSI/ASIS SPC.1-2009 Standard implementation requirements.

Primary Requirements for Standard	Subordinate Requirement Items	Section #	Requirement Items 4.4
Implementation and Operation		4.4	• Management shall ensure the availability of resources essential for the implementation and control of the OR management system. Resources include human resources and specialized skills, equipment, internal infrastructure, technology, information, intelligence, and financial resources. Roles, responsibilities, and authorities shall be defined, documented, and communicated in order to facilitate effective OR management.
	Structure and responsibility	4.4.1	• The organization's top management shall appoint (a) specific management representative(s) who, irrespective of other responsibilities, shall have defined roles, responsibilities, and authority for: • Ensuring that an OR management system is established, communicated, implemented, and maintained in accordance with the requirements of this Standard; and • Reporting on the performance of the OR management system to top management for review and as the basis for improvement.

Exhibit 4.7   ANSI/ASIS SPC.1-2009 Standard implementation requirements. (continued)

65

Primary Requirements for Standard	Subordinate Requirement Items	Section #	Requirement Items 4.4
		4.4.1	• The organization shall establish: • An OR management team with appropriate authority to oversee incident preparedness, response, and recovery; • Logistical capabilities and procedures to locate, acquire, store, distribute, maintain, test, and account for services, personnel, resources, materials, and facilities produced or donated to support the OR management system; • Resource management objectives for response times, personnel, equipment, training, facilities, funding, insurance, liability control, expert knowledge, materials, and the time frames within which they will be needed from organization's resources and from any partner entities; and • Procedures for stakeholder assistance, communications, strategic alliances, and mutual aid
		4.4.1	• The organization shall develop financial and administrative procedures to support the OR management program before, during, and after an incident. Procedures shall be:

Exhibit 4.7 (continued)   ANSI/ASIS SPC.1-2009 Standard implementation requirements. (continued)

Primary Requirements for Standard	Subordinate Requirement Items	Section #	Requirement Items 4.4
			• Established to ensure that fiscal decisions can be expedited; and • In accordance with established authority levels and accounting principles.
	Training, awareness, competence	4.4.2	• The organization shall ensure that any person(s) performing tasks who have the potential to prevent, cause, respond to, mitigate, or be affected by significant hazards, threats, and risks are competent (on the basis of appropriate education, training, or experience) and retain associated records. • The organization shall establish, implement, and maintain (a) procedure(s) to ensure persons working for it or on its behalf are aware of: • The significant hazards, threats, and risks, and related actual or potential impacts, associated with their work and the benefits of improved personal performance; • The procedures for incident prevention, deterrence, mitigation, self-protection, evacuation, response, continuity, and recovery;

Exhibit 4.7 (continued) ANSI/ASIS SPC.1-2009 Standard implementation requirements. (continued)

67

Primary Requirements for Standard	Subordinate Requirement Items	Section #	Requirement Items 4.4
			• The importance of conformity with the OR management policy and procedures and with the requirements of the OR management system; • Their roles and responsibilities in achieving conformity with the requirements of the OR management system; • The potential consequences of departure from specified procedures; and • The benefits of improved personal performance.
	Communication	4.4.3	• The organization shall build, promote, and embed an OR management culture within the organization that: • Ensures the OR management culture becomes part of the organization's core values and organization governance; and • Makes stakeholders aware of the OR management policy and their role in any plans. • Documenting, recording, and communicating changes in documentation, plans, procedures, the management system, and results of evaluations and reviews; • Internal communication between the various levels and functions of the organization;

Exhibit 4.7 (continued)   ANSI/ASIS SPC.1-2009 Standard implementation requirements. (continued)

Primary Requirements for Standard	Subordinate Requirement Items	Section #	Requirement Items 4.4
			• External communication with partner entities and other stakeholders;
			• Receiving, documenting, and responding to communication from external stakeholders;
			• Adapting and integrating a national or regional risk or threat advisory system or equivalent into planning and operational use;
			• Alerting stakeholders potentially impacted by an actual or impending disruptive incident;
			• Assuring availability of the means of communication during a crisis situation and disruption;
			• Facilitating structured communication with emergency responders;
			• Assuring the interoperability of multiple responding organizations and personnel;
			• Recording of vital information about the incident, actions taken, and decisions made; and
			• Operations of a communications facility.
	Documentation	4.4.4	• The OR management system documentation shall include:
			• The OR management policy, objectives, and targets;
			• Description of the scope of the OR management system;

Exhibit 4.7 (continued)   ANSI/ASIS SPC.1-2009 Standard implementation requirements. (continued)

69

Primary Requirements for Standard	Subordinate Requirement Items	Section #	Requirement Items 4.4
			• Description of the main elements of the OR management system and their integration with related documents;
			• Documents, including records, required by this Standard; and
			• Documents, including records, determined by the organization to be necessary to ensure the effective planning, operation, and control of processes that relate to its significant risks
	Document control	4.4.5	• The organization shall establish, implement, and maintain (a) procedure(s) to:
			• Approve documents for adequacy prior to issue;
			• Review, update and re-approve documents as necessary;
			• Ensure that changes and the current revision status of documents are identified;
			• Ensure that relevant versions of applicable documents are available at points of use;
			• Establish document retention and archival parameters;
			• Ensure that original and archival copies of documents, data, and information remain legible and readily identifiable;

Exhibit 4.7 (continued)   ANSI/ASIS SPC.1-2009 Standard implementation requirements. (continued)

Primary Requirements for Standard	Subordinate Requirement Items	Section #	Requirement Items 4.4
			• Ensure that documents of external origin determined by the organization to be necessary for the planning and operation of the OR management system are identified and their distribution controlled; • Identify as obsolete all out-of-date documents that the organization is required to retain; and • Ensure the integrity of the documents by ensuring they are tamperproof, securely backed-up, accessible only to authorized personnel, and protected from damage, deterioration, or loss.
	Operational control	4.4.6	• The organization shall identify and plan those operations that are associated with the identified significant risks and consistent with its ORM policy, risk assessment, impact analysis, objectives, and targets, in order to ensure that they are carried out under specified conditions, by:

Exhibit 4.7 (continued)   ANSI/ASIS SPC.1-2009 Standard implementation requirements. (continued)

Primary Requirements for Standard	Subordinate Requirement Items	Section #	Requirement Items 4.4
			• Establishing, implementing, and maintaining procedures related to the identified hazards, threats and risks to the activities, functions, products, and services of the organization and communicating applicable procedures and requirements to suppliers (including contractors);
			• Establishing, implementing, and maintaining (a) documented procedure(s) to control situations where their absence could lead to deviation from the ORM policy, objectives, and targets; and
			• Stipulating the operating criteria in the documented procedures.
			• The operational control procedures shall address reliability and resiliency, the safety and health of people, and the protection of property and the environment impacted by a disruptive incident.

Exhibit 4.7 (continued)   ANSI/ASIS SPC.1-2009 Standard implementation requirements. (continued)

Primary Requirements for Standard	Subordinate Requirement Items	Section #	Requirement Items 4.4
	Incident prevention, preparedness and response	4.4.7	• The organization shall establish, implement, and maintain (a) procedure(s) to identify potential disruptive incidents that can have (an) impact(s) on the organization, its activities, functions, services, stakeholders, and the environment. The procedure(s) shall document how the organization will prevent, prepare for, and respond to them. The organization shall prepare for and respond to actual disruptive incidents to prevent or mitigate associated adverse consequences.
		4.4.7	• When establishing, implementing, and maintaining (a) procedure(s) to prepare for and respond to a disruptive incident expeditiously, the organization should consider each of the following actions: • Preserve life safety; • Protect assets; • Prevent further escalation of the disruptive incident; • Reduce the length of the disruption to operations; • Restore critical operational continuity;

Exhibit 4.7 (continued) ANSI/ASIS SPC.1-2009 Standard implementation requirements. (continued)

Primary Requirements for Standard	Subordinate Requirement Items	Section #	Requirement Items 4.4
			• Recover normal operations (including evaluating improvements); and
			• Protect image and reputation (including media coverage and stakeholder relationships).
		4.4.7	• It is the responsibility of the organization to develop (an) incident prevention, preparedness and response procedure(s) that suits its particular needs. In developing its procedure(s), the organization should address its needs with regard to:
			• The nature of onsite hazards (e.g., ammable and toxic materials, storage tanks and compressed gases) and measures to be taken in the event of a disruptive incident or accidental releases;
			• The nature of local, nearby, or other external hazards with a potential impact on the organization;
			• The most likely type and scale of a disruptive incident;
			• The most appropriate method(s) for mitigation and emergency response to a disruptive incident to avoid escalation to a crisis or disaster;

Exhibit 4.7 (continued) ANSI/ASIS SPC.1-2009 Standard implementation requirements. (continued)

Primary Requirements for Standard	Subordinate Requirement Items	Section #	Requirement Items 4.4
			• Procedures to prevent environmental damage,
			• Command and control procedures for and structure of pre-defined chain of command, (an) emergency operations center(s), and/or (an) alternate worksite(s);
			• Procedures and authority to declare an emergency situation, initiate emergency procedures, activate plans and actions, assess damage, and make nancial decisions;
			• Internal and external communication plans including notication of appropriate authorities and stakeholders.
			• Procedures to acquire and/or provide appropriate medical care;
			• The action(s) required to minimize human casualties, and physical and environmental damage;
			• The action(s) required to secure vital information, information systems, facilities, and people;
			• Mitigation and response action(s) to be taken for different types of disruptive incident(s) or emergency situation(s);

Exhibit 4.7 (continued)   ANSI/ASIS SPC.1-2009 Standard implementation requirements. (continued)

Primary Requirements for Standard	Subordinate Requirement Items	Section #	Requirement Items 4.4
			• The need for (a) process(es) for post-event evaluation to establish and implement corrective and preventive actions;
			• Periodic testing of incident and emergency management and response procedure(s) and processes;
			• Training of incident and emergency response personnel;
			• A list of key personnel and aid agencies, including contact details (e.g., re department, emergency medical services, law enforcement, hazardous material clean-up services);
			• Evacuation routes and assembly points including lists of personnel and contact details;
			• The potential for (a) disruptive incident or emergency situation(s) to affect or be affected by critical infrastructure (e.g., electricity, water, communications, transportation);
			• The possibility of mutual assistance to and from neighboring organizations; and

Exhibit 4.7 (continued)   ANSI/ASIS SPC.1-2009 Standard implementation requirements. (continued)

Primary Requirements for Standard	Subordinate Requirement Items	Section #	Requirement Items 4.4
			• Procedure(s) and action(s) required to recover each critical activity within the organization's recovery time objective and the resources that it requires for recovery.
		4.4.7	• The organization shall periodically review and, where necessary, revise its incident prevention, preparedness, and response procedures—in particular, after the occurrence of accidents or incidents that can escalate into an emergency, crisis, or disaster.

Source: ANSI/ASIS SPC.1-2009, page 8-13

Exhibit 4.7 (continued)   ANSI/ASIS SPC.1-2009 Standard implementation requirements.

Primary Requirements for Standard	Subordinate Requirement Items	Section #	Requirement Items 4.5
Checking and Corrective Action		4.5	• The organization shall evaluate OR management plans, procedures, and capabilities through periodic assessments, testing, post-incident reports, lessons learned, performance evaluations, and exercises. Significant changes in these factors should be reflected immediately in the procedures. • The organization shall keep records of the results of the periodic evaluations.
	Monitoring and measurement	4.5.1	• The organization shall establish, implement, and maintain performance metrics and (a) procedure(s) to monitor and measure, on a regular basis, those characteristics of its operations that have material impact on its performance (including partnership and supply chain relationships). The procedure(s) shall include the documenting of information to monitor performance, applicable operational controls, and conformity with the organization's OR management objectives and targets. • The organization shall evaluate and document the performance of the systems which protect its assets, as well as its communications and information systems.

Exhibit 4.8   ANSI/ASIS SPC.1-2009 Standard implementation requirements. (continued)

78

Primary Requirements for Standard	Subordinate Requirement Items	Section #	Requirement Items 4.5
	Evaluation of compliance	4.5.2.1	• The organization shall evaluate compliance with other requirements to which it subscribes including industry best practices. The organization may wish to combine this evaluation with the evaluation of legal compliance referred to above or to establish (a) separate procedure(s). The organization shall keep records of the results of the periodic evaluations.
	Exercise and testing	4.5.2.2	• The organization shall test and evaluate the appropriateness and efficacy of its OR management system, its programs, processes, and procedures (including partnership and supply chain relationships). • The organization shall validate its OR management system using exercises and testing that: • Are consistent with the scope of the OR management system and objectives of the organization; • Are based on realistic scenarios that are well planned with clearly defined aims and objectives; • Minimize the risk of disruption to operations and the potential to cause risk to operations and assets;

Exhibit 4.8 (continued) ANSI/ASIS SPC.1-2009 Standard implementation requirements. (continued)

Primary Requirements for Standard	Subordinate Requirement Items	Section #	Requirement Items 4.5
			• Produce a formalized postexercise report that contains outcomes, recommendations, and arrangements to implement improvements in a timely fashion;
			• Are reviewed within the context of promoting continual improvement; and
			• Are conducted at planned intervals, and from time to time on a non-periodic basis as determined by the management of the organization, as well as when significant changes occur within the organization and the environment it operates in.
	Nonconformity, corrective and preventive action	4.5.3	• The organization shall establish, implement, and maintain (a) procedure(s) for dealing with actual and potential nonconformity(ies) and for taking corrective action and preventive action. The procedure(s) shall define requirements for:
			• Identifying and correcting nonconformity(ies) and taking action(s) to mitigate their impacts;
			• Investigating nonconformity(ies), determining their cause(s), and taking actions in order to avoid their recurrence;

Exhibit 4.8 (continued)   ANSI/ASIS SPC.1-2009 Standard implementation requirements. (continued)

Primary Requirements for Standard	Subordinate Requirement Items	Section #	Requirement Items 4.5
			• Evaluating the need for action(s) to prevent nonconformity(ies) and implementing appropriate actions designed to avoid their occurrence; • Recording the results of corrective action(s) and preventive action(s) taken; and • Reviewing the effectiveness of corrective action(s) and preventive action(s) taken. • Actions taken shall be appropriate to the impact of the potential problems, and conducted in an expedited fashion. • The organization shall identify changed risks, and identify preventive action requirements focusing attention on significantly changed risks. • The priority of preventive actions shall be determined based on the results of the risk assessment and impact analysis. • The organization shall make any necessary changes to the OR management system documentation.
	Records	4.5.4	• The organization shall establish and maintain records to demonstrate conformity to the requirements of its OR management system and of this Standard and the results achieved.

Exhibit 4.8 (continued)   ANSI/ASIS SPC.1-2009 Standard implementation requirements. (continued)

81

Primary Requirements for Standard	Subordinate Requirement Items	Section #	Requirement Items 4.5
			• The organization shall establish, implement, and maintain (a) procedure(s) to protect the integrity of records including access to, identification, storage, protection, retrieval, retention, and disposal of records. • Records shall be and remain legible, identifiable, and traceable.
	Internal audits	4.5.5	• The organization shall conduct internal ORM system audits at planned intervals, and from time to time on a non-periodic basis (as determined by the management of the organization) to determine whether the control objectives, controls, processes, and procedures of its ORM system: • Conform to the requirements of this Standard and relevant legislation or regulations; • Conform to the organization's risk management requirements; • Are effectively implemented and maintained; and • Perform as expected.

Exhibit 4.8 (continued)   ANSI/ASIS SPC.1-2009 Standard implementation requirements. (continued)

Primary Requirements for Standard	Subordinate Requirement Items	Section #	Requirement Items 4.5
			• An audit program shall be planned, taking into consideration the status and importance of the processes and areas to be audited, as well as the results of previous audits. The audit criteria, scope, frequency, and methods shall be defined. The selection of auditors and conduct of audits shall ensure objectivity and impartiality of the audit process. Auditors shall not audit their own work.
			• The responsibilities and requirements for planning and conducting audits, and for reporting results and maintaining records, shall be defined in a documented procedure.
			• The management responsible for the area being audited shall ensure that actions are taken without undue delay to eliminate detected nonconformities and their causes. Follow-up activities shall include the verification of the actions taken and the reporting of verification results.

Source: ANSI/ASIS SPC.1-2009, page 14-16

Exhibit 4.8 (continued) ANSI/ASIS SPC.1-2009 Standard implementation requirements.

Primary Requirements for Standard	Subordinate Requirement Items	Section #	Requirement Items 4.6
Management Review		4.6.1	• Management shall review the organization's OR management system at planned intervals to ensure its continuing suitability, adequacy, and effectiveness. This review shall include assessing opportunities for improvement and the need for changes to the OR management system, including the OR management system policy and objectives. The results of the reviews shall be clearly documented and records shall be maintained.
	Review input	4.6.2	• The input to a management review shall include: • Results of ORM system audits and reviews; • Feedback from interested parties; • Techniques, products, or procedures that could be used in the organization to improve the ORM system performance and effectiveness; • Status of preventive and corrective actions; • Results of exercises and testing; • Vulnerabilities or threats not adequately addressed in the previous risk assessment; • Results from effectiveness measurements; • Follow-up actions from previous management reviews; • Any changes that could affect the ORM system; • Adequacy of policy and objectives; and

Exhibit 4.9 ANSI/ASIS SPC.1-2009 Standard implementation requirements. (continued)

Primary Requirements for Standard	Subordinate Requirement Items	Section #	Requirement Items 4.6
			• Recommendations for improvement.
	Review output	4.6.3	• The output from the management review shall include any decisions and actions related to the following:
			• Improvement of the effectiveness of the OR management system;
			• Update of the risk assessment, impact analysis, and incident preparedness and response plans;
			• Modification of procedures and controls that effect risks, as necessary, to respond to internal or external events that may impact on the OR management system, including changes to:
			• Business and operational requirements; Risk reduction and security requirements; Operational conditions processes effecting the existing operational requirements; Regulatory or legal requirements; Contractual obligations; and Levels of risk and/or criteria for accepting risks.
			• Resource needs; and
			• Improvement to how the effectiveness of controls is being measured.

Exhibit 4.9 (continued) ANSI/ASIS SPC.1-2009 Standard implementation requirements. (continued)

Primary Requirements for Standard	Subordinate Requirement Items	Section #	Requirement Items 4.6
	Maintenance	4.6.4	• Top management shall establish a defined and documented OR management system maintenance program to ensure that any internal or external changes that impact the organization are reviewed in relation to the OR management system. It shall identify any new critical activities that need to be included in the OR management system maintenance program.
Continual Improvement		4.6.5	• The organization shall continually improve the effectiveness of the OR management system through the use of the OR management policy, objectives, audit results, analysis of monitored events, corrective and preventive actions, and management review.

Source: ANSI/ASIS SPC.1-2009, page 16-17

Exhibit 4.9 (continued) ANSI/ASIS SPC.1-2009 Standard implementation requirements.

ESTABLISHING A RISK AND RESILIENCE MANAGEMENT PROGRAM

All organizations, and people, for that matter, manage risk and resilience, either planned or unplanned. ORM moves risk and resilience management away from an ad-hoc nature to a well-executed planned, integrated, and comprehensive approach. Therefore, all risk-oriented departments need to establish and maintain programs connected with the various plans that they use to address risk, keeping their eyes on the target of supporting the overarching objectives of the organization. A plan establishes the fundamentals of how to address the particular plan topic; the program establishes the structure to conduct the activities necessary to maintain the plan. The program allows a project to become routine, with goals, policies, and requirements to maintain the plan connected to the program. Plans that are not associated with a program are subject to irrelevancy; the plan becomes a bookend on a shelf and quickly outdated. Programs ensure the regular review, currency through a maintenance schedule, and are valued as an important part of the organization.

Programs and plans are dynamic and evolve with time, lessons learned, and an ever-changing environment. Mature risk and resilience management programs in an organization leverage all the disciplines that contribute to managing risk in order to achieve the organization's objectives. Many organizations have the building block of ORM, but legacy programs are typically reactive, siloed, and discipline specific. Your business continuity plans may be the domain of the business continuity management (BCM) manager, while the security plans are the purview of the security manager. There may be a disconnect and duplicity between the security and continuity plans. Part of evaluating the efficiency of the risk and resilience management program envisioned in the ANSI/ASIS SPC.1-2009 is the consolidation of these plans into a comprehensive multidisciplinary approach. The objective is to efficiently address the array of risks the organization faces to better meet its objective. As stated above, it is not just about the plans, but about the planning.

Our discussions surrounding the goal of achieving OR has included building positive relationships with all risk stakeholders, increasing the holistic perspective of the stakeholders with respect to the interdependencies of risk issues within the organization, and the desirability of creating a culture of risk management through organizational resilience management. The value of the program is that it helps create a culture of risk management. It helps establish the importance of the subject within the

87

minds of employees and managers alike, and ensures that there is senior management governance.

Programs are reviewed for effectiveness and conformance with standards or requirements. Implementing the Standard is not a tick-box exercise. It is about effectiveness and the interrelationships between the standard's elements. Therefore, auditing the management of organizational resilience is crucial to both the conformance with the Standard, but also to establishing an expectation of an ongoing review of the OR program. Audits, as prescribed by the Standard, are used as a self-assessment tool to measure both conformance and effectiveness. The performance of the audit in connection with the project and the program is not necessarily complex. The development of an audit program surrounding ORM helps ensure the continuation of the OR goal, and fulfills a requirement of the Standard. The organization should use trained auditors (perhaps from its Internal Audit program) familiar with the audit procedure of the ISO 19001 standard for management system auditing. This way it will be possible to create a routine review of all components connected with ANSI/ASIS SPC.1-2009. To ensure impartiality and objectivity, those involved in the audit should not evaluate their own work. The audit should do a comparison between what is in place and what should be in place in accordance with the Standard. Keep in mind that the Standard explains *what* is required. The organization decides *how* to implement the requirement tailored to its needs. Determining the effectiveness of a plan is not the same as determining if there is plan. Therefore, the determination of the level of effectiveness of the items under review is incumbent upon the organization.

5

Implementing the ANSI/ ASIS.SPC.I Standard

RECOGNIZING THE TOOLS IN THE TOOLBOX

As explained in the previous chapter, most organizations have some type of risk and resilience management process in place, even if it is ad hoc in some cases. To manage risk effectively, you will need to make sure you have all the tools in your toolbox. How you arrange all the tools in your toolbox is largely a function of how you and your organization work and the organization's culture. The Standard will provide you a catalog of what you need in your toolbox. You will decide how you arrange these tools to effectively and efficiently meet your organization's needs within your business model.

When you begin implementing the ANSI/ASIS.SPC.1 Standard, you need to understand you are not simply following some simple formula where you can check boxes. This is no simple linear process; implementing a standard is a complicated iterative process where the interaction between the elements is as important as the elements themselves. You want to understand the parts as well as the whole. Are your continuity and security plans directly linked to your risk assessment, definition of targets, training and awareness programs, and communications programs? You may have the pieces of the puzzle, but do you understand how they fit together?

As you start the implementation of the ANSI/ASIS.SPC.1 Standard, you must keep in mind that you are not a security manager, a crisis manager, or a business continuity manager, but rather you are first and foremost a business manager. You are not managing risk and resilience as an end in itself; you are managing risk and resilience because it helps the organization achieve its objectives. The Exhibits 4.4 to 4.9 in Chapter 4 identify each requirement from ANSI/ASIS SPC.1-2009, by section, and the meaning of each element, so that anyone attempting to implement the standard can see the requirements in easy to digest portions. While these tables provide a concise listing of the requirements, implementation of this material is still a considerable undertaking and is provided in more detail in tabulated form in Exhibits 5.1 to 5.6. The requirements of the Standard must be considered in conjunction with the business needs of the organization. It is not the intent of this book to assume that blind adherence to the Standard is mandatory or desirable. The implementation of any aspect of ANSI/ASIS SPC.1-2009 must be justified through a business advantage (a need), not simply because the perception that a standard conformance certificate on the wall justifies the need. The development of the Standard was accomplished with that understanding in mind, and the details contained within the ANSI/ASIS SPC.1-2009 Standard are intended to benefit and protect the organization. The requirements within the Standard are general enough to be applicable to nearly any organization. While the requirements were developed to apply to all organizations, each requirement was carefully discussed and considered. This Standard contains essential best practices aimed at achieving the goal of organizational resilience through the implementation of an organizational resilience management system. Implementation decisions need to be based on sound business judgment—a best practice is what is best for the business.

The ANSI/ASIS SPC.1-2009 ORM (organizational resilience management) system flow diagram is an iterative, process-oriented approach to implementing the Standard. Although the flow diagram in the Standard depicts a simple cycle, in reality there is no start or finish or a truly cyclical process. All the elements interrelate and interact with each other, and each element itself can be viewed as an individual PDCA (Plan-Do-Check-Act) cycle. The topical elements of the standard are presented in the flow diagram as illustrated in Exhibit 3.3 and displayed here as bullet points (ANSI/ASIS SPC.1-2009, p. 4). Comments have been entered after certain items to provide further clarification:

Primary Requirements for Standard	Subordinate Requiremen Items	Section #	Implementation Guidance Section A.1
General Requirements		A.l	• The implementation of an organizational resilience (OR) management system specified by this Standard is intended to result in improved security, preparedness, response, continuity, and recovery performance. • Therefore, this Standard is based on the premise that the organization will periodically review and evaluate its OR management system to identify opportunities for improvement and their implementation.
	Define scope and boundaries for preparedness, response, continuity and recovery management program	A.l	• This Standard requires an organization to: • Establish an appropriate OR management policy; • Identify the hazards and threats related to the organization's past, existing, or planned activities, functions, products, and services to determine the risk, consequences, and impacts of significance; • Identify applicable legal requirements and other requirements to which the organization subscribes; • Identify priorities and set appropriate OR management objectives and targets • Establish a structure and (a) program (s) to implement the policy and achieve objectives and meet targets;

Exhibit 5.1   ASIS SPC.1-2009 Standard implementation guidance. (continued)

Primary Requirements for Standard	Subordinate Requiremen Items	Section #	Implementation Guidance Section A.1
			• Facilitate planning, control, monitoring, preventive and corrective action, and auditing and review activities to ensure both that the policy is complied with and that the OR management system remains appropriate; and • Be capable of adapting to changing circumstances.
	Identify critical objectives, operations, functions, products and services	A.1	• An organization with no existing OR management system should establish its current position with regard to its critical assets and potential risk scenarios by means of a review. • The review should cover four key areas: • Identification of risks, including those associated with normal operating conditions, abnormal conditions including start-up and shut-down, and emergency situations and accidents. • Identification of applicable legal requirements and other requirements to which the organization subscribes. • Examination of existing risk management practices and procedures, including those associated with procurement and contracting activities. • Evaluation of previous emergency situations and accidents. • The organization should define and document the scope of its OR management system.

Exhibit 5.1 (continued) ASIS SPC.1-2009 Standard implementation guidance. (continued)

Primary Requirements for Standard	Subordinate Requiremen Items	Section #	Implementation Guidance Section A.1
			• Scoping is intended to clarify the boundaries of the organization to which the OR management system will apply, especially if the organization is a part of a larger organization at a given location. • OR management involves issues and actions before, during, and after a disruptive incident. Therefore, this Standard encompasses prevention, avoidance, deterrence, readiness, mitigation, response, continuity, and recovery.

Source: ANSI/ASIS SPC.1-2009, page 20-21

Exhibit 5.1 (continued)   ASIS SPC.1-2009 Standard implementation guidance.

93

Primary Requirements for Standard	Subordinate Requirement Items	Section #	Implementation Guidance Section A.2
Policy	Management commitment	A.2	• This policy should therefore reflect the commitment of top management to: • Comply with applicable legal requirements and other requirements; • Prevention, preparedness, and mitigation of disruptive incidents; and • Continual improvement.
	Commitment to protection of critical assets and continuous improvement	A.2	• It is essential that top management of the organization sponsors, provides the necessary resources, and takes responsibility for creating, maintaining, testing, and implementing a comprehensive OR management system. This will insure that management and staff at all levels within the organization understand that the OR management system is a critical top management priority.

Source: ANSI/ASIS SPC.1-2009, page 21-22

Exhibit 5.2 ASIS SPC.1-2009 Standard implementation guidance.

Primary Requirements for Standard	Subordinate Requirement Items	Section #	Implementation Guidance Section A.3
Planning	Risk Assessment and impact analysis	A.3.1	• An organization should conduct a comprehensive risk assessment and impact analysis within the scope of its OR management system, taking into account the inputs and outputs (both intended and unintended) associated with: • Its current and relevant past activities, products, and services; • Planned or new developments, or new or modified activities, functions, products, and services; • Relations with stakeholders; • Interactions with the environment and community; and • Critical infrastructure.
		A.3.1	• The risk assessment and impact analysis should: • Give consideration to risks related to and criticality of the organization's activities, functions, products, and services and their potential for direct or indirect impact on the organization's operations, people, property, assets, compensation, image and reputation, prot, credit, and/or environment. • Use a documented quantitative or qualitative methodology to estimate likelihood or probability of the identified potential risks and significance of their impacts if they are realized. • Be based on reasonable criteria by giving due consideration to all potential risks it recognizes to its operations.

Exhibit 5.3   ASIS SPC.1-2009 Standard implementation guidance. (continued)

Primary Requirements for Standard	Subordinate Requirement Items	Section #	Implementation Guidance Section A.3
			• Consider its dependencies on others and others dependencies on the organization, including critical infrastructure and supply chain dependencies and obligations.
			• Consider data and telecommunications integrity and cyber security.
			• Evaluate the consequences of legal and other obligations which govern the organization's activities.
			• Consider risks associated with stakeholders, contractors, suppliers, and other affected parties.
			• Analyze information on risks, and select those risks which may cause significant consequences and/or those risks whose consequence is hard to be determined in terms of significance.
			• Analyze and evaluate the level of resilience of each hazard or threat and each critical asset.
			• Evaluate risks and impacts it can control and influence. (However, in all circumstances it is the organization that determines the degree of control and its strategies for risk acceptance, avoidance, management, minimization, tolerance transfer, and/or treatment.)
	Legal and other requirements	A.3.2	• The organization needs to identify the legal requirements that are applicable to activities and functions. These may include:

Exhibit 5.3 (continued) ASIS SPC.1-2009 Standard implementation guidance. (continued)

Primary Requirements for Standard	Subordinate Requirement Items	Section #	Implementation Guidance Section A.3
			• National and international legal requirements;
			• State/provincial/departmental legal requirements; and
			• Local governmental legal requirements.
			• Examples of other requirements to which the organization may subscribe include, if applicable:
			• Agreements with public authorities;
			• Agreements with customers;
			• Non-regulatory guidelines (e.g., Incident Command System/ Unified Command);
			• Voluntary principles or codes of practice;
			• Voluntary labeling or product stewardship commitments;
			• Requirements of trade associations;
			• Agreements with community groups or non-governmental organizations;
			• Public commitments of the organizationor its parent organization; and/or
			• Corporate/company
	Objectives and targets	A.3.3	• The objectives and targets should be specific and measurable wherever practicable. They should cover short- and long-term issues. Programs should define the strategic means for achieving objectives and targets.

Exhibit 5.3 (continued) ASIS SPC.1-2009 Standard implementation guidance. (continued)

97

Primary Requirements for Standard	Subordinate Requirement Items	Section #	Implementation Guidance Section A.3
			• The creation and use of one or more programs is important to the successful implementation of an OR management system. Each program should describe how the organization's objectives and targets will be achieved, including timescales, necessary resources, and personnel responsible for implementing the program(s). • The program should include, where appropriate and practical, consideration of all stages of an organization's activities and functions....
		A.3.3	• Prevention, preparedness, and mitigation programs should consider removal of people and property at risk; relocation, retrofting, and provision of protective systems or equipment; information, data, document, and cyber security; establishment of threat or hazard warning and communication procedures; and redundancy or duplication of essential personnel, critical systems, equipment, information, operations, or materials, including those from partner agencies. • The organization should plan for incident response and recovery, ... there are three generic and interrelated management response steps that require preemptive planning and implementation in case of a disruptive incident:

Exhibit 5.3 (continued)   ASIS SPC.1-2009 Standard implementation guidance. (continued)

Primary Requirements for Standard	Subordinate Requirement Items	Section #	Implementation Guidance Section A.3
			• Emergency response: The initial response to a disruptive incident usually involves the protection of people and property from immediate harm.
			• Continuity: Processes, controls, and resources are made available to ensure that the organization continues to meet its critical operational objectives.
			• Recovery: Processes, resources, and capabilities of the organization are re-established to meet ongoing operational requirements.

Source: ANSI/ASIS SPC.1-2009, page 22-26

Exhibit 5.3 (continued) ASIS SPC.1-2009 Standard implementation guidance.

Primary Requirements for Standard	Subordinate Requirement Items	Section #	Implementation Guidance Section A.4
Implementation and Operation		A.4	• The successful implementation of an OR management system calls for a commitment from all persons working for the organization or on its behalf. Roles and responsibilities therefore should not be seen as confined to the risk management function, but can also cover other areas of an organization, such as operational management or staff functions other than risk management, security, preparedness, continuity, and response.
	Structure and responsibility	A.4.1	• … top management should establish the organization's OR management policy, and ensure that the OR management system is implemented. As part of this commitment, the top management should designate (a) specific management representative(s) with defined responsibility and authority for implementing the OR management system. • It is necessary that an appropriate administrative structure be put in place to effectively deal with crisis management during a disruptive incident. An organization should have a Crisis Management Team to lead incident/event response. • The Crisis Management Team may be supported by as many Response Teams as appropriate.… • Management should also ensure that appropriate resources are provided to ensure that the OR management system is established, implemented, and maintained.

Exhibit 5.4 ASIS SPC.1-2009 Standard implementation guidance. (continued)

Primary Requirements for Standard	Subordinate Requirement Items	Section #	Implementation Guidance Section A.4
			• Roles, responsibilities, and authorities should also be defined, documented and communicated for coordination with external stakeholders.
	Training, awareness, competence	A.4.2	• The organization should identify the awareness, knowledge, understanding, and skills needed by any person with the responsibility and authority to perform tasks on its behalf.
			• This Standard states that:
			• The importance of conformity with the OR management policy and procedures and with the requirements of the OR management system;
			• The significant hazards, threats, and risks, and related actual or potential impacts, associated with their work and the benefits of improved personal performance;
			• Their roles and responsibilities needed to achieve conformity with the requirements of the OR management system;
			• The procedures for incident prevention, deterrence, mitigation, self-protection, evacuation, response, and recovery; and
			• The potential consequences of departure from specified procedures.
		A.4.2	• Awareness and education programs should be established for internal and external stakeholders potentially impacted by a disruptive incident.

Exhibit 5.4 (continued)   ASIS SPC.1-2009 Standard implementation guidance. (continued)

Primary Requirements for Standard	Subordinate Requirement Items	Section #	Implementation Guidance Section A.4
			• Management should determine the level of experience, competence, and training necessary to ensure the capability of personnel, especially those carrying out specialized OR management functions.
			• All personnel should be trained to perform their individual responsibilities in case of a disruptive incident or crisis.
			• The Crisis Management and Response Teams should be educated about their responsibilities and duties including interactions with first responders and stakeholders.
			• It is recommended that any external resources that may be involved in a response – such as Fire, Police, Public Health, and third-party vendors – should be familiar with relevant parts of the response plans.
	Communication and response	A.4.3	• Internal communication is important to ensure the effective implementation of the OR management systems.
			• Arrangements should be made for communication and warnings internally and externally for normal and abnormal conditions.
			• Organizations should implement a procedure for receiving, documenting, and responding to relevant communications from stakeholders and interested parties.

Exhibit 5.4 (continued)   ASIS SPC.1-2009 Standard implementation guidance. (continued)

Primary Requirements for Standard	Subordinate Requirement Items	Section #	Implementation Guidance Section A.4
			• The organization may wish to plan its communication taking into account the decisions made on relevant target groups, the appropriate messages and subjects, and the choice of means. Methods for external communication can include annual reports, newsletters, websites, warnings, and community meetings.
			• Effective communication is one of the most important ingredients in crisis management.
			• Preplanning for communications is critical.
			• A potential disruptive incident should be identified, understood, and addressed and – in doing so – avoided or prevented.
			• Prevention can include proactive steps to coordinate with intelligence, law enforcement, and public agencies; establish information sharing agreements; physical protection of key assets; access controls; awareness and readiness training programs; warning and alarm systems; and practices to reduce the threat.
			• Organizational culture, operational plans, and management objectives should motivate individuals to feel personally responsible for prevention, avoidance, deterrence, and detection.

Exhibit 5.4 (continued)   ASIS SPC.1-2009 Standard implementation guidance. (continued)

Primary Requirements for Standard	Subordinate Requirement Items	Section #	Implementation Guidance Section A.4
			• Deterrence and detection can make a disruptive act or activity more difficult to carry out against the organization or significantly limit, if not negate, its impact. • Physical security planning includes protection of perimeter grounds, building perimeter, internal space and content protection.
		A.4.7	• Cost-effective mitigation strategies should be employed to prevent or lessen the impact of potential crises. • The organization should establish procedures to recognize when specic dangers occur that necessitate the need for some level of response. • A potential disruptive incident, once recognized, should be immediately reported to a supervisor, a member of management, or another individual tasked with the responsibility of crisis notication and management. • Problem assessment (an evaluative process of decision making that will determine the nature of the issue to be addressed) and severity assessment (the process of determining the severity of the crisis and what any associated costs may be in the long run) should be made at the outset of a crisis.

Exhibit 5.4 (continued) ASIS SPC.1-2009 Standard implementation guidance. (continued)

104

Primary Requirements for Standard	Subordinate Requirement Items	Section #	Implementation Guidance Section A.4
			• The point at which a situation is declared to be an emergency or crisis should be clearly defined, documented, and fit very specific and controlled parameters.
			• Preparedness and response plans should be developed around a "worst case scenario," with the understanding that the response can be scaled appropriately to match the actual crisis.
		A.4.7	• People are the most important aspect of any preparedness and response plan.
			• Logistical decisions made in advance will impact the success or failure of a good preparedness and response plan.
			• Once the Crisis Management Team has been activated, the damage should be assessed and carefully documented.
			• If appropriate, existing funding and insurance policies should be examined, and additional funding and insurance coverage should be identified and obtained.
			• Transportation in a time of crisis can be a challenge.
			• Critical vendor or service provider agreements should be established as appropriate and their contact information maintained as part of the preparedness and response plan.

Exhibit 5.4 (continued)   ASIS SPC.1-2009 Standard implementation guidance. (continued)

Primary Requirements for Standard	Subordinate Requirement Items	Section #	Implementation Guidance Section A.4
			• Mutual aid agreements identify resources that may be shared with or borrowed from other organizations during a crisis, as well as mutual support that may be shared with other organizations.
		A.4.7	• Strategic alliances identify delivery partners with which it has an interdependent relationship with other organizations to produce and supply products and services and share risk.
			• Once the extent of damage is known, the process recovery needs should be prioritized and a schedule for resumption determined and documented.
			• Once the processes to be restored have been prioritized, the resumption work can begin with processes restored according to the prioritization schedule.
			• Once the critical processes have been resumed, the resumption of the remaining processes can be addressed.
			• The organization should seek to bring the organization "back to normal." If it is not possible to return to the pre-crisis "normal," a "new normal" should be established.

Source: ANSI / ASIS SPC.1-2009, page 26-36

Exhibit 5.4 (continued)   ASIS SPC.1-2009 Standard implementation guidance.

Primary Requirements for Standard	Subordinate Requirement Items	Section #	Implementation Guidance Section A.5
Checking and Corrective Action	Monitoring and measurement	A.5.1	• Data collected from monitoring and measurement can be analyzed to identify patterns and obtain information. • Knowledge gained from this information can be used to implement corrective and preventive action. • Metrics should be established to measure success of the OR management system. • Key characteristics are those that the organization needs to consider to determine how it is managing its significant risks and impacts, achieving objectives and targets, and improving security, preparedness, response, continuity, and recovery performance. • When necessary to ensure valid results, measuring equipment should be calibrated or verified at specified intervals, or prior to use, against measurement standards traceable to international or national measurement standards.
	Evaluation of compliance	A.5.2.1	• The organization should be able to demonstrate that it has evaluated compliance with the legal requirements identified including applicable permits or licenses. • The organization should be able to demonstrate that it has evaluated compliance with the identified other requirements to which it has subscribed.
	Exercises and Testing	A.5.2.2	• Testing scenarios should be designed using the events identified in the risk assessment and impact analysis.

Exhibit 5.5 ASIS SPC.1-2009 Standard implementation guidance. (continued)

Primary Requirements for Standard	Subordinate Requirement Items	Section #	Implementation Guidance Section A.5
			• Testing can keep response teams and employees effective in their duties, clarify their roles, and reveal weaknesses in the OR management system that should be corrected.
			• The first step in testing should be the setting of goals and expectations.
			• Lessons learned from previous tests, as well as actual incidents experienced, should be built into the testing cycle for the OR management system.
			• The responsibility for testing the OR management system should be assigned.
			• A test schedule and timeline as to how often the plan and its components will be tested should be established.
			• The scope of testing should be planned to develop over time.
			• All participants should understand their roles in the exercise, and the exercise should involve all participants.
			• After completion, the exercises and tests should be critically evaluated.
			• Design of tests should be evaluated and modified as necessary.
			• Exercise and test results should be documented.

Exhibit 5.5 (continued) ASIS SPC.1-2009 Standard implementation guidance. (continued)

Primary Requirements for Standard	Subordinate Requirement Items	Section #	Implementation Guidance Section A.5
	Nonconformity, corrective and preventive action	A.5.3	• Depending on the nature of the nonconformity, in establishing procedures to deal with these requirements, organizations may be able to accomplish them with a minimum of formal planning, or it may be a more complex and long-term activity. Any documentation should be appropriate to the level of action.
	Control of Records	A.5.4	• Management system records can include, among others: • Compliance records; • Training records; • Process monitoring records; • Inspection, maintenance, and calibration records; • Pertinent contractor and supplier records; • Incident reports; • Records of incident and emergency preparedness tests; • Audit results; • Management review results; • External communications decision; • Records of applicable legal requirements; • Records of significant risk and impacts; • Records of management systems meetings; • Security, preparedness, response, continuity, and recovery performance information; • Legal compliance records; and

Exhibit 5.5 (continued)   ASIS SPC.1-2009 Standard implementation guidance. (continued)

109

Primary Requirements for Standard	Subordinate Requirement Items	Section #	Implementation Guidance Section A.5
			• Communications with stakeholders and interested parties.
			• Proper account should be taken of confidential information.
			• Organizations should ensure the integrity of records by rendering them tamperproof, securely backed-up, accessible only to authorized personnel, and protected from damage, deterioration, or loss.
			• Legal authority within the organization should determine the appropriate period of time documents should be retained.
	Internal audits	A.5.5	• Internal audits of an OR management system can be performed by personnel from within the organization or by external persons selected by the organization, working on its behalf.

Source: ANSI/ASIS SPC.1-2009, page 36-38

Exhibit 5.5 (continued) ASIS SPC.1-2009 Standard implementation guidance.

Primary Requirements for Standard	Subordinate Requirement Items	Section #	Implementation Guidance Section A.6
Management Review		A.6	• The management review should cover the scope of the OR management system, although not all elements of the OR management system need to be reviewed at once and the review process may take place over a period of time. • The OR management system should be regularly reviewed and evaluated. The following factors can trigger a review and should otherwise be examined once a review is scheduled: • Risk assessment and impact analysis • Sector/industry trends • Regulatory requirements • Event experience • Test and exercise results.
	Continual Improvement and Maintenance	A.6	• Continual improvement and OR management system maintenance should reflect changes in the risks, activities, functions, and operation of the organization that will affect the OR management system. The following are examples of procedures, systems, or processes that may affect the plan: • Policy changes; • Hazards and threat changes; • Changes to the organization and its business processes; • Changes in assumptions in risk assessment and impact analysis; • Personnel changes (employees and contractors); • Supplier and supply chain changes; • Process and technology changes;

Exhibit 5.6   ASIS SPC.1-2009 Standard implementation guidance. (continued)

111

Primary Requirements for Standard	Subordinate Requirement Items	Section #	Implementation Guidance Section A.6
			• Systems and application software changes;
			• Critical lessons learned from testing;
			• Issues discovered during actual implementation of the plan in a crisis;
			• Changes to external environment; and
			• Other items noted during review of the plan and identied during the risk assessment and impact analysis.

Source: ANSI/ASIS SPC.1-2009, page 39-40

Exhibit 5.6 (continued) ASIS SPC.1-2009 Standard implementation guidance.

- *Know your organization*: Before any project can begin, it is necessary to fully understand the organization, its objectives, the individual business units, and the context in which it operates.
- *Identify critical objectives, operations, functions, products, and services*: What creates value for the organization? As noted above, understanding the business units, what they do, and how they do it to ensure organizational success is absolutely necessary if the ORM project is to reach the desired level of success. Without this knowledge, the project team will not know what is important and where to focus their collective efforts.
- *Preliminary determination of likely risk scenarios and consequences*: An organization will often know what its usual or typical risks are and the threats it faces. Documenting the common risks will help provide a starting point for the discussion on all threats and risks, but don't forget to also consider the less common risks as well. A key question is asking what risks there are to my organization's critical objectives and what activities create the most value.
- *Define the scope and boundaries for security, preparedness, response, continuity, and recovery management program*: Establish the scope and limits of the organization's ORM efforts. It is important to define manageable boundaries.
- *Policy*: Senior management must clearly make the decision and support the effort to protect the tangible and intangible assets of the organization.
- *Management commitment*: Senior management must commit to the necessary activities of implementing organizational resilience management. This commitment must be inculcated within the culture of the organization and be seen as a philosophical principle of doing business.
- *Commitment to protection of critical assets and continuous improvement*: Senior management must clearly make the decision to protect the tangible and intangible assets of the organization and to promote the continual improvement of all approved measures so as to maintain the resilience of the organization.
- *Commitment of resources*: Management must provide the necessary resources to achieve organizational resilience. Wanting a resilient organization is not the same as actively pursuing one.
- *Planning*: The organization must plan for organizational resilience management and devise a plan for achieving its organizational

resilience objectives. Planning should clearly identify the strategy for ORM and managing risk.

- *Risk assessment and impact analysis*: Involves understanding the risks in order to prioritize and manage them. This includes assessments of the business processes, functions, necessary resources to achieve successful business functionality, and ongoing analyses of the threats and impact to the business if these processes and resources are interrupted—keeping in mind that prevention is often less costly than the cure.
- *Legal and other requirements*: The organization must understand the legal and other requirements under which it operates and it is expected to make every effort to achieve compliance in order to avoid regulatory violations.
- *Objectives and targets*: Define what your overarching risk treatment goals are. Documenting the objectives and targets of concern are necessary to provide guidance to the planners, management, and participants involved in implementing the measures to achieve the requirements of ORM. This becomes part of the milestones of the project plan to implement ORM.
- *Strategic prevention, preparedness, and response programs (before, during, and after an undesirable or disruptive event)*: The development of risk treatment programs designed to achieve and maintain ORM at the various levels within the organization are necessary to assist in institutionalizing the philosophy of ORM. Remember, this is a cyclical process and not a terminal project.
- *Implementation and operation*: Defining the tactical measures needed to achieve the strategic goals of ORM. The organization needs to develop precise action plans for how it will conduct its ORM programs. The organization must provide the personnel and property resources (including finances) necessary to achieve ORM.
- *Structure and responsibility*: The appropriate managerial assignment and facilitation must be coordinated to allow the implementation of ORM. Specific personnel shall be tasked with the responsibility and held accountable for the success of coordinating and implementing the ORM project. You are defining who does what, when, and how, and with what resources.
- *Training, awareness, competence*: Properly trained personnel shall be assigned to assist in the development and implementation of the ORM system. Trained staff will make the difference between success and failure in this project; the key stakeholders are the

leaders who will ensure the initial success, but everyone else in the organization must be trained to an acceptable level to ensure the maintenance of the established success. You achieve a cultural change in the organization when everyone working on behalf of the organization understands their roles as risk takers, risk makers, and risk managers.

- *Communication*: Communication is always a two-way street. Communication is the single most important practice in preventing and managing potentially disruptive events. From the reporting of situational assessments to the planning process involving multiple stakeholders to informing the organizational community of an emergency, communication makes the difference between resilience and chaos.
- *Documentation*: It is necessary to have a documented approach to establishing and maintaining ORM within the organization.
- *Document control*: The integrity of information is essential to the survival of any business. The appropriate personnel shall be assigned to properly document and update ORM documents. The maintenance of these documents is critical to ensuring a dynamic and living system.
- *Operational control*: Well-established plans and resources, an effective and tested command structure, and procedural responses to the risks facing the organization are necessary components in a compliant ORM.
- *Incident prevention, preparedness, and response*: It is necessary to have established, effective, and flexible action plans and procedures to address undesirable and disruptive events that may affect the organization *before* they happen. The common priorities and concerns should be addressed.
- *Checking and corrective action*: Process evaluation is critical to understand if the management system and its procedures are effective and efficient. This is an opportunity to ensure continual improvement of the ORM program, which includes all plans and procedures.
- *Monitoring and measurement*: Defining metrics and regular evaluation of the plans, procedures, and responses are necessary to provide documented evidence of the effectiveness and value of the ORM.
- *Evaluation of conformance and system performance*: Periodic reports and evaluations to include evaluation of legal compliance, after-action reports, pre- and posttests, and scheduled reviews of the

conformance of the ORM at the organization against the approved elements of the ANSI/ASIS SPC.1-2009 are desirable.

- *Nonconformity, corrective, and preventive action*: There should be continuous monitoring of the management system to identify potential nonconformances. Actions should be taken to remedy each nonconformance as well as to analyze its root cause and take steps to prevent a recurrence.
- *Records*: Maintenance of records is important to establish referential documentation of accomplishments and improvements. Records provide the documentary evidence to ensure you have your back covered.
- *Internal audits*: A thorough audit of the management system will identify what is working properly as well as opportunities for improvement. The audit is not just about whether an element is there, but if it is effective.
- *Management review*: This management review is necessary to ensure that senior management stays informed and involved in the ORM program. Is the management system adequate, and what are the opportunities for improvement?
- *Adequacy and effectiveness*: Because the organization has invested considerable resources into the ORM project, it is expected that senior management shall require regular reviews of the ORM. All plans and procedures must be adequate and effective in addressing the risks facing the organization.
- *Need for changes*: The ORM system is dynamic; therefore, change is inherent in the process. Changes in the operating environment coupled with the effectiveness or adequacy of the plans or procedures must be considered to modify, adjust, and enhance the plans and procedures.
- *Opportunities for improvement*: Continual improvement is a fundamental component of ORM and all opportunities for improvement must be considered. Again, this is a living process and not a terminal project.

ESTABLISHING THE CONTEXT AND SCOPE

The environment that the organization operates in will have a profound effect on the design and implementation of the management system. The internal and external factors that influence an organization, or even a facility within an organization, will determine how risk and resilience need to be managed. Which factors will affect the organization in its quest to achieve its objectives?

When establishing the context you need to consider the organization's objectives, its stakeholders (internal and external), and its dependencies and interdependencies (including supply chain and critical infrastructure), as well as the factors that make up its natural, political, social, cultural, economic, and competitive environment. When defining the context, understanding the value chain for the organization is important. Typically organizations have multiple activities, products, and services. Not all activities, products, and services are as critical to the survival of the organization, nor are the timeframes for their resilience the same. Which of these create the most value and are the most critical for the organization's survival? Are these nodes of value generation internal or external to the organization? What types of uncertainties are there in achieving these value generation objectives, not just the usual suspects, but any type of risk that might prevent the organization from reaching its goals?

The context for ORM should contain the same factors you would need to define for the organization's business environment when planning any aspect of business management. ORM is just part of the nexus of quality, environmental, occupational health, and safe management linking together the risks of potentially undesirable and/or disruptive events.

You need to understand how risk is managed in your organization. Yes, the objective is to have a holistic, multidisciplinary approach to managing risk and resilience in the organization, but is this your current structure or your aspiration structure? How are the decisions made in the organization that will support the determination of the level of risk? You need to understand what the basis is for analyzing and evaluating risk. It's easy to say that "our risk criteria are that we do not accept risk," but this is seldom reality. Risks to the organization cannot be eliminated; rather they must be managed in the most business-sensible manner using a balanced approach to addressing issues before, during, and after undesirable and disruptive events. Therefore, you need to understand the context in which the level of risk will be measured, determined, and expressed.

Once the context of the organization is understood, you are ready to define a scope for the management system. For the mathematicians and engineers in the audience, you define the boundary conditions. Every activity, product, and service that is within the scope is part of the management system. So, think carefully about what is included and what is excluded. The ANSI/ASIS.SPC.1 Standard gives you the flexibility to define the scope as the whole or a part of the organization, or along discipline or product or service lines. Remember, most people are humans (contrary to the beliefs of those readers with teenage children), so pace your implementation of the standard to provide achievable goals and reinforcement about the value of the endeavor. Consider doing a pilot project when defining the scope for the first time, and then expand the scope throughout the organization to get the most value out of the framework you build in the pilot.

POLICY AND MANAGEMENT COMMITMENT

For projects in an organization to thrive and be successful, there is a need for a clear mandate and commitment from senior management. There is little rationale for pursuing a business management project if there is not buy-in and provision of adequate resources by the management. You may take it for granted that senior management is naturally inclined to identify, understand, and take action to manage risk, but you need to realize that many managers take an ostrich's perspective on the world. They either bury their heads in the sand or consider identifying risks as questioning the conduct of their jobs. Senior management needs to recognize that this is a team effort and they are both the club owners and coaches. They need to set a clear policy establishing the mandate for the management system that articulates and communicates what are the high level risk and resilience management objectives.

The policy statement is backed up by a commitment of resources to support the management system. Resources are human, physical, and financial. The resources should include the designation of a champion of the management system who oversees the process—the team cheerleader. Commitment includes walking the walk and talking the talk. Senior management must be seen as actively engaged in the implementation of the management system to send the message to all persons working on behalf of the organization that managing risk and resilience is a priority for the organization.

Senior management must support the initiative for anything to happen. Without the support of the seniormost leaders, the project is destined to fail. This should be established as early in the project as possible. Yes, you may be able to get the project off the ground without the senior leaders giving their support, but moving beyond the early stages without that support is a mistake. Gaining that support depends on convincing the management responsible for allocating resources that establishing an

ORM system will protect and create value for the organization. It may not be a direct profit generator, but you need to show how it supports activities that are providing critical services and profit generators. You need to make a business case how the ORM system will improve business management and the organization's ability to achieve its objectives. Every organization is different; therefore, the presentation of materials needs to be tailored to the target audience as well as who will be making the presentation. Do you have direct access to the appropriate decision makers or will someone else be making the pitch? Regardless of the presenter, to get management buy-in, your focus should be on how you can help the management team create value and better provide the goods and services that are the value generators for the organization. Rightfully, management is usually more interested in creating value and profit than worrying about what might happen. Management buy-in is won by you showing them that you can cost effectively solve a problem that they recognize as negatively impacting the business. You want to show how you can lower risk while supporting business objectives.

Seek allies in your quest for management support. Who are the key stakeholders that will benefit from ORM? By coordinating environmental, safety, security, and continuity management, will the organization be able to solve problems that have been identified by all these disciplines? For example, stockpiling hazardous materials on an industrial site might not be a convincing argument for a management system if pitched from a business continuity perspective, but it becomes a compelling argument when management sees how it also impacts security, environmental health, and safety. You might just find that this is actually an accounting, procurement, and production issue. By building a team of all stakeholders, you may just discover that the organization lacks a means of managing life-cycle risks and is purchasing chemicals in bulk because the procurement costs are separate from the disposal costs. The risks can be reduced by life-cycle analysis of the hazardous materials are coupled with changing procurement and engineering policies.

Once you have management buy-in, they need to remain engaged to make the management system achieve its objectives. For example, they should be actively engaged in setting risk criteria, determining risk treatment priorities, evaluating performance (particularly exercise debriefings), and management review. You know that management is effectively engaged when the ORM system is an agenda item for management meetings discussing the value-generating activities of the organization.

PLANNING

The management system is the structure you are building to effectively manage risk. As with any structure, it stands strong and sturdy only if it is built on a solid foundation. The planning stage provides the foundation for the ORM. The risk assessment process is informed by the context of the organization and the legal and other requirements to which the organization subscribes. The risk assessment supports the decisions whether to treat risks and how. Therefore, planning together with an understanding of the internal and external context of the organization (including its supply chain and dependencies) provide the foundation for developing and evaluating all the other elements of the ORM system.

A risk assessment goes beyond thinking about what goes thump in the night. The risk assessment should enhance the organization's adaptive capacity and agility. The risk assessment supports the business mission of the organization and is a business management tool. Therefore, the analysis of risk is anchored in understanding what is of value to the organization, including both the tangible and intangible assets. A risk assessment includes an impact analysis, threat analysis, and a vulnerability analysis. It should be considered as something to complement other business management tools, such as SWOT analysis (strengths, weaknesses, opportunities, and threats).

Few modern organizations are totally self-reliant. Almost all organizations depend on a supply chain as well as have critical dependencies and interdependencies (e.g., water, electricity, and telecommunications). Risk assessments that only look inward are not sufficient to protect an organization against undesirable and disruptive events. Risk analysis should include identifying risks at critical nodes of the supply chain as well. It should also include the organizations reliance on outside factors to produce its goods and services. A detailed discussion of supply chain analysis is beyond the scope of this book. However, recent major disruptive events, such as the 2011 Fukushima earthquake in Japan and Hurricane Sandy, which devastated coastal New York and New Jersey in October 2012, have demonstrated that there is a need to map the value generation chain of your organization to identify multitiered choke points, as well as have a clear understanding of the critical infrastructure dependencies and your organization's access to these vital resources should a community-wide event occur.

From the discussion above, it should be clear that the planning element of the ORM system is a participatory activity. Communication and consultation throughout the process is key to success. Planning is a multiway conversation among the owners of risk, risk takers, generators of value, and managers of risk. It is an exercise in determining how everyone can work together to achieve the objectives of the organization. Planning is not about you sitting in your room writing plans, it about you facilitating the discussion to protect and create value for the organization.

The ANSI/ASIS SPC.1 Standard requires the organization to establish, implement, and maintain a formal and documented risk assessment and impact analysis process. One of the pitfalls of risk leading to poor risk assessments is the lack of a clearly defined process. The ISO 31000 provides an excellent model for risk assessments. However, you also should remember to carefully document your methodology, including risk criteria, stakeholders consulted, assumptions, methods, and scope.

The output from the risk assessment will provide the basis for decisions on the necessary risk treatment strategy. What is the correct balance of minimizing both the likelihood and consequences of an undesirable or disruptive event? Obviously, preventing an event is better than dealing with the aftermath. Unfortunately, no prevention plan is 100% effective; therefore, the organization also should prepare to mitigate the consequences of an event should it occur. Security and continuity management are not competing disciplines; in the ORM model, they are complementary, working together to find the most cost-effective strategy to support the organization's business objectives. To be agile and resilient, the organization needs to leverage all the disciplines that contribute to managing risk. Cost-effectively managing risk will require balanced strategies to adaptively, proactively, and reactively address the opportunities and minimize the likelihood and consequences of potential, undesirable, and disruptive events. Always remember, organizations do risk management to support the business, not the other way around.

Another important output of the planning phase is allocation of necessary resources. Most organizations view managing risks as a cost, not a profit generator. Therefore, when developing your strategy for managing risks, it is necessary to provide management with accurate and specific information about resources and timeframes. A proper risk assessment evaluates the process and functionality to identify the risks which will provide an understanding of the gaps between what is in place and what is needed.

After you are armed with a good risk assessment and strategic approach for managing risks, you need to present the results from the perspective that building a resilient organization is part of any good business management strategy. Explain how your strategy will make the organization agile in order to adapt, thrive, and survive in an ever-changing environment. All senior managers have their own priorities and perhaps projects that will now compete for common resources. You need to explain how the risk assessment and strategic approach for managing risks helps them address their priorities and achieve their goals. The presentation needs to be tailored to the audience. Different people respond to different messages and information—you want to capture as many supporters as possible. Focus on the benefits that result from the ORM implementation, particularly how ORM will benefit a specific audience. It is possible that each message will have very different benefits, but all of the benefits should be clearly linked to the overall organization's objectives, survival, and protection. Examples of the many benefits of ORM for a typical organization and which may be useful in promoting the project with the respective audiences include:

- Systematically identifying risks and problems to address them before something happens
- Methods for accomplishing identified objectives
- Protection of tangible and intangible assets (particularly personnel and property) from harm
- Fewer surprises
- More effective risk management planning, performance, and effectiveness to reduce costs
- Improved information for decision making
- Minimizing accidents, undesirable events, and problems
- More effective targeted training for incident prevention and management
- Preventing incidents from escalating into an emergency, crisis, or disaster situation
- Enhanced incident mitigation, response and recovery—shorter response and down times
- Improved stakeholder relationships (particularly with supply chain partners and the community)
- Promoting accountability, assurance, and good governance
- Cost savings

Managing risks with an ORM system is complex and will require considerable resources to implement throughout the organization. It is necessary to accept the realization that both the project and the forthcoming program are long-term initiatives. The project should be developed in accordance with approved business project plans indicating the organization's specific requirements that are approved for implementation. All facets of the project and the implementation of the ANSI/ASIS SPC.1 Standard are intended to benefit the organization as business requirements. The planning phase should indicate the business value for implementing specific components of the standard, as well as for providing performance indicators and metrics to measure success. Remember, it also may require time to determine the actual value of some parts of the standard with respect to the organization. Performance metrics based on the risk assessment and selection of treatment options should be carefully selected and not overly optimistic. Keep in mind that one of the basic premises of risk is that you are addressing many unknowns and not everything is within your control.

IMPLEMENTATION AND OPERATION

Implementation involves the tactical measures needed to achieve the strategic goals of ORM and managing risk. Implementation of the ANSI/ASIS SPC.1 is not an add-on; it is integrated into an organization's day-to-day activities. Like the antivirus program in your computer, it works quietly in the background, draining as few resources as possible from the value creation functions, while constantly monitoring and providing protection. It works with other programs; it doesn't take over the operations of other programs. You did not buy your computer so that you could run an antivirus program; the antivirus helps your computer function well and your computer is supposed to make you more productive.

The "Implementation and Operation" sections of the ANSI/ASIS SPC.1 Standard address the major tactical elements you need to translate your risk management strategy into dynamic action plans. Action plans are sets of procedures and work instructions explaining why and what needs to be done, when, by whom, with what resources, and measures of performance. All the procedures and work instructions developed are a direct outcome of the planning phase of the ORM system. They should be addressing risks and critical asset protection needs identified in the risk assessment and impact analysis. They are filling in the details of your strategic plans for managing risks. Therefore, the plans should reflect the multidisciplinary approach to make the organization agile and resilient in order to adapt, thrive, and survive in an ever-changing environment.

123

The procedures developed in the "Implementation and Operation" sections of the ANSI/ASIS SPC.1 Standard should be developed with input from the stakeholders that will be executing them. You are providing support for the business activities; therefore, the procedures and work instructions need to be tailored to the stakeholder needs. The point of the ORM system is not to develop procedures so you can tick off boxes that you have security plans, contingency plans, communication plans, and education plans. The point is to establish effective security, effective contingencies, effective communications, and effective training in the organization. The procedures should be clearly linked to the planning and performance evaluations sections of the ANSI/ASIS SPC.1 Standard.

To support any normal activity in the organization, there is a need to establish roles, responsibilities, authorities, and allocate resources. The standard requires these be established, documented, and communicated to the appropriate stakeholders. Preemptively defining and communicating roles, responsibilities, authorities, and allocating resources is even more critical when addressing issues surrounding potential undesirable and disruptive events. If all persons understand their role in managing risks to prevent and respond to events, they are much better prepared to identify the signs of trouble and respond expeditiously. Without the preparation of the ORM system your organization is largely at the mercy of individuals within an organization, hoping that heroes will step forward at any signs of trouble. As you know from your own experience, surprises can be quite stressful and you don't always respond as expected.

Command and control before, during, and after an event includes defining roles, responsibilities, authorities, and allocating resources. It is more effective to proactively determine the roles in establishing crisis management teams and establish incident response centers with adequate resources. Leadership is essential for a smooth and coordinated response. Leadership roles for a crisis situation are not necessarily the same as those during normal operations; therefore, clearly defining roles and testing the leadership capabilities of the assigned individuals is critical. Preparations should include the protection of assets as well as the continuity of operations. The ORM system calls for the coordinated response of all the disciplines that can contribute to managing risks in an orderly fashion.

Financial administration is another factor that needs to be considered during a crisis situation. Who has the authority to quickly designate the expenditure of funds to address developing events and how will these funds be accounted for? Resource limitations are inherent in any crisis situation of significance. It is not uncommon that individuals with ready cash go to the front of the line. Also, it is common that organizations that can document their expenditures and losses have quicker access to insurance reimbursements, so plan for how you are going to make a claim before you need to do so.

Competence, training, and awareness are central to any ORM system. They also are perhaps the most cost-effective tools for protecting an organization and establishing an ORM culture. A well-designed training and awareness program will engage stakeholders and help them understand their roles in being both risk owners and managers. This serves to identify potential events and respond appropriately. The standard requires the organization to identify necessary competences, develop and deliver appropriate training and awareness programs, and the test for competence. The goal of any training and awareness program is to instill a sense of ownership in all the participants. It is more than educating people about what they have to do; they need to understand why they are doing it to achieve the cultural shift. They need to feel that ORM is an integral part of everything they are doing.

Effective communications and consultation is a two-way street with both internal and external stakeholders. Recent tsunamis, earthquakes, hurricanes, terrorist events, and other major disruptions have clearly demonstrated the need for effective and robust communication. This goes well beyond the need for information sharing between persons and organizations before, during, and after an event. Organizations that have a relationship and strategy with the public media weather the storm of reputational damage better than organizations that think they can deal with the media on the fly. Remember that effective communications are not only about *what* you say, but also *how* you say it. This pertains to both the message and mode of delivery. When developing the communications strategy for your organization, keep in mind the risks that are inherent in all modes of communication and your dependencies on critical infrastructure. Plan your communications strategy based on how you would want to be communicated with.

A management system is also an information system. Therefore, documentation plays a significant effort in implementing any management system standard. Documentation should help you successfully execute all the other elements of the standard. It is not an exercise in compiling large stagnant manuals. It is about creating a dynamic information system of useful information. It is supported by procedures to protect the integrity of information and assure access only to the appropriate persons.

Central to managing risk is having preemptive plans to anticipate, prevent, protect, mitigate, respond, and recover from potentially undesirable and disruptive events. Plans, procedures, and work instructions should be the direct tactical output from your strategic risk management plans. Developing plans is a multidisciplinary activity. When developing your plans, keep in mind the timeframes for the various procedures. Many functions related to anticipation, prevention, protection, and mitigation are continuous activities, while response and recovery functions are activated by the onset of an event. The balance between adaptive, proactive, and reactive strategies will depend on the risk and what is the most cost-effective way to manage it. How will the identified risks affect your organization? How will loss of assets, activities, and functions affect your organization? You need to develop procedures recognizing that few preventative measures are 100% successful all the time. Risk can seldom be eliminated. Therefore, do you have a contingency plan? On the other hand, many contingency planners take a fatalistic view that because risk cannot be eliminated and prevention is not 100%, why bother. As the old saying goes, 28 grams of prevention is worth 0.454 kilograms of cure. The risk treatment strategy should consider both reputational and physical harm and be based on what is the best protection for the organization and to best assure the uninterrupted flow of goods and services.

The senior leaders are the key stakeholders in deciding the fate and success of the ORM project; success depends on their direct support and involvement. While the senior leaders may not be the ones directly performing many of the actual duties associated with implementation, they are the force behind the inertia necessary to promote an ORM culture in the organization. All members of the organization must view organizational resilience as critical to the ongoing survival of the organization. Implementation plans support the business objectives of the organization. For senior management and owners of value-generating processes in the organization to support the resilience plans and procedures, they need to clearly understand how the procedures support their day-to-day activities. The ORM system should not be seen as an additional burden, but rather something that supports normal organizational functions. It is necessary to understand the importance of the commitment from everyone to ensure success.

The development of the actual implementation plans and procedures should be based on achievable goals that are clearly specified, with time frames for execution, and with defined performance indicators to determine if the goals have been accomplished.

PERFORMANCE EVALUATION

Good business management practice includes performance evaluations. There is a common saying that "if you can't measure it, you can't manage it." The ORM system is no exception. You will need to justify the expenditure on ORM and provide a basis for continuing expenditures. This is especially true given that ORM is not a direct profit generator and a successful ORM strategy means nothing bad happening, or limiting the damage should something happen. Therefore, metrics should be considered within the context of the ORMS helping the organization achieve its objectives of providing goods and services. Fewer incidents and accidents, faster response times, and shorter downtimes all help the organization's bottom line.

Is the organization meeting its legal and regulatory obligations? Is the organization meeting its contractual obligations and needs of its supply chain partners? Are risk treatment objectives set in the planning phase being met? Are people working for the organization more aware of the risks faced by the organization and actively participating in the protection of the organization? Is there an ORM culture in the organization? All these questions provide indicators to the effectiveness of the ORM system.

Ongoing monitoring of the ORM system and the treatments to control risk provides a basis for determining the effectiveness of measures put in place. Ongoing monitoring also helps identify areas of potential nonconformances within the management system and measures to treat risk, therefore, enabling the organization to take corrective actions. When a nonconformance is discovered it should be viewed as an opportunity for improvement, not a failure. It should be analyzed to discover the root cause of the nonconformance and actions need to be taken to address the root cause in order to prevent a recurrence.

Exercise and testing the management system and the risk treatment methods provides an excellent tool for increasing awareness, validating the risk assessment, testing the effectiveness of treatment methods before an event, and reducing response times. Remember, the ORM system is not a linear process; some people use an exercise as a starting point, as a training and awareness exercise, and as a method to brainstorm to identify risks. Likewise, if an exercise highlights problems within the ORM system, they should be addressed expeditiously. As with all aspects of the ORM system, exercises should include all stakeholders in the organization from the top to the bottom rungs. Active engagement of management sends the message that the ORM system has high priority in the organization and provides a direct channel to those responsible for the opportunities of improvement.

Internal auditing is another tool for evaluating performance. Auditing an ORM system is not an inspection checking if elements are in place and ticking off a bunch of boxes. Auditing is about checking if all the elements are in place and whether or not they are effective. It's not about looking to see if a set of procedures are in a manual, but rather if people are aware of their role in the procedure and do they understand how to execute the procedure. Are they competent to carry out the tasks they have been assigned? Having a manual on the shelf cataloging security and business continuity procedures does not protect an organization; having a competent staff that knows how to put the procedures into action does.

The internal audit should be used as a means of identifying opportunities for improvement. A good internal audit by someone who understands the business objectives of the organization, while not auditing his/her own work, should dig for root causes of nonconformances and focus on how ORM is helping the organization achieve its business objectives.

MANAGEMENT REVIEW

Identifying deviations from plans and changing internal and external context should be seen as a learning experience and pave the way for the organization to adapt its ORM plans, and possibly even change its business management approach to meet new challenges. Challenges are opportunities for improvement. Change is one of the few constants in life; to thrive and survive organizations must be agile and adapt to internal and external changes. Monitoring and anticipating changes are an important part of change management and they help the organization preemptively adapt. At other times, organizations need to learn from their experiences and adapt based on lessons learned. Some adaptations may be minor, while others may require significant adaptation of the organization's nature, character, purpose, or structure, even to the point of reinventing itself.

Management review considers all the outputs from all of the elements of the ORM system and determines the adequacy of the ORM system, the effectiveness of risk treatment measures, the appropriateness of risk criteria and objectives, new priorities, and the budgets for ORM. Because change is constant and the risks facing an organization are always subject to change, it is necessary to periodically review all aspects of the ORM elements within an organization as well as the supply chain associated with the organization in order to ensure it is up to date. It is a requirement and fundamental underpinning of ANSI/ASIS SPC.1-2009. Too often plans are written and placed on a shelf only to become quickly outdated. This is a waste of valuable resources and establishes a mindset of accepting of the status quo, or worse, the ORM system is a simple paper exercise. Improvement of the processes by the business units are likely to occur because with improvements come cost savings. With these process changes occurring, it is absolutely necessary to seek continual improvement of the plans and documents to remain current with the organization.

Some people delude themselves by assuming that because there were no disruptive events over the past year there is no need for management reviews; obviously, the security and business continuity plans worked. This attitude is an indicator of inverted priorities. It's not about the event; it's about the business objectives of the organization. Management review of the ORM system is done within the context of overall objectives and risk profile of the organization. Assumptions, criteria, and priorities should be revisited within the context of overall business management review.

Once opportunities for improvement are identified, priorities set, and new issues added to the ORM system, management can also revisit the scope and determine if the scoping definition is appropriate to meet the organization's objective. Frequently, organizations start the project with a more narrowly defined scope, using a pilot project approach, and then expand the scope as the benefits of the ORM system are recognized. However, management review is not the end of the process, it is the beginning of the ongoing cycle.

Exhibits 5.1 to 5.6 contained the guidance information for the implementation of ANSI/ASIS SPC.1-2009 from the text of the Standard. It was presented in tabulated form to help organize your implementation efforts.

6

Planning Tools

RISK ASSESSMENT

The effectiveness of the risk management approach will depend on the foundation set from identifying the context of the organization as well as a well-defined, comprehensive approach as outlined in the ISO 31000:2009. As with ANSI/ASIS SPC.1-2009, it is imperative to thoroughly understand the target organization from as many aspects as possible. For instance, there are internal considerations that must be determined, such as the organization's personnel and culture, the organizational structure, the organizational policies and procedures, all known stakeholders, and the environment within which the organization operates. There are also external considerations, such as the physical, social, political, economic, and cultural environment in which the organization operates. Supply chain consideration, including its dependencies and interdependencies, should be considered, such as the ability of vendors to provide resources necessary for the organization to achieve goals (products) and to move these products in accordance with the demands of organizational plans. This understanding is used to develop the risk management policy, which must show a clear purpose and alignment between the policies and objectives of the organization, along with the criteria used to define and evaluate the risk. The risk criteria, like the risk policy, should be aligned with one another in accordance with the values and objectives of the organization. The risk criteria provide the basis for evaluating the significance of risk. The risk criteria establish how the organization will assess, avoid, accept, or exploit risk (which depends on the organization's risk appetite). It provides the basis for evaluating the types of risk events, the likelihood

131

of occurrence, frequency, and consequences of risk events; what constitutes unacceptable risk; and the perspectives of the stakeholders. This is absolutely critical to understanding risk (ISO 3100:2009(E), p. 17). Simply listing the risks facing an organization is not sufficient to understanding the actual risks. The risk criteria should be based on achieving the organization's objectives, not merely listing events. When developing the risk criteria to evaluate the risks, there is a need for a robust understanding from multiple stakeholders concerning the acceptable level of risk, as well as agreed upon definitions of the methods for assessing likelihood, frequency, and consequences of the risk (ISO 3100:2009(E), p. 17). You cannot assess something if you don't understand what you are looking at or why it's important. Risk criteria should be developed before the risk assessment; however, they also should be revisited throughout the risk assessment and management processes to ensure they remain relevant and continue to reflect the values and objectives of the organization and its stakeholders.

The risk assessment process broadly involves three processes:

1. Risk identification: Recognizing what risks exist
2. Risk analysis: Considered in terms of likelihood and consequence, after considering current controls
3. Risk evaluation: Deciding how to prioritize the risks

Risk identification is necessary so that the organization has a comprehensive list of the known and likely sources of risk, the likelihood and consequences of the events, the actual causes of the consequences, and the areas of the organization affected by the consequences. Before any management of risks may take place, it is necessary to understanding the potential problems facing the organization. The stakeholders within the organization's risk environment (all of those involved in addressing risk issues internal and external to the organization) need to identify all the risks, large and small, along with the sources. This must be an inclusive activity to ensure that as many risks as possible are identified. The sources of risk will lead to the consequences and the organizational processes affected by the event. Expending resources on risk identification will prepare and allow you to effectively use your time to analyze those risks. It is important to comprehensively identify the risks so that you may understand the full risk picture facing the organization. Remember, simply identifying a risk does not mean that it will be necessary or advisable to do something to affect that risk. It is necessary, even desirable, to accept some risk.

The risk analysis takes the information gathered in the risk identification and allows the organization to gain an understanding of the risk: where does the risk come from, where does it lead, and what is the chance of an occurrence. "Risk analysis involves consideration of the courses and sources of risk, their positive and negative consequences, and the likelihood that those consequences can occur" (ISO 3100:2009(E), p. 18). Exhibit 4.1 in Chapter 4 provided a number of examples so that you would be able to begin to view the relationship between the source of the risk and how it affects the organization. Knowing the consequence of a risk does not provide the likelihood of the event or consequence occurring. For example, it is necessary to understand how a break-in may affect the organization's ability to meet a delivery deadline. Does the adversary have the motivation and capability to carry out a successful break-in? Are the security measures sufficient to deter, detect, and delay a break-in? What assets are vulnerable and how critical are they to meeting your delivery deadline? What is the potential nature of the break-in and its impacts? What is the level of risk based on the likelihood and consequences of a successful break-in?

Risk evaluation is the final stage in the risk assessment and uses of the information obtained through risk analysis to develop informed decisions. You are comparing the level of risk with the risk criteria to determine the necessary risk treatments.

Risk Identification

When identifying the risks to an organization, it is necessary to consider both the internal and external context of the organization. The internal context is the internal factors and environment that characterize how the organization is structured and operates. Examples include governance and organizational structure; the decision-making processes; attributes of the organization's culture; resources and capabilities; profit generators and processes; stakeholders and critical personnel; equipment necessary to achieve critical business functions; communications and information flow; and policies, standards, and rules within the organization. The external context is the external factors that characterize the organization's operating environment. External issues are those concerns that take place or are generated outside of the organization, frequently outside the organization's direct control. Examples include legislative, regulatory, and contractual obligations; political, social, economic, financial, and cultural factors; dependencies and interdependencies, including critical infrastructure; supply chain requirements; environment, climatic, and geological factors; the media; and demographic and community factors. The organization should consider a range of risks that could impact the organization's ability to achieve its objectives. This should go beyond the usual suspects and consider risks associated with its internal and external context. Risk identification should answer the following questions:

- Why could something happen? (A cause or factor creating risk; effectiveness of controls)
- Who could be involved? (Individuals or groups associated with threat, control of risk, and/or impacted by risk)
- How could it happen? (A source of risk)
- What could happen? (Potential event and consequences)
- When could something happen? (Timeframes that affect likelihood and consequence)
- Where could it happen? (Locations and variances)

Supply chain mapping is an important part of the risk identification process. Few organizations today operate as independent islands. The risks associated with your supply chain may differ from those internal to your organization. Many contingency plans have failed because of a lack of understanding of supply chain risks and by underestimating the timeframes for recovery of supply chain partners and critical infrastructure.

Also consider collateral risks, such as the nearby chemical or petroleum companies that may pose a threat, or the highway or train tracks that routinely have hazardous materials transported within close proximity to the company. Businesses that are near military bases should consider the possibility of air crashes from helicopters and airplanes; think about the air show that draws large numbers of people. Consider supply chain issues, such as the number of vendors providing services and issues that may affect their ability to fulfill their deliveries or pickups. Also think of cascading effects. If there is a serious snow or rainstorm and a common roadway is blocked, it may affect deliveries or how people get to work. It is very possible that the organization's building is perfectly fine, unaffected by a storm, but the roadway is blocked and the staff is not able to reach the building. Unless there are plans for alternative routes or telecommuting, operations may become disrupted.

Criticality Analysis
Every organization has certain functions or activities that are critical to the operation of the organization. All of these should be accurately documented. Without these functions, the organization is unable

to operate. When looking into the risks facing an organization, it is important to understand the activities and obligations that are taking place within and those that are external to the organization. While all of the activities are important, not all of them are critical to the operation and continuity of the organization. Typically, organizations create the bulk of their value from a few products and services; therefore, continuity of these functions is more critical than more marginal activities. Criticality is not just based on tangible value, but also intangible value. Loss of reputation or information can strongly influence the criticality. Whether the organization is public, private, or not-for-profit, it is necessary to consider activities and processes during both normal and abnormal conditions of operation, such as production (this includes whatever the organization does as a service or business), fundraising, payroll, finance (to include strategy, investments, etc.), accounts receivable/payable, supply chain management, distribution of products or services, and information technology (ANSI/ASIS SPC.1-2009, p. 22). Assistance may be obtained from the procurement, process, and sales departments in the organization to identify acceptable downtimes and recovery time objectives related to a business interruption. Also, please remember, personnel are the most critical resource an organization has and it is necessary to consider how the people will be involved in all of the above activities and processes. Do not forget to include the people in the risk calculations.

Threat Analysis
As part of a documented and actively reviewed risk management process, it is necessary to understand the difference between threats and risks. A threat is the potential cause of an undesirable or disruptive event, and a risk is the deviation from the expected outcome on objectives and may be either positive or negative (ANSI/ASIS SPC.1-2009, pp. 48–50). The threat is the source and cause of risks that may trigger an uncertainty in achieving the organization's objectives. With this association established, it is possible to appreciate the value and need for a threat analysis—the properties of a threat from the perspective for the organization. It is valuable to reference many different sources (internal and external) to gather the information on the threats. Some examples include:

- Financial records
- Stockholder reports
- Insurance records

135

- Internal and external security/crime reports
- Flood and storm data
- Technology-related issues
- Sources of human resources data
- Regulations
- Supply chain related issues
- Access control records (network access and facility access)

It is useful to associate threats to risks (cause and effect) so that the involved stakeholders understand and appreciate the connection between threats and risks. For instance, a simple threat is a severe storm, such as a hurricane, that may result in a power loss for the facility—the threat is the storm and the effect is the power loss. The electrical power loss may have a number of additional consequences, such as loss of network connectivity, loss of the telephone system, and loss of the HVAC system. The importance of this exercise is to consider what may happen from various causes so that they may be included in the risk assessment process. While you cannot prevent the storm, you can arrange to have a generator in place to address the electrical interruption.

Analysis of intentional threats is based on consideration of the capability and intent or motivation of the adversary. The capability will be dependent of the resources and knowledge available to the adversary. Intent and motivation are a function of the adversary's desire and confidence as well as the attractiveness of the target. When considering the likelihood of a threat, consider both the likelihood of a threat occurring and the likelihood of the threat successfully causing an impact.

Vulnerability Analysis
The vulnerability analysis identifies the potential weakness that can be exploited related to preventing the organization from achieving its objectives. Key to understanding vulnerabilities is to identify existing countermeasures and determine their effectiveness. Criticality, threat, and vulnerability analyses are not done in isolation. The degree of vulnerability should be determined relative to each asset and threat. Consider the interactions between the threat, assets, activities and functions of the organization, and measures that have been put in place to protect them. What opportunities are there for a threat to materialize? Is the asset made vulnerable by a single weakness or multiple weaknesses? Does the nature of the vulnerability make it difficult to exploit? Is the vulnerability of the asset lessened by multiple layers of protective measures?

Using the above example of the hurricane and the electrical power loss, we see the vulnerability to the facility as a weakness in the electrical backup capabilities for the facility. While we used a natural incident for our example, it is important to consider all vulnerabilities to the organization relative to all processes, activities and functions—don't forget the people.

Using a vulnerability analysis, the organization will have a comprehensive understanding of the threats, risks, and weaknesses associated with the organization. This understanding will allow the risk managers to consider ways to treat the issues and either prevent them from occurring, reduce the consequential effects, transfer the risk to another (insurance), or accept the risk as a tolerable issue.

Risk Analysis

The risk criteria and output from the risk identification are used as input into the risk analysis. The purpose of a risk analysis is to separate minor risks from major, and to understand the nature and level of risk in order to make decisions about risk treatment. When conducting a risk analysis it is important to keep in mind the level of subjectivity and reliability of the data and information on which it is based. As illustrated in Exhibit 6.1, risk analysis entails understanding the sources and causes of risk identified during risk identification, their likelihood and consequences, particularly the likelihood that they will impact the organization's objectives, as well as the effectiveness of risk treatment measures.

Qualitative versus Quantitative Methods

There is a distinction between qualitative and quantitative methods used to understand data in risk analysis. Likelihood and consequences can be determined by either qualitative or quantitative methods. While many people like to debate that one method is better than the other, we will venture some simple advice: Pick whichever method is better understood by the senior management that needs to make decisions on risk treatments. The qualitative approach involves understanding and appreciating the nuances in substantive nonnumeric value differences in data; there are no numeric values attached to data. Instead of assigning numeric values, a perceived ranking is assigned a qualitative value of the data (e.g., low, medium, high, and extreme). In essence, you are looking to identify the subjective importance of each item. It is possible to assign numeric values to qualitative data, but the values only apply to the particular data set and will not have meaning outside of the subjective assignment. For instance,

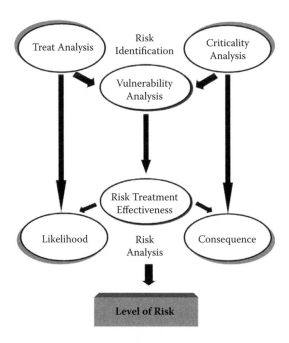

Exhibit 6.1   Risk analysis relationships.

the ranking of two risks have subjective value in that one risk is more important to the organization than the other risk, or one is more serious than another, but it would be a mistake to say that one risk is four times greater than another risk. That sort of conclusion is best made through a quantitative analysis where you are able to determine the specific cost of a consequence and the claim that one risk is four times more costly to the organization has a valid numeric value.

Quantitative methods involve the use of numeric values assigned to the data to determine the objective placement of data. A particular risk may cost the organization $100,000 in damages and another risk may cost $10,000. This is a quantitative comparison and it has an objective value to say that the first is 10 times more costly than the second. This comparison may be used against other values apart from this data set as long as the other data are determined the same way; the values are objective and, therefore, useable in other analyses. Likelihood is typically expressed in terms of probability or frequency. Keep in mind that likelihood is also a function of time, so care must be taken to be consistent in timeframe considerations.

In some cases, analysis will be done using a combination of qualitative and quantitative analysis. For instance, the value derived in a company contributing pro bono services to a community group consists of both qualitative and quantitative values. There is great subjective value attributed to company personnel providing services to the community, such as reputation, networking, and public relations. There is also objective value derived from such activities like tax deductions for services rendered and the monetary value of the resulting benefit from the services.

When using complex quantitative or semiquantitative models, beware of a false sense of confidence in their outputs. If there is large uncertainty in the inputs, there will be large uncertainty in the outputs. Therefore, simpler models may provide more acceptable approximations

Risk Evaluation

Before we can begin a discussion on the cost-benefit considerations of risk evaluations, we must briefly review the meaning of a cost-benefit analysis. A cost-benefit analysis is a means to measure the cost of various alternatives against the benefits gained by each alternative. Cost-benefit analysis is a very common management tool to determine the most acceptable and beneficial alternative for the money. While it may appear desirable to equate each alternative with a specific value, it may be very difficult to determine the cost of some risks because the risk may not have a monetary value attached to it. For instance, the reputation of an organization is priceless. You may not be able to affix a cost to that.

Risk evaluation uses the risk criteria and outputs from the risk identification and risk analysis steps to determine what risk levels are acceptable and which require risk treatments. The level of risk determined during risk analysis will indicate the priorities for risk treatment. Risk evaluation considers the cost and benefits of different treatment options. Care should be taken during the risk evaluation stage to make sure treating one risk is not creating another risk.

Risk evaluation considerations include:

- Objectives of projects and opportunities
- Tolerability of risks to others
- Whether a risk needs treatment
- Deciding whether risk can be tolerated
- Whether an activity should be undertaken
- Priorities for treatment

Using a Criticality Assessment as a Refinement Tool

The risk evaluation will identify risks which you can treat. There may be risks that need further consideration to develop contingency plans. A criticality assessment (CA), also known as a business impact analysis, is a structured approach to gaining information about the processes and associated necessary resources of an organization and information about what is important during an interruption of the business. Through the careful evaluation of these processes and what is necessary to achieve them, a determination is made as to the most critical processes and the resources (assets) that are requirements to achieve the process outcome. The critical processes are the ones that must be operational to maintain an acceptable level of business functionality during and immediately following an unacceptable business interruption. The CA is a logical undertaking and is extremely useful in understanding an organization. Important policy decisions must be made concerning focusing resources and the CA is the best way to collect the information necessary for an informed decision. An in-depth CA is often time-consuming and resource intensive, but unavoidable if you wish to really understand the organization. It is not uncommon for senior managers to suggest not performing a CA and just "getting" the job done. This is synonymous with making a decision without any information. The value of the CA is that it provides critical information to make a decision that may affect the survival of the organization. You also may have suggestions to use anecdotal information as the basis of the CA. While some anecdotal information may be useful in thinking about threats and risks facing an organization, it is a mistake to base your CA on stories that have been handed down. Perform a comprehensive analysis of the organization with as many stakeholders involved in the development and analysis of the process as possible for a valuable work product. Remember, involving as many key stakeholders throughout the project and into the program development will allow for the best opportunity at success and a more resilient organization.

Because one of the goals of this book is to provide a concise and simple explanation of how to achieve the implementation of organizational resilience management (ORM), we will focus on the basic CA categories of qualitative and quantitative data and leave the more exhaustive discussions of data analysis to other books. The qualitative CA involves collecting information that has a substantive or value-oriented nature. There are certain value-oriented functions or processes that are difficult to quantify; activities related to reputation, life-safety, and product/organizational trust are normally considered "priceless" and, therefore, extremely difficult to equate with a monetary value. While it may be difficult to place a financial value on something, it does not mean we cannot determine the criticality of that process. This qualitative determination is just as valid as a quantitative decision. An excellent example of management making a qualitative assessment can be seen in product recalls. Management is placing the trust and quality of a product over the money that is lost from a recall of the questionable product. The senior managers realize that gaining public trust is extremely important to the success of the company and, once lost, they may not be able to regain that trust. Customer or client trust has been qualitatively assessed as critical to the organization. This determination is closely connected to the culture of the organization and the ethical stance that is taken concerning the products and quality control principles of the organization.

The quantitative CA involves placing a numeric value on a process or activity. Finance people love to assign a monetary value to everything because that is a solid method to justify the resources necessary for a function or process. The quantitative approach is an easily understood example aligned with our earlier discussion concerning the connection between business requirements and resources. Viewing the cost or revenues of a business function allows for a straightforward decision concerning its criticality.

The collection of the data is one part of the analysis effort. The most important piece of the puzzle is the interpretation of the data into information. There are certain assumptions that the organization's leadership shall have to consider. For instance, on the CA template that is provided in Exhibits 6.2 to 6.7, there are classifications that categorize the data and assist in making quicker decisions. These classifications of data are based on decisions made by management, such as the monetary values necessary for certain ranges in calculations and substantive values resulting from calculations. See Exhibit 4.9 in Chapter 4 for a better understanding of this example.

There are three basic ways to conduct a CA:

1. Have a consultant perform it
2. Perform the CA internally
3. A combination of the above two options

The best way is the one that works for your organization. The available resources will make that determination more clear: the number of staff actually performing the CA: the time available to complete the work; the budget, if any, to perform the CA; and the expertise of the internal

Criticality Assesment Survey
This Criticality Assessment (CA) survey is designed to identify the critical business processes required for a business unit to operate. Through completion of this survey you will be able to determine the financial impact to your operation; the important processes that are related to reputation, legal/regulatory compliance, and other qualitative considers; the necessary infrastructure dependencies; recovery time objectives; and the resumption prioritization, from the business unit's perspective, during an unacceptable business interruption. The critical decision of determining which processes to recover and in which order, if at all, is a management decision derived through analysis of the aforementioned information.
Section 1—Project Cover Sheet
Business Unit Surveyed:
Survey Respondent:
Business Unit Manager:

Exhibit 6.2 Critical assessment (CA) template cover sheet.

staff leading the effort. If you are lucky enough to have a large budget and the consultant is a viable option—congratulations, you are probably in the minority. Using the consultant approach is an excellent way to achieve the goal of completing a quality CA in a reasonable time period. It is always a good idea to follow established company procedures for bringing in a consultant. Ensure that you do your "due diligence" and that the consulting firm has experience performing successful CAs.

The rest of our readers are probably looking to either perform the CA in-house or have a consultant help get the process started. Again, the quality of the consultant should be verified to ensure that you do not waste critical resources; one poor vendor could jeopardize the project.

There are simple ways to collect the desired information for a CA. If you are planning on using a consultant, a CA from the consultant is an option. There are plenty of examples on the Internet, but caution should be taken to ensure that the survey that is obtained from the Web is going to produce the results that are expected. That should be a concern regardless of where the CA is obtained. The actual CA document

CA Survey/"Process Assessment & Impact Analysis" Section 2—Processes, Recovery Time Objectives (RTOs), and Business Resumption Sequence					
Refer to Appendix A.5 for detailed steps and sample responses.					
Complete columns A through F as they pertain to your business unit based on the following denitions:					
A "Primary Business Activity" is a fundamental high-level activity (or family of related activities) that are critical to the continuity of business, regulatory compliance, business/process controls and reporting requirements, adherence to applicable Company policies, and the overall survival of the company. A Primary Business Process is made up of one or several subset activities.					
"Functional Processes" are supporting processes that, along with other supporting processes, contribute to the execution and completion of a company Core Business Process.					
Recovery Time Objective (RTO) is the business unit's expectation for recovering from a business interruption and resuming a specific business process/function. RTOs are subject to justication, management approval, and proper funding of the associated recovery solution.					
Primary Business Activity	**Functional Processes**	**Critical RTO**	**Desired RTO Range**	**Preferred Business Resumption Sequence (Specify 1,2,3>>)**	**Routine Work Location**
Building Security	Facility Access Control Management	24 hrs	24 to 48 hours	2	1 Main St. Anywhere, USA
Corporate Security Investigations	Investigative Reporting Tool	72 hrs	48 to 72 hours	3	1 Main St. Anywhere, USA
Crisis Management	Incident Command Management Process	N\A	0 to 2 hours	1	1 Main St. Anywhere, USA

Exhibit 6.3 Critical assessment (CA) processes and recovery time objectives.

143

CA Survey/"Process Assessment & Impact Analysis"
Section 3—Financial Impacts on Unit Operation

Refer to Appendix A.5 for detailed steps and sample responses.

| Primary Business Activity (autofilled from Section 2) | Functional Processes (autofilled from Section 2) | Financial impact estimate for each identified process in your business operation of the Criticality Assessment Survey. Provide worst-case estimates for the busiest day of the week/month/year. | | | Financial Impact Risk Score 5 4 3 2 1 | Financial Impact Financial Loss Range $1,000,000 > $500,000 to 999,999 $100,000 to 499,999 $25,001 to 99,999 < $25,000 | Describe how financial estimates were reached (production volume, requirements, expenses/revenues, calculations, etc.). |
		Daily Incurred Costs/Expenses ($)	Daily Lost Revenues ($)	Daily Regulatory Penalties ($)	Row Total (auto-calculated)	Financial Impact Risk Score (automatically computed)	
Building Security	Facility Access Control Management	3,240	0	0	3,240	1	$27*24 hours*5 Guards to secure a building.
Corporate Security Investigations	Investigative Reporting Tool	0	0	0	0	1	
Crisis Management	Incident Command Management Process	0	0	0	0	1	
#REF!	#REF!	0	0	0	0	1	
#REF!	#REF!	0	0	0	0	1	

Exhibit 6.4 Critical assessment (CA) financial impacts.

CA Survey/"Process Assessment & Impact Analysis"
Section 4—Nonfinancial Impacts
Estimate the extent of "nonfinancial" impacts based on the choices below.

This will provide a quantitative understanding for operational issues not realizing a financial impact.

Primary Business Activity (autofilled from Section 2)	Functional Processes (autofilled from Section 2)	Functional Operations Risk Score (autofilled from Section 2)	Risk Impact Score (Non-financial Impact)	Reputation Risk Score (Non-financial Impact)	Total CA Impact Score (sum of 3 preceding scores)	Business Critically Rating (Defined by CA Score)	Describe how the "nonfinancial" impacts were determined—justify answer
			Impact Score Ranges 4 to 5 = High Impact 3 = Moderate Impact 1 to 2 = Minimal Impact			Criticality Score 11 to 15 = Critical 6 to 10 = Important 3 to 5 = Deferrable	
Building Security	Facility Access Control Management	1	3	3	7	Important	System necessary for access to controlled areas.
Corporate Security Investigations	Investigative Reporting Tool	1	1	1	3	Deferrable	Necessary for reports on security incidents. Manual work-around available for short term.
Crisis Management	Incident Command Management Process	1	5	5	11	Critical	Incident Command does not rely on one system—manual work-arounds available.

Exhibit 6.5 Critical assessment (CA) nonfinancial impacts.

CA Survey/"Process Assessment & Impact Analysis" Section 5—IT Applications Required						
For each process, indicate the IT Application required.						
Primary Business Activity (autofilled from Section 2)	Functional Processes (autofilled from Section 2)	Appli- cation 1	Appli- cation 2	Appli- cation 3	Appli- cation 4	Appli- cation 5
Building Security	Facility Access Control Management	C-Cure 800				
Corporate Security Investigations	Investigative Reporting Tool					
Crisis Management	Incident Command Management Process	Outlook- Email				

Exhibit 6.6   Critical assessment (CA) IT applications.

should be easy to understand by the people expected to complete the form. It is advisable to have an instructional booklet to assist in explaining the CA, but it is ill advised to have a survey that is so complicated that people need to constantly refer to the instructions. The instructions should explain what you expect people to do during the completion of the survey—the meaning of certain words that may not be common language, the type of answers, or the automatic population of cells from previous calculations/spreadsheets. It is also a good idea to have brief meetings with the participants to explain the survey form. The example provided in Appendix 5 is fairly self-explanatory, but even that survey would benefit from an explanation.

The project team should reach out to the appropriate departments and bring them into the discussion of the CA. Through a unified effort of the various departments, it should be possible to develop a good criticality assessment survey (tool) that will provide the desired information. Each business unit will have to complete the CA survey. It is important that each operational unit be involved to ensure that an accurate reflection of the processes of those units is established. The best resource for gaining

CA Survey/"Process Assessment & Impact Analysis" Section 6—Other Critical Applications, Shared Drives, etc.			
Examples: MS-Word, MS-Excel, MS-PowerPoint, Visio, etc..			
Examples: Z:\Shared\Security\Projects\Reports; Be specific as to the path, folder name(s), file names, etc.			
Primary Business Activity (autofilled from Section 2)	**Functional Processes (autofilled from Section 2)**	**Applications, Shared Drives, etc. (list in order of importance)**	**Comments**
Building Security	Facility Access Control Management	C-Cure 800:\\ CCURE800\Shared\ Corporate_Security	C-Cure dedicated server in Administration Bldg Datacenter, rack 12
Corporate Security Investigations	Investigative Reporting Tool	Incident Reporting Tool: \\XYZ\Shared\ Corporate_Security\ Reporting_Made_Easy	Application on server 25 in Administration Bldg Datacenter, rack 12
Crisis Management	Incident Command Management Process	N/A	Refer to the Crisis Management Plan (hard copy)— network resources are unnecessary

Exhibit 6.7 Critical assessment (CA) other critical applications.

an understanding of the actual processes involved in an operation shall be obtained from those actually performing the functions. The CA template in Appendix 5 is a typical example of many surveys in use. It is simple, direct, and uses MS Excel® as the application. The value of using this sort of survey is that it does not require any expense other than the staff time involved, but that would be needed regardless of the application, and the results will be presented in a consistent report. The use of a spreadsheet to gather survey results is directly related to the end results. They are based on uniform calculations and consistent questions. The survey should be augmented with an opportunity to interview the managers of the business units to ensure that the data reflected in the survey are correctly presented. Remember, the survey results will be the basis of decisions affecting the resources that are provided for recovery and crisis management efforts.

The following exhibits show the CA template with test data so that the reader will have a better understanding of the formulae and spreadsheet commands. Further explanations of the template pages are presented in Appendix 5. You should be able to create a similar document for your use, but remember to ensure that the CA that is used achieves the desired goals of your organization. If you choose to use this template, it may be necessary to customize it in accordance with your needs. Modify it as necessary and incorporate any other templates/suggestions that are appropriate. The goal is to develop a document that will provide the results that best serve the organization.

A reasonable approach to conducting a CA is to schedule training sessions for those staff members who will be tasked with performing the actual work of completing the survey forms. This training is not intended to make any of the staff experts, but rather to ensure that they have the necessary understanding of the forms, to answer any questions about definitions, to explain how to go about thinking about the processes, and the goal of the CA. It is important for these people to really appreciate the value of the work involved in completing the CA. As stated earlier, the CA does not have to be complicated or fancy, but it does have to document the information that you need to make informed decisions. It may be necessary to directly assist a department in completing its CA form(s) to ensure that the surveys are done correctly.

After the survey forms have been completed, it will be necessary to have a meeting with the participants to review the answers. The information on the forms must be understandable by the reviewer and meet whatever standards have been applied for the CA completion. Remember, the goal of the CA is to document the processes of the organization; the determination of what is critical comes afterwards. Some of the determination can be built into the survey as noted on the examples, but any autocalculations must be verified with the Finance Department to ensure that the information is correct. Process criticality is very likely to be expensive, both as a routine process (revenues) and as an item for recovery. The organization will have to decide what constitutes a critical process, an important process, and a deferrable process. The processes that are considered critical will likely require technology and Disaster Recovery preparations to ensure acceptable recovery time objectives. Therefore, the goal of the CA is twofold: (1) to determine processes necessary to maintain the viability of the organization, and (2) the CA provides information to the IT staff to accommodate the technological needs of the aforementioned processes.

Exhibits 6.8 through 6.13 provide further explanation of the important components of the example criticality assessment. The balloon comments provide information to allow the reader to construct a simple CA document for use in his or her organization. As stated earlier, the CA does not have to be complicated, but it does have to be effective. Ensure that all stakeholders are involved in the development and review of the CA creation and interpretation to ensure accuracy. The Business Continuity and Disaster Recovery staff professionals are probably very familiar with a CA and may have templates to use.

Criticality Assessment Survey
This Criticality Assessment (CA) survey is designed to identify the critical business processes required for a business unit to operate. Through completion of this survey you will be able to determine the financial impact to your operation; the important processes that are related to reputation, legal/regulatory compliance, and other qualitative considers; the necessary infrastructure dependencies; recovery time objectives; and the resumption prioritization, from the business unit's perspective, during an unacceptable business interruption. The critical decision of determining which processes to recover and in which order, if at all, is a management decision derived through analysis of the aforementioned information.
Section 1—Project Cover Sheet
Business Unit Surveyed:
Survey Respondent:
Business Unit Manager:

Enter the appropriate information to identify that business unit, manager, and the person completing the forms.

Exhibit 6.8 Critical assessment (CA) template cover sheet.

CA Survey/ "Process Assessment & Impact Analysis" Section 2—Processes, Recovery Time Objectives (RTOs), and Business Resumption Sequence					
Refer to Appendix A.5 for detailed steps and sample responses.					
Complete columns A through F as they pertain to your business unit based on the following definitions:					
A "Primary Business Activity" is a fundamental high-level activity (or family of related activities) that are critical to the continuity of business, regulatory compliance, business/process controls and reporting requirements, adherence to applicable Company policies, and the overall survival of the company. A Primary Business Process is made up of one or several subset activities.					
"Functional Processes" are supporting processes that, along with other supporting processes, contribute to the execution and completion of a company Core Business Process.					
Recovery Time Objective (RTO) is the business unit's expectation for recovering from a business interruption and resuming a specific business process/function. RTOs are subject to justification, management approval, and proper funding of the associated recovery solution.					
Primary Business Activity	**Functional Processes**	**Critical RTO**	**Desired RTO Range**	**Preferred Business Resumption Sequence (Specify 1,2,3>>)**	**Routine Work Location**
Building Security	Facility Access Control Management	24 hrs	24 to 48 hours	2	1 Main St. Anywhere, USA
Corporate Security Investigations	Investigative Reporting Tool	72 hrs	48 to 72 hours	3	1 Main St. Anywhere, USA
Crisis Management	Incident Command Management Process	N\A	0 to 2 hours	1	1 Main St. Anywhere, USA

Enter business name and process	Business leader determines RTO	Business leader determines order of recovery for process

Exhibit 6.9   Critical assessment (CA) processes and recovery time objectives.

CA Survey/"Process Assessment & Impact Analysis"
Section 3—Financial Impacts on Unit Operation

=IF(F6<25000,1,IF(F6<100000,2,IF(F6<500000,3,IF(F6<1000000,4,5)))) Command to reflect the value of Row Total in cell F6 ($3240) as an impact Risk Score

Refer to Appendix A.5 for detailed steps and sample responses.

This is entered as a formula so that adjustments can be made with clarity maintained. =SUM(27*5*24)

Financial impact estimate for each identified process in your business operation of the Criticality Assessment Survey. Provide worst-case estimates for the busiest day of the week/month/year.

Financial Impact Risk Score — Financial Loss Range:
5 — $1,000,000 > $500,000 to 999,999
4 — $100,000 to 499,999
3 —
2 — $25,001 to 99,999
1 — < $25,000

Describe how financial estimates were reached (production volume, requirements, expenses/revenues, calculations, etc.).

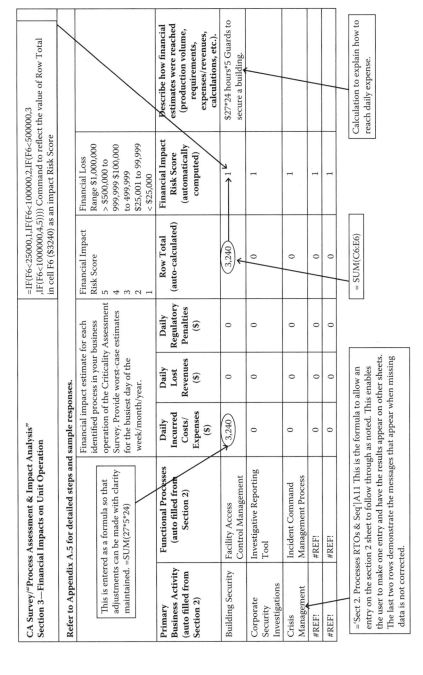

Primary Business Activity (auto filled from Section 2)	Functional Processes (auto filled from Section 2)	Daily Incurred Costs/ Expenses ($)	Daily Lost Revenues ($)	Daily Regulatory Penalties ($)	Row Total (auto-calculated)	Financial Impact Risk Score (automatically computed)	Describe how financial estimates were reached (production volume, requirements, expenses/revenues, calculations, etc.).
Building Security	Facility Access Control Management	3,240	0	0	3,240	1	$27*24 hours*5 Guards to secure a building.
Corporate Security Investigations	Investigative Reporting Tool	0	0	0	0	1	
Crisis Management	Incident Command Management Process	0	0	0	0	1	
#REF!	#REF!	0	0	0	0	1	
#REF!	#REF!	0	0	0	0	1	

='Sect 2. Processes RTOs & Seq'!A11 This is the formula to allow an entry on the section 2 sheet to follow through as noted. This enables the user to make one entry and have the results appear on other sheets. The last two rows demonstrate the messages that appear when missing data is not corrected.

= SUM(C6:E6)

Calculation to explain how to reach daily expense.

Exhibit 6.10 Critical assessment (CA) financial impacts.

CA Survey/"Process Assessment & Impact Analysis"
Section 4—NonFinancial Impacts
Estimate the extent of "nonfinancial" impacts based on the choices below.

This will provide a quantitative understanding for operational issues not realizing a financial impact.

Primary Business Activity (auto filled from Section 2)	Functional Processes (auto filled from Section 2)	Functional Operations Risk Score (auto filled from Section 2)	Risk Impact Score (Non financial Impact)	Reputation Risk Score (Non financial Impact)	Total CA Impact Score (sum of 3 preceding scores)	Business Critically Rating (Defined by CA Score)	Describe how the "non-financial" impacts were determined—justify answer
		Auto filled with this command: = 'Sect 3. Financial Impacts' !G6	Impact Score Ranges 4 to 5 = High Impact 3 = Moderate Impact 1 to 2 = Minimal Impact			Criticality Score 11 to 15 = Critical 6 to 10 = Important 3 to 5 = Deferrable	The number is based on the value to the left
Building Security	Facility Access Control Management	1	3	3	7	Important	System necessary for access to controlled areas.
Corporate Security Investigations	Investigative Reporting Tool	1	1	1	3	Deferrable	Necessary for reports on security incidents. Manual work-around available for short term.
Crisis Management	Incident Command Management Process	1	5	5	11	Critical	Incident Command does not rely on one system—manual work-arounds available.

Exhibit 6.11 Critical assessment (CA) nonfinancial impacts.

CA Survey/"Process Assessment & Impact Analysis" Section 5—IT Applications Required						
For each process, indicate the IT Application required.						
Primary Business Activity (auto filled from Section 2)	**Functional Processes (auto filled from Section 2)**	**Application 1**	**Application 2**	**Application 3**	**Application 4**	**Application 5**
Building Security	Facility Access Control Management	C-Cure 800				
Corporate Security Investigations	Investigative Reporting Tool					
Crisis Management	Incident Command Management Process	Outlook- Email				

List applications for the auto filled business activity and process—allows IT to know required resources for recovery.

Exhibit 6.12   Critical assessment (CA) IT applications.

153

CA Survey/"Process Assessment & Impact Analysis" Section 6—Other Critical Applications, Shared Drives, etc.
Examples: MS-Word, MS-Excel, MS-PowerPoint, Visio, etc..
Examples: Z:\Shared\Security\Projects\Reports; Be specific as to the path, folder name(s), file names, etc.

Primary Business Activity (auto filled from Section 2)	Functional Processes (auto filled from Section 2)	Applications, Shared Drives, etc. (list in order of importance)	Comments
Building Security	Facility Access Control Management	C-Cure 800:\\ CCURE800\Shared\ Corporate_Security	C-Cure dedicated server in Administration Bldg Datacenter, rack 12
Corporate Security Investigations	Investigative Reporting Tool	Incident Reporting Tool: \\XYZ\Shared\ Corporate_Security\ Reporting_M ade_Easy	Application on server 25 in Administration Bldg Datacenter, rack 12
Crisis Management	Incident Command Management Process	N/A	Refer to the Crisis Management Plan (hard copy)—network resources are unnecessary

Auto filled from earlier sheets

Network path information for resources explanation of the device.

Exhibit 6.13   Critical assessment (CA) other critical applications.

Risk Treatment

The risk treatment is essentially what is going to be done to modify the risk. Using the risk assessment process, the organizational leaders are now in a position to make decisions relating to the risks. They have an understanding of the risks and may now determine the best course of action to treat the risk. An important thing to remember when considering treatments for risks, is that these treatments are not necessarily intended to be used individually; you may want to consider applying as many as possible so that there is an overlapping or dove-tailing effect. This will reduce the risk and increase the confidence that the organization can achieve its objectives. Obviously, preemptive and proactive treatment methods are preferred. It is always better to avoid a problem whenever possible. While it may be desirable to remove the source of the risk, it may not always be possible. For instance, if you have identified the public entering your facility as a source of risk, you should consider preventing the public from entering. If the facility is a private organization and there is no business reason to allow entry, you may want to remove that source of risk. If the facility is a public building, you may not have that ability, but there are other options to consider.

You may decide to temporarily halt the activities that generate the risk, thereby avoiding the risk. Closing the building for the above example is a possible treatment and results in avoiding the risk because the public is unable to access the facility. Avoiding the risk is a good way to address the risk if avoidance is possible. Not all organizations will be able to avoid a risk because that risk in an inherent part of doing business.

Another approach to treating a risk is to reduce the likelihood of the risk. Reducing the likelihood of the risk occurring involves clearly understanding what causes the risk and removing as many causes as possible. Establishing or updating the control measures (procedures) for various risks issues is an effective way to reduce or remove the likelihood of occurrence.

Removing or reducing harmful consequences is an excellent approach if you are not able to reduce the likelihood of occurrence. The risk remains, but the consequences have been addressed through reduction or removal. If this approach is used, it is extremely important to maintain an accurate and current understanding of the risk issues. If the risks change, it is possible that the treatment that once was effective will no longer produce the same results.

Sharing the risk with other parties, including risk insurance, is an extremely common approach and one that most of us understand very well. Auto insurance is a perfect example of how the risk is transferred to another party. As with the other treatment options, it is highly advisable to seek a multiple treatment approach if feasible and warranted by the business objectives. Often the risk treatment approaches will produce an additive effect in that there is a benefit, albeit minor, from each approach and the cumulative value is synergistic in effect. Keep in mind that risk is never truly transferred, only shared.

Retaining risk by informed decision is an acceptable and viable option when reducing the risk is cost prohibitive to address otherwise or the consequence is relatively minor. For instance, if the risk is very unlikely to occur or the consequence is minor in effect, it may not be

155

worth spending the money to treat the risk; the benefit does not outweigh the cost. If you are guided by Hollywood movies you should be convinced that a meteor is destined to hit the Earth and destroy life as we know it. Who knows, perhaps Bruce Willis is on retainer to NASA. The meteor scenario is a good example of something that an organization will not have the resources to affect. Allowing this risk to go unattended is a good business decision. The cost to develop something to deflect or destroy the meteor is almost certainly cost prohibitive for any single organization. While this is assuredly a silly example, it is clearly an excellent one showing how a cost prohibitive issue is a valid reason in making a decision *not* to treat the risk.

7

Implementation Tools

ROLE, RESPONSIBILITIES, AND AUTHORITIES

All organizations operate through the assignment of roles and responsibilities along with the necessary authority to carry out these assigned duties. ORM (organizational resilience management) implementation is no different. Selecting the right people to perform assignments is of obvious importance and will often be a deciding factor in the successful planning and implementation of ORM. Those leaders tasked with the responsibility to accomplish the implementation of an organizational resilience management program must receive their authority from the most senior leadership in the organization; they must be empowered to communicate the message of developing the culture of risk management that we have discussed throughout this book. While the senior management leaders are required to play important roles, they are not the ones who will actually perform the day-to-day activities. The assigned leaders performing the management functions associated with the ORM implementation effort must ensure they have developed an ongoing system that conforms to ANSI/ASIS SPC.1-2009. They are responsible for developing, communicating, implementing, and maintaining the requirements of the aforementioned standard (ANSI/ASIS SPC.1-2009, p. 9). An important part of the system that will allow for the successful conformance with SPC 1-2009 is a reporting structure that keeps the senior management leaders both informed and involved. ORM is a top-down initiative and it is imperative to maintain the interest and involvement of the senior leaders as a vital part of the effort. It will mean the difference between failure and success. It is common practice to report on the progress of a project to

157

senior management so that the expenditure of resources is justified. The ANSI/ASIS SPC.1-2009 Standard requires that senior management be kept informed of the progress, but not just because of resource justification; improvements can't be made if there is no understanding of the journey (ANSI/ASIS SPC.1-2009, p. 9). Making improvements is not an option, but is a requirement of the standard to ensure that the measures and practices instilled in the organization are kept relevant.

TRAINING AND AWARENESS

The quality of the personnel involved in performing the myriad tasks associated with addressing the issues surrounding the sorts of incidents discussed in this book, as well as developing, implementing, and maintaining the conformance of ANSI/ASIS SPC.1-2009 at an organization, should be educated and trained to perform those tasks. While formal education centering on resilience-oriented disciplines is extremely important and valuable, training specifically designed to provide the necessary knowledge to perform the tasks of conforming to the standard is critical. You must have people performing the tasks who know what they are doing; achieving resilience will not occur by accident. In addition to a general knowledge of risk management and ORM, personnel must understand their respective organization and the current risks. It also is crucial to ensure that the regular employees of the organization understand their importance to ORM. They must be trained and prepared for active involvement in the success of organizational resilience. You must ensure that the culture of organizational resilience management is identified as a core value of the organization (ANSI/ASIS SPC.1-2009, p. 10). All members of the organization, including both internal and external stakeholders, must understand their importance and they must understand what is necessary to accomplish and conform to ANSI/ASIS SPC.1-2009; training shall communicate that information. We have discussed the critical value of instilling risk management and organizational resilience into the very culture of the organization. Training is a fundamental method to achieve that goal. You have heard that mathematics is not a spectator sport; the same can be said for ORM—you must learn it and live it every day.

It is important to clarify the difference between training and exercising within the context of ORM. Training is the process of teaching material to the people who must clearly understand and use that knowledge. In this case, all stakeholders require a certain level of training. Exercising is the coordinated demonstration of how well the people learned the material from the training. There is a certain level of learning that takes place from exercising, but it is incorrect to equate exercising with training.

Training is necessary to achieve organizational resilience and an absolute if OR is to be maintained. Awareness training can be in the form of posters, brief announcements as the computer logs into the network, brochures or pamphlets, and any other form of quick reminders. Quick reminder-oriented training is great to keep all organizational personnel informed on important issues. This is a common form of training that is used by network and physical security professionals. Providing training to personnel and the scheduling of exercises is a constant challenge for organizations, but is an issue that actually makes the difference between a managed crisis and an event that is made more chaotic. Properly trained and prepared personnel shall have the greatest chance of managing an incident, and poorly trained personnel shall have the greatest chance of the incident overwhelming them. Conducting analyses and developing plans are only worth the amount of time and effort expended on training personnel. Having prepared and knowledgeable personnel is the single most valuable resource during an emergency. Fostering a traditional perspective of training (a specific period of time and conditions surrounding activities, e.g., sitting in a class, reading a manual, listening/watching a video presentation, etc.) without considering the inherent value of routine events as training opportunities is a failure to recognize the possibilities of developing a more dynamic vision of training. Traditional training approaches are valuable and should be used, but there is a tremendous opportunity to train personnel from the beginning of the project and this realization is necessary to prevent wasted opportunities. Everything involved with the project of implementing ORM is an opportunity for training. People learn to work together, they learn to communicate more effectively and in a timely fashion, they learn different perspectives surrounding risk, they discover what is important to the organization and why, and they learn from their mistakes. These examples are hidden opportunities for training that exist if you acknowledge the possibility of expanding the traditional concept of training. It is not necessary to gather all stakeholders in a classroom for a briefing to conduct training. A classroom training session may be great, but it is not the only form of training. Any opportunity to learn is training; it does not need to be complex and time-consuming. A common excuse not to have training is that people are too busy, which is a poor and defeatist excuse that only shows the limited vision of the people involved. Building training into the actual philosophy of the resiliency approach will allow routine events to become opportunities for training. Any chance to increase the effectiveness of communication practices and techniques is a valuable training experience for all of those involved.

The following is an example of an opportunity for training that was missed and what could have been done to train the responders and managers. At company X, security officers on patrol discovered a water leak in a large meeting room during the early hours (0400) of the morning. Security notified the maintenance on-call person of the problem; the technician responded at 0500 and took responsibility for addressing the problem. Instead of addressing this as an incident with potential far-reaching consequences, the maintenance tech considered it just another maintenance call and began working on the problem in a routine fashion. The technician did not know that the CEO had a meeting in that room scheduled for first thing in the morning (0800). While the technician thought he was doing the right thing in handling the water leak—stop the water, look for the cause and correct the identified cause, and repair any damage—his failure to report this to his supervisor created a more significant problem. The maintenance tech was not trained to inform others of a leak in case it might affect other aspects of the organization. This was a failure of management to consider the training opportunities that are afforded in routine problems. The incident was not communicated beyond the first level of resolution. The risk-oriented managers/stakeholders were not notified, thereby preventing the crisis management or business recovery/disaster recovery personnel from rescheduling the meeting. While the water leak by itself was not a crisis, it fell to someone to explain to the CEO that his presentation had to be rescheduled at the last minute because of a water leak that had been identified four hours earlier (the event planners didn't know about the water leak and the damage to the room until they arrived for the presentation). Telling the boss that people failed to consider options of this sort can easily become a crisis for those involved.

This example is rather simple and common, but illustrates the problems that typically face incident responders when missed opportunities for training are not identified. The command and control element of the preparedness operation is critical to achieving resiliency and must be routinely exercised if it is to remain viable and dynamic. ANSI/ASIS SPC.1-2009 requires that those individuals involved in implementing and performing the functions associated with ORM are properly trained and certified in their respective areas of responsibility. Again, training is often viewed as a luxury that is not really needed because the organization has plans and procedures in place to handle an incident. This is a perfect plan for failure. Personnel need to know what the plans and procedures are for them to be implemented.

The fundamental opportunity for training from either of the afore-mentioned examples is taking advantage of routine problems and using them to train personnel. After an incident, you can review how the incident was handled and evaluate if it could be done better in the future. This is ad hoc- or opportunity-based training because it does not require any planning other than the willingness to use the event to perform realistic and practical training. This approach, as all the others, must be part of the strategy to increase resiliency within the organization. If key emergency personnel assigned to leadership positions on the organization's Incident or Crisis Command team require training, it is possible to gain experience and training by using routine issues as an opportunity to train personnel. Incidents such as weather events are great for allowing decision makers to interact and practice making decisions quickly in a much less stressful situation. Naturally, it will be difficult for the functional level managers to explain to senior level managers that training is needed. Senior managers may consider themselves ready to manage any incident because they hold a senior position. Building opportunity training into the basic ORM project plan is a good way to create the expectation that everyone will be involved in training regardless of position. Having the CEO of the organization approve and support the ORM strategy is another great way to ensure the involvement of the senior level managers.

Self-study is an extremely simple approach to providing training and is accomplished through multimedia presentations or written manuals/books. A self-study does require dedication and discipline from the individual to complete the training, but it is usually inexpensive and less invasive on the employee's time while at work. Of course, that assumption is based on the employee performing the self-study at home. Salaried employees will be able to perform the training at home, but hourly workers are a different issue. Providing time at work to attend this training is both wise and cost-effective for the organization. Some people do not perform well with this type of training and caution is advised to prevent reliance on a method that may not be as effective as it should be. As noted above, discipline is required for this type of training and the ability to process the information without the benefit of interaction with an instructor may be ineffective for some people, depending on their learning style. The development of stakeholders through training is best achieved with a blending of various methods like self-study, classroom, tabletops, and full exercises.

Classroom training is the traditional approach to conveying information and certainly serves an important purpose. Through PowerPoint® presentations and assorted training aids, the participants receive a structured presentation of information. The feasibility of this sort of training for higher-level managers may be questionable because of time constraints, but it is an excellent method for presenting information and does not necessarily require anything fancy. If the organization has in-house expertise, it may be possible to conduct the training without any expense other than the time of the personnel. For classroom training to be effective, it must be well developed and presented by an experienced lecturer capable of engaging the participants. The ability to hold the attention of the participants is critical. Some of this material is rather dry, and this may become a problem. Don't let students/participants become bored due to the lecture material being dry; creativity in the presentation of the material will keep the students involved. The use of creative visuals and practical examples instead of a regular, spoken cadence of material will also help increase the interest of the attendees.

Structured workshops or educational sessions provided by external organizations may be a valuable teaching approach if people have the resources to attend. There are excellent training opportunities from established organizations to establish a knowledge base or foster a greater understanding of relevant material, e.g., ASIS International, Disaster Recovery Institute International, International Consortium for Organizational Resilience, Federal Emergency Management Agency, National Fire Protection Association, Project Management Institute, etc. These organizations offer both traditional classroom instruction and self-study courses. Regular training from professional organizations is a great way to maintain a current understanding of knowledge that is necessary to achieve organizational resilience. There also is the need to consider training opportunities that represent and incorporate many disciplines, because achieving organizational resilience entails accepting the reality that many stakeholders and specialties are involved in OR. The better rounded an organization's risk managers are, the better they will be able to participate in achieving organizational resilience. Therefore, it is valuable for these risk managers to acquire training outside of their primary functional area of responsibility.

COMMUNICATIONS

One of the most difficult activities of any initiative or project is effective communications to the right audience. There are many different audiences and each has a specific interest that the message must address. It is unlikely that any single message will achieve the desired level of effectiveness. A general audience may only want a very broad discussion, while specialists would expect and demand a more detailed message. Using communication techniques to inform an organization about either a particular project or an emergency requires an understanding of the desired message, the audience, the desired outcome, and the probable interference between the message and the audience. Understanding the various audiences will allow you to craft the correct message, with the correct level of detail and focus. It is not uncommon to send several messages to the subsets of the organizational audience targeting those recipients with a tailored message. It also is necessary to send reminder or update messages over a period of time. Remember, the message must be kept accurate to be of value and there will be changes in any project over time.

It is necessary to establish procedures to address communications before, during, and after an incident so that any effort is organized and effective. Any change that affects the efforts connected to the ORM system (any crisis, security or business continuity plans, response procedures, training documents or exercise evaluations, etc.) must be documented and maintained for accuracy (ANSI/ASIS SPC.1-2009, p. 10).

OPERATIONAL CONTROLS

Operational controls consist of documented and maintained procedures developed under the auspices of the ORM policy and associated objectives to address the various organizational risks identified through the risk management process. The procedures are an important part of the conformance with ANSI/ASIS SPC.1-2009. The procedures are typical to incident prevention, preparedness, and response as identified as the below noted actions (ANSI/ASIS SPC.1-2009, p. 12):

- Preserve life safety
- Protect assets
- Prevent further escalation of the disruptive incident
- Reduce the length of the disruption to operations
- Restore critical operational continuity

- Recover normal operations (including evaluating improvements)
- Protect image and reputation (including media coverage and stakeholder relationships)

The use of procedures is a standard approach in addressing any matter that requires an organized and standardized course of action. Security practitioners have procedural manuals designed to provide the instructions necessary for in-depth protective response. A layered series of protective measures allows for a carefully designed, proactive treatment of risks. A commonly used heuristic is deter, deny, delay, detect, and respond. This is especially true in the layered approach to risk, which is described below.

The outer layer is deterrence: fences, dogs, active security monitoring patrols, lights, and open areas. You basically try to scare an intruder off before a problem develops. The fences, locked doors, and similar physical barriers deny access to sensitive areas or assets. They also delay access, allowing detection from other measures, such as cameras or patrols. Response is the inner most layer of protective measure, but should not be viewed as failure if used. Having personnel or a technological response is a part of the protective philosophy and is necessary. An important facet of protective measures is recovering from an incident and the acceptance that improvement may be necessary. Continual improvement is a valuable and critical part of resiliency and not just a buzz phrase from a business textbook. Systems by their very nature are subject to change from the constituent components of that system, and as things change, improvements must be made.

8

Evaluation Tools

EXERCISES AND TESTING

The importance of evaluating the established plans, procedures, and the personnel, both internal and external, associated with the organizational resilience management (ORM) system should be obvious. Conformance with ANSI/ASIS SPC.1-2009 requires the validation of the system through exercises to ensure that the effectiveness of the plans, procedures, and processes operate as expected and that they achieve the desired outcome (ANSI/ASIS SPC.1-2009, p. 14). A brief description and proposed value for several types of exercises are provided below for consideration. The important point to remember about exercises or evaluations is that they are designed to test performance against set criteria or objectives. The criteria must be established before the exercise, and the criteria should be consistent with the requirements set forth by ANSI/ASIS SPC.1-2009. You are looking to test the ability of the organization and the ORM system to perform. This is a chance to see how successful your efforts have been at reaching for a resilient organization. Granted, an exercise is only a test and not the real thing, but an exercise is an excellent opportunity to identify weaknesses and discrepancies in conformance to the standard. Conformance will achieve resilience, and exercises are a necessary part of the journey.

Tabletop

A tabletop exercise is an opportunity for stakeholders to gather for an exercise without the involvement of a large number of participants. There is no predefined number of participants; this is strictly a function of the exercise and the involvement of the participants. The planners design a scenario that allows the participants to run through the exercise without having to leave the training room. Often the people sit around a table and simply explain what they would do during the event. It is possible to make this more involved and have external authorities (police and fire) attend and provide information that the internal personnel may not be as informed about. This may appear to be a waste of time, but it is an excellent chance for people to experience an exercise with more details and challenges than as a presentation in a classroom. The exercise moderator uses the scenario to allow the participants to make decisions and respond to issues.

A tabletop exercise is an excellent opportunity for different departments to conduct an evaluation that requires a clear demonstration of how the various participants would react to a given event. Granted, the "reaction" of the participants will be very calculated, but the other participants will see and hear what the other stakeholders would do during an incident, thereby providing a better understanding of what to expect. This form of exercise provides the participants with an opportunity to experience a controlled exchange of information from various perspectives without considerable resources (time and money). It will be obvious which participants are prepared and clearly understand their role in an emergency and which members need additional training or role clarification. Tabletop exercises should be conducted after there has been some form of basic training like a classroom presentation or self-study. A tabletop exercise is not helpful to the participants if there has been little initial training. The people must have the required contextual understanding to appreciate the issues associated with the training.

Small Team and Large Team

The team approach involves personnel that would be involved in handling an event. (The determination of small or large is dependent upon the size of the exercise.) The members may be from one department or from different groups; it really depends on the scope of the exercise and the complexity of detail. Team exercises may be short or long in duration, several hours or for several days and involving organizational resources from different states. The key to success with this type of exercise is to begin small and work up to a more complex and dynamic exercise with multiple problems and demands on the participants. A primary goal of any exercise is to evaluate and allow the participants to learn from mistakes, and also to learn what they have done correctly. Ensuring that people fail is not going to produce a positive outcome with any long-term results that benefit the organization. Building confidence in the participants is crucial to the long-term success of ORM.

Larger Team/Organizational with External Entities

Including external entities, such as the local fire department or police, will bring a level of realism to the exercise that will send a clear message on the seriousness of the evaluation. These external entities, which may be vendors to the organization, will increase the understanding of all involved through an increase in the perspectives providing information to the situation. For instance, during a real event, if governmental entities like the police or fire departments are called for assistance, they take command and the organization follows instructions from the command personnel. This is often a real surprise to organizational senior management accustomed to making decisions. A requirement to evacuate a building is not a suggestion, but an order and does not consider the importance of a scheduled business conference call. The preparedness groups (Business Continuity/Disaster Recovery, Crisis Management, etc.) should have arrangements in place to reduce the interruption from these sorts of events. Awareness training will help alert people to the need to prepare for alternate work arrangements. Evaluating the plans and understanding of key stakeholders is a great way to identify areas of concern requiring additional preparations to mitigate those issues.

Scenario Selection

The selection of a scenario should be based on the needs of the organization. It makes no sense to initiate an exercise for something that has nothing to do with the organization. For instance, a reasonable scenario for a Pennsylvania organization near Philadelphia would be severe weather involving snow or rain; preparing for a volcano would be a less useful exercise. The level of complexity for the scenario will likely be determined through the level of training and experience of the stakeholders. If the people in the organization have little experience, it is reasonable and appropriate to begin at a level that is not too complex. Allow the participants to gain an understanding and comfort level with handling emergencies before increasing the demands.

Scenarios should be as real as possible, within the context of the established session. Realism does not necessarily mean complexity. An exercise involving a test of the contact list is simple, but real if you require people to call into an established number by a certain time following notification. As personnel become more experienced, it will be possible to increase the level of complexity and demands on the decision makers. Scenarios should be designed to challenge and push personnel to experience the stress of a real situation. Expect mistakes in an exercise because that is the place to make them. Allow people to learn from their mistakes and remember to include those issues in the next training session as well as the next exercise. If the lesson was learned, the mistake should not reoccur.

Conducting Exercises

Time is the most difficult resource to obtain for training or exercising. Everyone has a reason why a certain time is not acceptable and the larger the group the more difficult the scheduling of the event will become. For this reason, smaller groups are much easier to manage, but it is possible to provide excellent opportunities through creative involvement of the personnel. The success of the exercise is always in the preparations and effort of those conducting the session. Identify the participants and their level of experience. Gauge the exercise to the audience and the intended outcome. Avoid trying to accomplish everything in a single session, especially if time is a serious constraint. Design the exercise with specific deliverables or evaluation objectives and focus on those issues, and ensure that the objectives are achieved during the exercise session.

Exercise Documentation

Evaluations are important documents to establish and maintain. Any evaluation becomes part of the ORM documentation and should contain who participated, what the exercise involved, where and when the event took place, the evaluation goals of the exercise, and the after action review indicating accomplishments and failures. It is important to establish an understanding in the beginning that the evaluation process is not intended to punish anyone, but is intended to assist in determining resource requirements, teaching weaknesses and future teaching needs, and basic achievement with the intended ORM goals. This will not be an easy sell and may not be accepted. The culture of the organization will probably be the deciding factor in how well evaluations are received.

It may be possible to change the attitude toward the evaluations after a number have been conducted and an emphasis is placed on successes. While it is important to focus on successes, it will be necessary to identify the failures or, perhaps more accurately phrased, items that need attention. Focusing on improving performance will take time. It also may be a political issue within the organization. As indicated earlier in this book, it is necessary to dissolve the silo approach, but that will take time and it is unwise to allow evaluations to become a cause of dissention. You don't want anyone looking bad in the early stages of this effort. Eventually, everyone involved will be held accountable, but it is crucial to allow people time to gain experience and understanding of the material.

Remember, there is no value in affixing blame or identifying a person as weak during or after an exercise. Exercises validate the training experience and seek weaknesses so that they may be corrected, but the harm from mishandling the weaknesses may be far-reaching more important than the actual weakness. For this reason, it is desirable to soften the description and avoid overt labels that may create tension. It is important to engender the need and desirability of evaluations in the organization. Viewing every routine event as an opportunity for training will create an expectation of regular feedback and review. Using a review template to allow for quick documentation, with diplomatic language, will be valuable in establishing a comfort level in receiving the reviews. People will become accustomed to the review form and the nonconfrontational language.

INTERNAL AUDITS

Internal audits, also known as first party audits, are an important part of achieving resilience within an organization. Most organizations conduct audits of some sort to ensure financial accountability, regulatory, or safety compliance, or one of a myriad of control measures to safeguard personnel and property assets of the organization. An audit of a management system is a planned process that must use acceptable approaches and techniques to ensure a valid result. Using "homegrown" audit methods is ill advised and may produce results that are questionable. ISO 19011-2011 *Guidelines for Auditing Management Systems* is well respected and detailed in providing the necessary information to accomplish a reliable and factual audit.

Most of us have been involved in inspections, either as participants or as the person conducting the inspection. You look for current plans and documents at the security posts and note any problems (e.g., electrical concerns, HVAC or water issues, faulty or nonworking equipment, etc.) as you walk around inspecting the facility. This sort of activity takes a few hours and does not take into consideration the complexity of a management system. An internal management system audit is about evaluating the effectiveness of the management system and the risk treatment measure to identify opportunities for improvement.

An audit, as stated above, is a carefully planned process of collecting factual evidence leading to an objective evaluation against established criteria which results in a conclusion of how well the organization has achieved conformance to the standard. It is necessary to understand that an audit is a careful, systematic evaluation that determines the level of conformance. An audit is not an inspection or a cursory review. Because a system is a complex series of interrelated processes, it is necessary to examine the processes of the system to determine if they are working. An audit normally takes up to approximately one week to conduct—you can't rush through a proper audit. It also is important to remember that an audit involves the leaders that are responsible for the management system. The organizational leadership drives a management system and an audit must reflect their performance in managing the system's performance.

The audit team consists of personnel possessing an acceptable level of audit experience/knowledge and who do not have a conflict of interest in the audit. A knowledgeable person that was not responsible for the work under audit review conducts an internal audit. It is never wise to have someone review his or her own work for conformance. Some organizations retain the services of companies that conduct first-party audits using the ISO 19001 in order to avoid conflicts and to have an external set of eyes look at the ORM system from a different angle. Objective and thorough audits should be conducted according to a schedule (both planned and irregular/sporadic) to verify that the objectives, control measures, processes, and procedures are still accurate and reflect the current state of the organizational risks (ANSI/ASIS SPC.1-2009, p. 15). Audits allow the organization to verify that the changes which have occurred over time have been incorporated into the risk management process and the continual improvement requirements identified in the ANSI/ASIS SPC.1-2009. An audit should not be viewed as an adversarial activity, but rather a positive and necessary safeguard for the organization. Managers may consider an audit to be a threat to their operation, but this is a mistake and educational awareness should be part of the communication efforts to build support for the ORM.

The audit process and activities should be documented and be made common knowledge to the entire organization. Do not hide what the auditors do; acceptance will only occur with an enlightened attitude and understanding toward the audit function. Documenting the audit criteria, purpose, scope, and structured methods for conducting an audit are necessary to educate the organization's employees on what to expect, but also to clearly show what is necessary to ensure an accurate and thorough audit (ANSI/ASIS SPC.1-2009, p. 16).

If the organization has the resources, it is advisable and highly valuable to have trained auditors as part of the organization. Some organizations feel that having an in-house team of certified lead auditors that operate independently using the same auditing standards as certification bodies is preferred over external, third-party certification. There are many training courses for auditors, but if becoming a certified resilience lead auditor is necessary or desirable for professional development, it is extremely important to select the correct training program. Not all programs will lead to a valid certification. It is wise to verify that the resilience lead auditor training course will qualify the candidate for an internationally recognized certification to audit. Be careful of the nuances of training providers. A certified course that issues a certificate is not the same as a certified course that leads to the path of becoming a certified auditor. Many people mistakenly take the former path only to discover that they need to start over again to achieve the title of certified lead auditor.

9

Maturity Model

WHAT IS A MATURITY MODEL?

Philip Crosby developed the concept of a maturity model in his 1979 book *Quality Is Free*, in which he presented a Quality Management Maturity Grid. Since then, maturity models have become valuable tools in quality assurance, business continuity, and a number of management systems on these topics and others.

ANSI/ASIS SPC.4-2012 presents a six-phase maturity model for measuring organizational resilience efforts within an organization that will allow for a more rational and effective approach to achieving ORM at an organization. ANSI/ASIS SPC.4-2012 correctly identifies that the phased approach recognizes that resilience must be achieved in balance with the business needs of the organization. Furthermore, there are time and financial constraints when building a system that is continually improving, growing, and maturing (ANSI/ASIS SPC.4-2012, p. 4). By using this maturity model, an organization has the greatest chance of implementing ORM and achieving organizational resilience within the business realities common in today's economy. A typical organization has very limited resources and attempting to implement ANSI/ASIS SPC.1-2009 through extensive use of unlimited resources is simply not reasonable. Remember, the common managerial phrase in current use is: "Do more with less." And, this applies to projects as well as regular job assignments. Depending on the organization and the experience of the personnel involved, it is possible to either start at phase one and move along, or start at a higher level to achieve the desired effect (ANSI/ASIS

SPC.4-2012, p. 5). Each organization shall have different levels of preparedness in place and the maturity model factors that into the evaluation stage. The maturity model clearly demonstrates that implementing the ANSI/ASIS SPC.1-2009 Standard is not an all-or-nothing proposition. The ANSI/ASIS SPC.1-2009 Standard acknowledges the need and appropriateness of implementing strategies that are necessary for an organization in accordance with the organization's business environment. The maturity model allows the organization to evaluate all risk-oriented preparedness measures against the phases indicated in the model. The evaluation is accomplished through the comparison between the standard and what the organization has in place—the Gap Analysis. An easy way to perform this comparison is to use the tables included herein as part of the Appendices (1, 2, and 3) section and to use the conformance matrix provided in Appendix 1. Once the evaluation is complete, the project team will be able to determine the appropriate maturity model phase through a comparison between what is in place and what still remains to be completed. It is not necessary for the organization to seek full conformance if there is no business justification. Seek conformance for the level that is appropriate for the organization.

Exhibit 9.1 documents the various maturity levels (stages) and their respective meaning. This maturity model is an excellent way to evaluate the current level of preparedness and conformance with the ANSI/ASIS SPC.1-2009 Standard. Determining which level an organization has attained may be very easy or a bit more obscure. As noted above, it is very possible that an organization will start at a higher level and only progress one or two levels. The level of progression is an organizational decision based on the needs and resources available. Senior management may consider moving beyond stage 5 as unnecessary because there is no business justification. Again, this is an organization-specific decision and what is appropriate for one organization does not necessarily equate as necessary for another organization. Exhibit 9.2 documents the phases for implementation of ANSI/ASIS SPC.1-2009 from the maturity model perspective. Chapter 5 contained detailed tables of the implementation conformance requirements to the ANSI/ASIS SPC.1-2009 Standard, and provided further guidance on implementation.

Phase	Explanation
Phase One: Pre-Awareness	Pre-awareness phase where the organization is not conducting pre-planning – no formal resilience management process is in place – lack of information about resilience management – may be viewed as "putting out res" – undesirable phase.
Phase Two: Project Approach	Beginning phase – senior management is willing to allow a trial or pilot project to explore the benefits of resilience management – small project focusing on core elements of OR Standard as a means to improve performance – critical to view this phase as a typical project requiring standard project management practices.
Phase Three: Program Approach	Expansion of the project phase from limited scope project to organization-wide issues – focuses on individual core elements rather than interrelationships and integration of elements – emphasis is on action plans to address critical issues.
Phase Four: Systems Approach	Putting the pieces together – core elements are paid special attention with the goal of identifying and addressing root causes with viable solutions – resilience management is continually improved through the Standard – it is understood that the process has built-in learning opportunities.
Phase Five: Management Approach	Organization can show conformance with Standard as the organizational resilience management system is fully implemented with a multi-year perspective by senior management – culture of resilience promoted to each member of organization – everyone is advised to take ownership of risk issues.
Phase Six: Holistic Management	The organization is prepared to go beyond the Standard and include external supply chain vendors to ensure a fully integrated resilience strategy – organization emphasizes enterprise-wide relationships with a well-developed culture of resilience management in all business units

Exhibit 9.1 Maturity model phases table.

Maturity Model for the Phased Implementation of the ANSI/ASIS SPC.1-2009 Organizational Resilience Standard				
ANSI/ASIS SPC.1 Standard Clause	**Core Element**	**Issues Addressed by Core Element (establish, implement, and maintain)**	**Preawareness (Phase One)**	**Project Approach (Phase Two)**
- Generic Concepts	- Key elemental theme	- Description of element.	- No formal organization al resilience management. - Risk and resilience management actions are reactionary in nature. - Not yet recognizing the importance and value of ORMS elements.	- Initiates a project to address specic issue(s) by partially implementing core elements. - Actions generally reactionary in nature, focusing on pre-identified issue(s). - Recognizes the importance of elements and the need for some preplanning. - Focus is on solving an identified problem(s) to demonstrate the business value of using the *Standard*.

Exhibit 9.2   Maturity model for phased implementation. (continued)

Maturity Model for the Phased Implementation of the ANSI/ASIS SPC.1-2009 Organizational Resilience Standard			
Program Approach (Phase Three)	**Systems Approach (Phase Four)**	**Management System (Phase Five)**	**Holistic Management (Phase Six)**
- Establishes a division- or organization-wide program to address organizational resilience issues by partially implementing core elements. - Recognizes the importance of elements and the need for preplanning; however, focus is on individual elements and not their interrelationship and integration (checklist approach). - May be in reaction to an incident or near miss or be driven by external concerns. - Risk management applications selected for their chances of demonstrating success.	- Organizational resilience management is viewed as a matter of strategic value to the organization. - Focuses on integration and interrelationships between core elements. - Focuses on mission-based management of risks to minimize both likelihood and consequences of a disruptive incident. - Organizational resilience management is viewed as part of a continual improvement process using PDCA model. - Managing risk is seen as important at all levels and individuals in organization.	- The organization is conformant with the requirements of the standard. - The organization establishes, documents, implements, maintains, and continually improves an ORMS in accordance with the requirements of the ORMS Standard. - Examines the linkages and interactions between the ORMS elements that compose the entirety of the system for the defined scope. - Manages risk using balanced strategies to adaptively, preemptively, and reactively address minimization of both likelihood and consequences of disruptive events.	- The organization goes beyond conformance to the standard to fully integrate organizational resilience management into its overall risk management strategy - The organization emphasizes enterprise-wide and supply chain relationships in all aspects of its ORMS. - The organization mentors other stakeholders (in its supply chain and community). The organization views its organizational resilience as an active integral part of community resilience.

Exhibit 9.2 Maturity model for phased implementation. (continued)

Maturity Model for the Phased Implementation of the ANSI/ASIS SPC.1-2009 Organizational Resilience Standard				
ANSI/ASIS SPC.1 Standard Clause	Core Element	Issues Addressed by Core Element (establish, implement, and maintain)	Preawareness (Phase One)	Project Approach (Phase Two)
4.1.1 Scope of OR Management System	- Understands the organization and its context. - Scope of ORMS.	- The internal, external, and risk management context of the organization. - Scope and boundaries for development and implementation of ORMS.	- No process to identify or internal and external context for organizational resilience. -No definition of scope.	- Projects of limited scope focusing on one or a limited number of issues viewed as having significant interest. - Internal, external, and risk management context limited to project scope definition.

Exhibit 9.2 Maturity model for phased implementation. (continued)

Maturity Model for the Phased Implementation of the ANSI/ASIS SPC.1-2009 Organizational Resilience Standard			
Program Approach (Phase Three)	**Systems Approach (Phase Four)**	**Management System (Phase Five)**	**Holistic Management (Phase Six)**
- Program driven by "Program Manager" who applies a program management approach.	- Integration and feedback loops of systems approach. - Organizational resilience management culture is developing and part of decision making.	- Organizational resilience management is demonstrably part of the routine management of projects and business processes.	- ORM culture is well-developed and considered an integral part of overall management and risk decision making. - ORM and ORMS principles are expanded to all areas of the organization and its activities.
- Programs are established to address core elements based on evaluation of the internal, external, and risk management context of all or part of the organization. - Scope defined based on protecting and preserving activities, functions, and services viewed as essential.	- Organization defines and documents the internal, external, and risk management context. - Operational objectives, assets, activities, functions, services, and products are defined. - Boundaries of scope are defined and documented based on protecting and preserving activities, functions, and services, as well as relations with stakeholders.	- Organization defines and documents the internal, external, and risk management context. - Boundaries of scope defined and documented, considering the organization's mission, goals, internal and external obligations, risk assessment, and legal responsibilities.	- Organization defines and documents the internal, external, and risk management context, as well as enterprise-wide risk management interactions and supply chain tiers, commitments, and relationships. Defining the organizational resilience internal, external, and risk management context related to community resilience.

Exhibit 9.2 Maturity model for phased implementation. (continued)

Maturity Model for the Phased Implementation of the ANSI/ASIS SPC.1-2009 Organizational Resilience Standard				
ANSI/ASIS SPC.1 Standard Clause	**Core Element**	**Issues Addressed by Core Element (establish, implement, and maintain)**	**Preawareness (Phase One)**	**Project Approach (Phase Two)**
4.2.1 Policy Statement	- Setting a policy framework	- Top management policy to provide a framework for setting objectives and provide the direction and principles for action.	- No defined ORM policy. - Lack of top level governance.	- Policy limited to addressing identified issue(s). - Driven by "Project Leader", may or may not have top management involvement beyond approval of project.

Exhibit 9.2   Maturity model for phased implementation. (continued)

Maturity Model for the Phased Implementation of the ANSI/ASIS SPC.1-2009 Organizational Resilience Standard			
Program Approach (Phase Three)	**Systems Approach (Phase Four)**	**Management System (Phase Five)**	**Holistic Management (Phase Six)**
	- Weighting of risk management strategies is defined.	- Scope of the ORMS defined in terms of and appropriate to the size, nature, and complexity of the organization from a perspective of continual improvement.	- Boundaries of scope defined and documented.
-Drafted by "Program Manager" and signed by top management. - Policy addresses organizational resilience management in divisions defined in scope. - Communicated to relevant divisions.	- Policy establishes framework for organizational resilience management by setting objectives and providing direction. - Supported by top management. - Communicated throughout organization.	- Policy establishes framework for organizational resilience management by setting objectives and providing direction. - Clear commitment to comply with applicable legal and other requirements. - Supported and promoted by top management. - Communicated throughout organization and to stakeholders, making them aware of content and meaning.	- Policy integrated into all management structures, levels, and individual responsibilities - Clear commitment to holistic ORM. - Communicated throughout organization, enterprise, and to external stakeholders (supply chain and community).

Exhibit 9.2 Maturity model for phased implementation. (continued)

181

Maturity Model for the Phased Implementation of the ANSI/ASIS SPC.1-2009 Organizational Resilience Standard				
ANSI/ASIS SPC.1 Standard Clause	**Core Element**	**Issues Addressed by Core Element (establish, implement, and maintain)**	**Preawareness (Phase One)**	**Project Approach (Phase Two)**
4.2.2 Management Commitment	- Management mandate and commitment.	- Top management commitment to meeting the requirements of organizational resilience management. - Top management provision of appropriate resources and authorities for ORMS.	- Management ambivalent or unreceptive. - Concerned that acknowledging risk and uncertainty. - No guidance from the top of organization. - Ostrich effect.	- Management authorization and resources provided to "Project Leader" to conduct project. - Resources restricted to address limited scope. - Resource allocation linked to perceived benefit. - Project aims to encourage more management support and buy-in.

Exhibit 9.2 Maturity model for phased implementation. (continued)

Maturity Model for the Phased Implementation of the ANSI/ASIS SPC.1-2009 Organizational Resilience Standard			
Program Approach (Phase Three)	**Systems Approach (Phase Four)**	**Management System (Phase Five)**	**Holistic Management (Phase Six)**
- Top management sponsorship. - Endorsement of established programs for ORM. - One or more individuals appointed as Program Manager. - Set prioritization and timeframes to address risks of disruptive events. - Resources allocated to support program.	- Top management participation - Active endorsement of ORMS by top management - Establishes an ORMS policy. - One or more individuals appointed to be responsible for ORMS. - Decides criteria for accepting risk, acceptable levels of risk. - Sets prioritization and timeframes for managing the risks of disruptive events. - Resources allocated to support ORMS.	- Documents evidence of its mandate and commitment to the establishment, implementation, operation, monitoring, review, maintenance, and improvement of the ORMS. - Defines and documents criteria to be used to evaluate the significance of risk, determination of appropriate risk treatments, and setting of timeframes for recovery. - Sufficient resources allocated and competencies assured.	- Documents evidence of its mandate and commitment to the establishment, implementation, operation, monitoring, review, maintenance, and improvement of the ORMS and its relationship to its external stakeholders (supply chain and community). - Sharing best practices with external stakeholders (supply chain and community). - Defines and documents criteria to be used to evaluate the significance of risk, determination of appropriate risk treatments, and setting of time-frames for manag-ing the risks of disruptive events of organization and relevant stakeholders.

Exhibit 9.2   Maturity model for phased implementation. (continued)

Maturity Model for the Phased Implementation of the ANSI/ASIS SPC.1-2009 Organizational Resilience Standard				
ANSI/ASIS SPC.1 Standard Clause	**Core Element**	**Issues Addressed by Core Element (establish, implement, and maintain)**	**Preawareness (Phase One)**	**Project Approach (Phase Two)**
4.3.1 Risk Assessment and Impact Analysis	- Risk Assessment (Identification, Analysis, Evaluation).	- Risk identification, analysis, and evaluation. - Threat, vulnerability, impact, and criticality analysis (including dependencies and interdependencies). - Evaluates the effect of uncertainty on the organization and its objectives (analyze likelihood and consequences of disruptive events).	- No process. - Indications of risks, problems, near misses, and warning signs identified retroactively.	- No formal process. - Reactive in nature with issue(s) targeted as problematic or requiring immediate attention. -A gap analysis to address project issues, rather than a risk assessment examining what is needed organizationally.

Exhibit 9.2 Maturity model for phased implementation. (continued)

Maturity Model for the Phased Implementation of the ANSI/ASIS SPC.1-2009 Organizational Resilience Standard			
Program Approach (Phase Three)	**Systems Approach (Phase Four)**	**Management System (Phase Five)**	**Holistic Management (Phase Six)**
- Develops and implements a procedure to identify, analyze, and evaluate essential assets, risks, and impacts. - Priorities based on outcomes of risk or impact analysis.	- Establishes, implements, and maintains an ongoing formal risk and impact assessment process. - Prioritized risks and impacts are taken into account in establishing, implementing, and operating the ORMS. -Risk assessment and impact analysis recognized as providing the foundation for elements of the ORMS and for organizational decisionmaking.	- Establishes, implements, and maintains an ongoing formal and documented risk assessment process. - Prioritizes and documents risks and impacts. - Periodically reviews whether ORM scope, policy, and risk assessment are still appropriate given the organizations' internal and external context. - Re-evaluates risk and impacts within the context of internal and external change.	- Establishes, implements, and maintains an ongoing formal and documented risk assessment process which includes external stakeholders (supply chain and community). - Establishes, implements, and maintains a formal and documented communication and consultation process with external stakeholders (supply chain and community) in the risk assessment process. - Establishes, implements, and maintains a formal and documented process for monitoring and reviewing the risk assessment process. - Integrate risk assessment processes with external stakeholders (supply chain and community).

Exhibit 9.2 Maturity model for phased implementation. (continued)

185

Maturity Model for the Phased Implementation of the ANSI/ASIS SPC.1-2009 Organizational Resilience Standard				
ANSI/ASIS SPC.1 Standard Clause	**Core Element**	**Issues Addressed by Core Element (establish, implement, and maintain)**	**Preawareness (Phase One)**	**Project Approach (Phase Two)**
4.3.2 Legal and Other Requirements	- Identifies and assesses legal, regulatory, and other requirements to which the organization subscribes.	- Identification of legal and other requirements. - Evaluation of internal and externa requirements pertinent to the organization. - Communication of relevant information on legal and other requirements to stakeholders.	- No process for identifying and understanding of legal and other requirements associated with ORM.	- Informal process initiated to identify legal and other requirements related to identified issue being addressed.

Exhibit 9.2 Maturity model for phased implementation. (continued)

Maturity Model for the Phased Implementation of the ANSI/ASIS SPC.1-2009 Organizational Resilience Standard			
Program Approach (Phase Three)	**Systems Approach (Phase Four)**	**Management System (Phase Five)**	**Holistic Management (Phase Six)**
- Legal requirements applicable to the activities, functions, and services in the scope of the program are identified.	- Establishes and maintains procedures to identify legal and other requirements. - Determines how the legal and other requirements apply to the organization. - Communicates requirements to appropriate parties. - Legal and other requirement considered in risk management process.	- Establishes and maintains documented procedures to identify legal and other requirements. - Determines how the legal and other requirements apply to the organization risks and obligations. - Ensures that applicable legal, regulatory, and other requirements are considered in developing, implementing, and maintaining its ORMS. - Documents information and keeps it up-to-date.	- Establishes and maintains procedures to identify legal and other requirements relevant to the organization and appropriate stakeholders (including supply chain partners and community). - Determines how the legal and other requirements apply to the organization and stakeholder risks and obligations.

Exhibit 9.2   Maturity model for phased implementation. (continued)

187

Maturity Model for the Phased Implementation of the ANSI/ASIS SPC.1-2009 Organizational Resilience Standard				
ANSI/ASIS SPC.1 Standard Clause	**Core Element**	**Issues Addressed by Core Element (establish, implement, and maintain)**	**Preawareness (Phase One)**	**Project Approach (Phase Two)**
4.3.3 Objectives, Targets, and Program(s)	- Select and prioritize risk treatment options.	- Prioritization of the issues identified as a result of the risk assessment and impact analysis. - Objectives and targets (including time frames) based on the prioritization of issues within the context of an organization's ORMS policy and mission. - Strategic plans for prevention, protection, preparedness, mitigation, response, continuity, and recovery. - Identification of resources needed. - Identification of roles, responsibilities, authorities, and their inter-relationships within the organization needed for ORM.	- No process to define objectives and targets. - No risk prioritization.	- Defines targets and objectives for demonstrating project success. - Develops targets, objectives, and strategic action plans to achieve immediate organizational resilience performance improvement related to identified issue(s) and to demonstrate business value. - Action plans for identified issues include required resources, responsibilities, and timescales.

Exhibit 9.2   Maturity model for phased implementation. (continued)

Maturity Model for the Phased Implementation of the ANSI/ASIS SPC.1-2009 Organizational Resilience Standard			
Program Approach (Phase Three)	**Systems Approach (Phase Four)**	**Management System (Phase Five)**	**Holistic Management (Phase Six)**
- Organizational resilience performance objectives for program management are set based on the risk assessment and impact analysis. - Strategic action plans designate actions, responsibilities, accountability, resources, and timeframes for achieving objectives and targets.	- Objectives are consistent with the ORM policy and risk assessment. - Documents objectives and targets to manage risks in order to avoid, prevent, protect, deter, mitigate, respond to, and recover from disruptive events. - Targets are measurable and derived from the objectives. - Establishes, implements, and maintains strategic programs (action plans) for prevention, protection, deterrence, mitigation, response, recovery, and continuity. - Strategic plans designate actions, responsibilities, accountability, resources, and timeframes for achieving objectives and targets.	- Documented objectives and targets are established to manage organizational resilience by avoiding, accepting, removing the source, changing the likelihood, changing the consequences, and sharing and/or retaining the risk. - Objectives provide a basis for selecting one or more options for managing risk including asset value, opportunities for reducing likelihood and/or consequences, cost/benefit, and tolerable levels of residual risk. - Targets are documented, measurable, achievable, relevant, and timebased.	- Documented objectives and targets establish internal and external expectations for the organization and its stakeholders (supply chain and community) that relate to mission accomplishment, product and service delivery, and functional operations.

Exhibit 9.2 Maturity model for phased implementation. (continued)

189

Maturity Model for the Phased Implementation of the ANSI/ASIS SPC.1-2009 Organizational Resilience Standard				
ANSI/ASIS SPC.1 Standard Clause	Core Element	Issues Addressed by Core Element (establish, implement, and maintain)	Preawareness (Phase One)	Project Approach (Phase Two)
		- Planning the operational processes for actions effecting how the objectives and targets are achieved.		
4.4.1 Resources, Roles, Responsibility, and Authority	- Availability and accountability of resources essential for the implementation of the ORMS and to facilitate effective OR management.	- Procedures, roles, and responsibilities to cover all normal operating conditions and disruptive events. - Techniques for management of functional, tactical, and strategic teams. - Provisions for adequate finance and administrative resources to support normal operating conditions and disruptive events. - Arrangements for supply chain obligations, mutual aid, and community assistance. - Determination of local, regional, and public authorities' roles, relationships, and interactions.	- Not defined. - No dedicated personnel for ORMS. - Needed resources not identified.	- Assigns roles and responsibilities to specific persons to address issue(s) in the limited scope. - Allocates adequate resources in accordance with action plan. - A "Project Leader" is designated to oversee the project. - Participation based on project scope.

Exhibit 9.2 Maturity model for phased implementation. (continued)

	Maturity Model for the Phased Implementation of the ANSI/ASIS SPC.1-2009 Organizational Resilience Standard		
Program Approach (Phase Three)	**Systems Approach (Phase Four)**	**Management System (Phase Five)**	**Holistic Management (Phase Six)**
		- Documents and maintains strategic programs (action plans) for risk treatment in order to achieve its objectives and targets - Documented risk treatment options.	
- Identifies and defines authorities, roles, responsibilities, and appropriate resources within the organization. - Identifies internal and external departments, division, business units, and partners that will play a role in addressing a disruptive event. - Identifies an ORM program team and leader. - Allocates adequate resources in accordance with the action plan.	- Top management appoints a specific management representative responsible for the ORMS. - Formal ORM responsibilities and relationships are defined and adhered to. - Teams with defined roles and adequate resources are established to support ORM action plans. - Establishes arrangements for stakeholder assistance, communication, strategic alliances, and mutual aid.	- Roles, responsibilities, and authorities are defined, documented, and communicated in order to facilitate effective ORM, consistent with the achievement of its ORM policy, objectives, targets, and programs. - Documented organizational resilience (security, crisis, response, and recovery) team(s) with defined roles, appropriate authority, and adequate resources.	- Roles, responsibilities, and authorities are defined, documented, and communicated in order to facilitate effective ORM within the organization, enterprise-wide and within the community consistent with achieving organization, and external stakeholders' (supply chain and community) objectives, targets, and programs.

Exhibit 9.2 Maturity model for phased implementation. (continued)

191

Maturity Model for the Phased Implementation of the ANSI/ASIS SPC.1-2009 Organizational Resilience Standard				
ANSI/ASIS SPC.1 Standard Clause	**Core Element**	**Issues Addressed by Core Element (establish, implement, and maintain)**	**Preawareness (Phase One)**	**Project Approach (Phase Two)**
4.4.2 Competence, Training, and Awareness	- Defining and addressing competence.	- Skills and competency requirements to support normal operating conditions and disruptive events.	- Lack of ORM cultural awareness. - Competencies and skills not identified. - No training program. - Little or no in-house expertise or experience.	- Competence, skills, and training needs identified to achieve project objectives and targets. - Conducts training with some measure of competence to achieve objectives and targets.

Exhibit 9.2 Maturity model for phased implementation. (continued)

Maturity Model for the Phased Implementation of the ANSI/ASIS SPC.1-2009 Organizational Resilience Standard			
Program Approach (Phase Three)	**Systems Approach (Phase Four)**	**Management System (Phase Five)**	**Holistic Management (Phase Six)**
		- Establishes and documents logistical capabilities and procedures to locate, acquire, store, distribute, maintain, test, and account for services, personnel, resources, materials, and facilities produced or donated to support the ORMS. - Formal and documented procedures for stakeholder assistance, communications, strategic alliances, and mutual aid..	
- Determines competence requirements that are necessary for activities defined in the program scope. - Develops and implements training, competence, and awareness procedures.	- Identifies competencies and training needs associated with achieving the ORMS objectives, targets, and programs. - Develops and implements procedures to address competence and training needs.	- Ensures that any person(s) performing tasks who have the potential to prevent, cause, respond to, mitigate, or be affected by significant hazards, threats, and risks are competent (on the basis of appropriate education, training, or experience).	- Builds, promotes, and embeds an ORM culture within the organization, enterprise, supply chain and community. - Sharing best practices with external stakeholders (supply chain and community).

Exhibit 9.2   Maturity model for phased implementation. (continued)

		Maturity Model for the Phased Implementation of the ANSI/ASIS SPC.1-2009 Organizational Resilience Standard		
ANSI/ASIS SPC.l Standard Clause	**Core Element**	**Issues Addressed by Core Element (establish, implement, and maintain)**	**Preawareness (Phase One)**	**Project Approach (Phase Two)**
		- Training and education program for the organization's personnel, contractors, and other relevant stakeholders. - Organizational awareness and culture to support ORM. - Organizational interface protocol, identification and training requirements. - Tools to enhance situational awareness.	- Workforce unaware of risk management needs and lacks training to adequately take ownership and control risks.	- Training and awareness focus on addressing the identified issue(s) in the scope.
4.4.3 Communication and Warning	- Identify and address internal and external communication requirements.	- Procedures, arrangements, and tools for communication to support normal operating conditions and disruptive events.	- No procedures. - Not coordinated internally or externally. - Reactive in nature. - Driven by demands for information.	- Communication procedures address project objectives, target, and scope.

Exhibit 9.2 Maturity model for phased implementation. (continued)

194

Maturity Model for the Phased Implementation of the ANSI/ASIS SPC.1-2009 Organizational Resilience Standard			
Program Approach (Phase Three)	**Systems Approach (Phase Four)**	**Management System (Phase Five)**	**Holistic Management (Phase Six)**
	- Assesses competence against requirements.	- Documents and retains associated training and competence records. - Ensures the OR management culture becomes part of the organization's core values and organization governance. - Makes stakeholders aware of the OR management policy and their role in any plans.	
- Identifies what will be communicated and to whom. - Determines communications and warning needs.	- Identifies what will be communicated and to whom regarding the ORM policy, risks, objectives, targets, and programs.	- Preplanning of communications for targeted audiences. - Develops and documents key messages and set communication targets, objectives, and performance indicators.	- Development of Net-Centric capacity for all communications with external stakeholders (supply chain and community).

Exhibit 9.2 Maturity model for phased implementation. (continued)

		Maturity Model for the Phased Implementation of the ANSI/ASIS SPC.1-2009 Organizational Resilience Standard		
ANSI/ASIS SPC.1 Standard Clause	**Core Element**	**Issues Addressed by Core Element (establish, implement, and maintain)**	**Preawareness (Phase One)**	**Project Approach (Phase Two)**
		- Exercises for plans to communicate information and warnings with stakeholders (including the media) to support normal operating conditions and disruptive events. - Reliable and tested communications and a warning capability in the event of a disruption.		- Develops communication procedures for internal and external stakeholders (including authorities and media) consistent with the project scope.

Exhibit 9.2 Maturity model for phased implementation. (continued)

196

Maturity Model for the Phased Implementation of the ANSI/ASIS SPC.1-2009 Organizational Resilience Standard			
Program Approach (Phase Three)	**Systems Approach (Phase Four)**	**Management System (Phase Five)**	**Holistic Management (Phase Six)**
- Establishes, implements, and maintains procedures for internal and external communications and warnings. - Establishes notification systems and roles in which to use them.	- Establishes internal, external, and Net-Centric communication procedures. - Identifies target audiences for communications and warnings to ensure effective two-way dialogue. - Determines information sharing and security needs. - Ensures ongoing communications capacity in the event of a disruptive event.	- Assigns and documents responsibilities and establish timelines for communications. - Establishes, documents, and maintains procedures for internal, external, and Net-Centric communications. - Communication on ORM issues occurs throughout the organization and with appropriate stakeholders. - Documents communication with emergency and first responders. - Sets and documents communications protocols for normal and for disruptive events. - Regularly exercises communications system and documents results.	- Determines reliability of external communications infrastructure, and to augment the system internally and externally in the event of a disruption.

Exhibit 9.2 Maturity model for phased implementation. (continued)

Maturity Model for the Phased Implementation of the ANSI/ASIS SPC.1-2009 Organizational Resilience Standard				
ANSI/ASIS SPC.1 Standard Clause	**Core Element**	**Issues Addressed by Core Element (establish, implement, and maintain)**	**Preawareness (Phase One)**	**Project Approach (Phase Two)**
4.4.4 Documentation	- Identifying and addressing documentation	- Processes and procedures for management of documents which are essential to the ORMS. - Procedures, processes, work plans, and forms to support the ORMS and its elements, to support norma operating conditions and disruptive events.	- Informal, if any.	- Develops documented procedures to support action plans. - Maintains documentation to support project scope. - Documentation supports elements addressed in project.

Exhibit 9.2 Maturity model for phased implementation. (continued)

Maturity Model for the Phased Implementation of the ANSI/ASIS SPC.1-2009 Organizational Resilience Standard			
Program Approach (Phase Three)	**Systems Approach (Phase Four)**	**Management System (Phase Five)**	**Holistic Management (Phase Six)**
- Develops a document management program. - Documentation supports elements addressed in program action plans.	- Establishes organizational resilience management documentation system. - Determines security, sensitivity, and information integrity needs and takes appropriate steps to protect information documentation.	- Documentation system is consistent with document control requirements. - Prepares a formal manual documenting the structure of the ORMS.	- Evaluates document and information needs of external stakeholders (supply chain and community) for sharing of documentation best practices.

Exhibit 9.2   Maturity model for phased implementation. (continued)

199

Maturity Model for the Phased Implementation of the ANSI/ASIS SPC.1-2009 Organizational Resilience Standard				
ANSI/ASIS SPC.1 Standard Clause	**Core Element**	**Issues Addressed by Core Element (establish, implement, and maintain)**	**Preawareness (Phase One)**	**Project Approach (Phase Two)**
4.4.5 Control of Documents	- Developing and implementing documentation control.	- Processes and procedures for control of documents and records. (including back-up). - Protection of the integrity of essential information.	- No document control system other than that used in general organizational operations.	- Document control with some procedures developed to help demonstrate success and business benefit. - Limited back-up of critical information.

Exhibit 9.2 Maturity model for phased implementation. (continued)

200

Maturity Model for the Phased Implementation of the ANSI/ASIS SPC.1-2009 Organizational Resilience Standard			
Program Approach (Phase Three)	**Systems Approach (Phase Four)**	**Management System (Phase Five)**	**Holistic Management (Phase Six)**
- Establishes processes and procedures for control of documents and records in the scope of the program	- Establishes processes and procedures for control of documents and records in the scope of the management system, including access, backup condentiality, storage, retention, archiving, and destruction.	- Formally documents processes and procedures for control of documents and records, including information security and protection and document integrity.	- Implementing best practice document control with external stakeholders (supply chain and community).

Exhibit 9.2   Maturity model for phased implementation. (continued)

201

Maturity Model for the Phased Implementation of the ANSI/ASIS SPC.1-2009 Organizational Resilience Standard				
ANSI/ASIS SPC.1 Standard Clause	**Core Element**	**Issues Addressed by Core Element (establish, implement, and maintain)**	**Preawareness (Phase One)**	**Project Approach (Phase Two)**
4.4.6 Operational Control	- Developing and implementing operational control.	- Operational control measures and procedures needed to implement the ORM during normal operating conditions and disruptive events. - Risk avoidance, mitigation, reduction, sharing, and treatment procedures to minimize the likelihood and consequences of a disruptive event.	- Procedures and processes are undefined. - Some individuals may address perceived disruptive events on an ad hoc basis.	- Operational controls and procedures established to achieve objectives and targets addressed within the project scope.

Exhibit 9.2   Maturity model for phased implementation. (continued)

202

Maturity Model for the Phased Implementation of the ANSI/ASIS SPC.1-2009 Organizational Resilience Standard			
Program Approach (Phase Three)	**Systems Approach (Phase Four)**	**Management System (Phase Five)**	**Holistic Management (Phase Six)**
- Risk or impact analysis is used to determine proper operational controls within the scope of the program.	- Operational controls for risk reduction are based on the risk assessment, objectives, targets, and programs. - Considers ways of minimizing risk in day-to-day operations, including engineering controls, administrative controls, technical specications, and contractual agreements. - Priority is given to preemptive approaches.	- Establishes, implements, maintains, and documents adaptive and pre-emptive procedures for those operations that are associated with the identified significant risks, consistent with its organizational resilience management policy, risk assessment, supply chain requirements, objectives, and targets. - Control procedures are written and/or reviewed by persons involved in operations and communicated effectively to others including external stakeholders.	- Demand signals are incorporated in capacity planning. - Priority is given to adaptive approaches. - Processes are in place to validate supplier responses.

Exhibit 9.2 Maturity model for phased implementation. (continued)

Maturity Model for the Phased Implementation of the ANSI/ASIS SPC.1-2009 Organizational Resilience Standard				
ANSI/ASIS SPC.1 Standard Clause	**Core Element**	**Issues Addressed by Core Element (establish, implement, and maintain)**	**Preawareness (Phase One)**	**Project Approach (Phase Two)**
4.4.7 Incident Prevention, Preparedness, and Response	- Procedures for prevention, protection, preparedness, mitigation, response, and recovery.	- Risk avoidance, mitigation, reduction, sharing, and treatment procedures to minimize the likelihood and consequences of a disruptive event. -Prevention and protection techniques to minimize risk. - Techniques for a response structure. - Action plans for increased threat levels. - Recovery strategies and plans based on risk and impact assessment and conditions of the disruptive event.	- Little or no defined or documented procedures. - Dependence on the reactive behavior of individuals in the organization (and hope for the best).	- Defines procedures to achieve objectives and targets of issue(s) addressed within the scope of the project. - Develops procedures to support action plans including measures to reduce likelihood and/or consequences. - Develops procedures based on identfiied issue(s) - may be predominately reactive in nature given that no formal risk assessment was conducted.

Exhibit 9.2 Maturity model for phased implementation. (continued)

204

Maturity Model for the Phased Implementation of the ANSI/ASIS SPC.1-2009 Organizational Resilience Standard			
Program Approach (Phase Three)	Systems Approach (Phase Four)	Management System (Phase Five)	Holistic Management (Phase Six)
- Develops and implements procedures, that prevent (if possible), respond to, and recover from potential disruptive events within the program scope. - Considers measures that emphasize minimizing consequences.	- Develops and implements procedures linked to the risk assessment, objectives, targets and programs, with detailed work plans how the organization will prevent, prepare for, respond to and recover from disruptive events. - Periodically reviews and, where necessary, revises its incident prevention, preparedness, response and recovery procedures.	- Establishes, implements, maintains, and documents procedures to avoid, prevent, protect from, mitigate, respond to and recover from a disruptive event and continue its activities based on organizational resilience objectives developed through the risk assessment process. - Ensures that any persons performing incident prevention and management measures on its behalf are competent - Establishes, documents and implements procedures for a management structure to prevent, prepare for, mitigate, and respond to a disruptive event.	- Incident prevention, preparedness, response, and recovery is integrated with external stakeholders (supply chain and community).

Exhibit 9.2 Maturity model for phased implementation. (continued)

205

Maturity Model for the Phased Implementation of the ANSI/ASIS SPC.1-2009 Organizational Resilience Standard				
ANSI/ASIS SPC.1 Standard Clause	Core Element	Issues Addressed by Core Element (establish, implement, and maintain)	Preawareness (Phase One)	Project Approach (Phase Two)
4.5.1 Monitoring and Measurement	- Performance evaluation.	- Metrics and mechanisms by which the organization assesses its ability to achieve its objectives and targets on an ongoing basis.	- No formal monitoring. - No formal measurement	- Progress against specific indicators are assessed periodically with persons involved in relevant activities defined within project scope. - Project indicators and metrics are established and monitored to demonstrate progress and performance improvement.

Exhibit 9.2   Maturity model for phased implementation. (continued)

206

Maturity Model for the Phased Implementation of the ANSI/ASIS SPC.1-2009 Organizational Resilience Standard			
Program Approach (Phase Three)	**Systems Approach (Phase Four)**	**Management System (Phase Five)**	**Holistic Management (Phase Six)**
		- Establishes detailed procedures for how the organization will recover or maintain its activities to a predetermined level, based on management-approved recovery objectives.	
- Identifies and implements key characteristics that need monitoring and measuring within the program scope.	- Establishes, implements, and maintains performance metrics and procedures to monitor and measure, on a regular basis, those characteristics of its operations that have material impact on its organizational resilience performance.	- Documents procedures that monitor performance, applicable operational controls, and conformity with the ORMS objectives and targets. - Documents procedures to measure the performance of the systems which protect assets, communications, and information systems.	- Monitoring and measurement integrated with external stakeholders and the community.

Exhibit 9.2 Maturity model for phased implementation. (continued)

Maturity Model for the Phased Implementation of the ANSI/ASIS SPC.1-2009 Organizational Resilience Standard				
ANSI/ASIS SPC.1 Standard Clause	**Core Element**	**Issues Addressed by Core Element (establish, implement, and maintain)**	**Preawareness (Phase One)**	**Project Approach (Phase Two)**
4.5.2.1 Evaluation of Compliance	Compliance evaluation.	- Legal and regulatory compliance performance evaluation on an ongoing basis.	- No formal procedures established beyond those already in place as part of normal operations.	- Compliance evaluated and demonstrated related to the project scope.
4.5.2.2 Exercises and Testing	- Assessing and validating ORMS elements.	- Process to measure and evaluate appropriateness and efficacy of the ORMS: its programs, processes, and procedures to drive it. - An exercise program. - Continual improvement plan reviewed with and agreed to by top management to ensure appropriate action is taken.	- Limited or no exercising or testing.	- Exercising and testing are planned and conducted as required by project scope. - Results of exercises and tests demonstrate project OR performance improvement, and business benefits.

Exhibit 9.2 Maturity model for phased implementation. (continued)

Maturity Model for the Phased Implementation of the ANSI/ASIS SPC.1-2009 Organizational Resilience Standard			
Program Approach (Phase Three)	**Systems Approach (Phase Four)**	**Management System (Phase Five)**	**Holistic Management (Phase Six)**
- Compliance evaluated and demonstrated related to program scope.	- Establishes, implements, and maintains procedure(s) for periodically evaluating and demonstrating compliance with applicable legal and other requirements.	- Documents procedures and records and reports the results of the evaluation with corrective measures and recommendations for improvement.	- Integrate compliance evaluation with stakeholders and community.
- Exercising and testing are planned and conducted as required by program scope. - Results of exercises and tests demonstrate program OR performance improvements, and business benefits.	- Tests and exercises designed to validate appropriateness and effectiveness of action plans and procedures, as well as interrelationship of elements in ORMS – including appropriate external parties (e.g., first responders) and stakeholders	- Comprehensive documentation of exercises and tests. - Produces a formalized post-exercise report that contains accountable outcomes, recommendations, and arrangements to implement improvements in a timely fashion.	- Integrate exercise and tests with stakeholders and community

Exhibit 9.2 Maturity model for phased implementation. (continued)

209

Maturity Model for the Phased Implementation of the ANSI/ASIS SPC.1-2009 Organizational Resilience Standard				
ANSI/ASIS SPC.1 Standard Clause	**Core Element**	**Issues Addressed by Core Element (establish, implement, and maintain)**	**Preawareness (Phase One)**	**Project Approach (Phase Two)**
4.5.3 Non-conformity, Corrective Action, and Preventive Action	- Monitor and address non-conformities	- Process to identify nonconformities and their root cause. - Mechanisms for eliminating the causes of detected nonconformities both in the ORMS and the operational processes. - Mechanisms for instigating action to eliminate potential causes of non-conformities in both the ORMS and the operational processes.	- Minimum required by law.	- Deviations from action plans, programs, objectives, and targets within the project scope are evaluated for opportunities for improvement. - Adequate corrective and preventative actions taken (if necessary) to ensure the projec progresses according to plan.
4.5.4 Control of Records	- Developing and implementing records control.	- Records to demonstrate conformity to the requirements of the ORMS and the results achieved.	- Only as required by normal business practices.	- Collects and retains evidence addressing project implementa-tion and results.

Exhibit 9.2   Maturity model for phased implementation. (continued)

Maturity Model for the Phased Implementation of the ANSI/ASIS SPC.1-2009 Organizational Resilience Standard			
Program Approach (Phase Three)	**Systems Approach (Phase Four)**	**Management System (Phase Five)**	**Holistic Management (Phase Six)**
- Deviations from action plans, programs, objectives, and targets within the program scope are evaluated for opportunities for improvement. - Establishes a corrective and preventative action process.	- Establishes procedures to determine nonconformities in the ORMS, risk assessment, objectives, targets, programs, action plans, and their implementation. - Evaluates actual and potential non-conformances to eliminate the causes and prevent their occurrence or recurrence.	- Establishes, implements, and maintains documented procedures for dealing with actual and potential nonconformities and for taking corrective action and preventive action. - Reviews effectiveness of corrective actions and take preventative actions.	- Integrate nonconformity, corrective, and preventive actions with stakeholders and community
- Collects and retains evidence addressing program implementation and results.	- Collects and retains evidence addressing ORMS implementation and results.	- Establishes, implements, and maintains documented procedures to collect and retain evidence addressing ORMS implementation and results.	- Establish shared record controls with stakeholders and community

Exhibit 9.2 Maturity model for phased implementation. (continued)

211

Maturity Model for the Phased Implementation of the ANSI/ASIS SPC.1-2009 Organizational Resilience Standard				
ANSI/ASIS SPC.1 Standard Clause	Core Element	Issues Addressed by Core Element (establish, implement, and maintain)	Preawareness (Phase One)	Project Approach (Phase Two)
4.5.5 Internal Audits	- Conducts management system audits.	- Internal audits of system and programs. - Audit reports reviewed by top management.	- Not conducted for ORM.	- Performance of project audited informally. - Project Leader oversees development of audit procedures.

Exhibit 9.2 Maturity model for phased implementation. (continued)

Maturity Model for the Phased Implementation of the ANSI/ASIS SPC.1-2009 Organizational Resilience Standard			
Program Approach (Phase Three)	**Systems Approach (Phase Four)**	**Management System (Phase Five)**	**Holistic Management (Phase Six)**
- Conducts audit of program within defined scope, including all elements of the program.	- Determines what needs to be audited. - Plans and implements an audit program. - Reports audit findings to management and acts upon them.	- Establishes, implements, and maintains documented procedures for internal audits. - Responsibility of audit program assigned to an individual that has knowledge and understanding of audit principles. - Determines whether the control objectives, risk controls, processes, and procedures of ORMS are conducted properly and are achieving the desired results. - Identifies opportunities for improvement. - Ensures that actions are taken without undue delay to eliminate detected nonconformities and their causes	- Audit includes stakeholder and community interactions, as well as the supply chain.

Exhibit 9.2   Maturity model for phased implementation. (continued)

213

Maturity Model for the Phased Implementation of the ANSI/ASIS SPC.1-2009 Organizational Resilience Standard				
ANSI/ASIS SPC.1 Standard Clause	Core Element	Issues Addressed by Core Element (establish, implement, and maintain)	Preawareness (Phase One)	Project Approach (Phase Two)
4.6 Management Review	- Top management review.	- Management review of the ORMS's performance, adequacy, and effectiveness to identify opportunities for improvement. - Priorities, policy, objectives, and targets to support continual improvement.	- No management review of ORM	- Project Leader supervisor (and other, appropriate members of the management team) reviews the performance of project and reports to project sponsor
4.6.4 Maintenance	- ORM change management.	- Change management provisions for improvement of ORMS programs, systems, and/or operational processes.	- No ORMS to maintain or link to change management process.	- Project outcomes that improve organizational resilience performance become standard operating procedures.

Exhibit 9.2   Maturity model for phased implementation. (continued)

Maturity Model for the Phased Implementation of the ANSI/ASIS SPC.1-2009 Organizational Resilience Standard			
Program Approach (Phase Three)	**Systems Approach (Phase Four)**	**Management System (Phase Five)**	**Holistic Management (Phase Six)**
- Program Leader (and other appropriate members of the management team) reviews the program performance and reports to program sponsor. - Uses review to demonstrate business case for ORMS and provide a basis to seek further efficiencies by linking core elements in a systems approach.	- Reviews integration of ORMS elements. - Reviews the suitability, adequacy, and effectiveness of the ORMS. - Top management reviews the policies, objectives, evaluation of program implementation, audit results and changes resulting from preventive and corrective actions	- Top management participates in documented reviews of the ORMS at planned intervals to ensure its continuing suitability, adequacy, and effectiveness. - Assesses opportunities for improvement and the need for changes to ORMS, including the ORMS policy and objectives, targets and risk criteria.	- Integrates review with overall risk management and fiscal review processes. - Review includes evaluation of suitability, adequacy, and effectiveness with regard to stakeholders, community, and supply chain. - Top management promotes OR with external stakeholders (supply chain and community).
- Program and action plans outcomes that improve organizational resilience performance become standard operating procedures.	- Any internal or external changes (including outputs from exercises, audits, and reviews) that impact the organization are reviewed in relation to the ORMS.	- Establish documented change management procedures for ORMS tied to other change management programs.	- Integrate change management for ORMS with external stakeholders (supply chain and community).

Exhibit 9.2 Maturity model for phased implementation. (continued)

215

Maturity Model for the Phased Implementation of the ANSI/ASIS SPC.1-2009 Organizational Resilience Standard				
ANSI/ASIS SPC.1 Standard Clause	**Core Element**	**Issues Addressed by Core Element (establish, implement, and maintain)**	**Preawareness (Phase One)**	**Project Approach (Phase Two)**
4.6.5 Continual Improvement	- Evaluate and implement opportunities for improvement.	- Continual improvement process for the ORMS, risk management, and organizational resilience performance.	- No ORMS to link to continual improvement process	- Opportunities for improvement identied for use in other projects.

Exhibit 9.2 Maturity model for phased implementation. (continued)

Maturity Model for the Phased Implementation of the ANSI/ASIS SPC.1-2009 Organizational Resilience Standard			
Program Approach (Phase Three)	**Systems Approach (Phase Four)**	**Management System (Phase Five)**	**Holistic Management (Phase Six)**
- Implement procedures for continuous improvement of program	- Continually improves the effectiveness of ORMS through the use of the organizational resilience management policy, objectives, audit results, analysis of monitored events, corrective and preventive actions, and management review.	- Continual improvement is a part of the organization's culture, demonstrated at all levels.	- Integrate continual improvement of ORMS with external stakeholders (supply chain and community).

Source: ANSI/ASIS SPC.4-2012, page 9-24.

Exhibit 9.2 Maturity model for phased implementation.

WHY USE A MATURITY MODEL?

The value of using an organizational resilience maturity model (ORMM) in achieving ORM lies in the development of a shared understanding of where the organization currently is and what is necessary to get the organization to where it wants to be. As noted earlier in this book, achieving organizational resilience (OR) through the development and implementation of organizational resilience management requires considerable effort and resources. To achieve the desired goals you must have a good plan to meet these goals and using the maturity model is an excellent method. Through the ORMM, the organization is able to measure its current placement against the established goals with a clear balance between the full scope of implementation of ORM and the limited resources available for the project. As stated above, implementation of ANSI/ASIS SPC.1-2009 is not an all-or-nothing proposition. ORMM allows an organization to identify a starting point based on a plan that takes into consideration the history of the organization and the problems encountered through routine operations. Using previously identified risks provides valuable knowledge and evidence for the need to seek organizational resilience.

How It Works

The application of the maturity model during the development of the project plan in conjunction with the review of the ANSI/ASIS SPC.1-2009 implementation requirements allows for the consideration of where to begin the project. As discussed earlier, the maturity model is a tool to determine the organizational resilience efforts in place. The following bullet points are provided as a review of the basic phases of the model (ANSI/ASIS SPC.4-2012, p. x–xi):

- *Phase One*: Preawareness is where the organization is not conducting preplanning. There is no formal resilience management process in place and there is a lack of information about resilience management. This is similar to the very undesirable practice of "putting out fires" as the normal course of business.
- *Phase Two*: Project Approach is really the beginning phase of implementing ORM. Senior management is willing to allow a trial or pilot project to explore the benefits of resilience management. This may result in a small project focusing on core elements of the OR standard as a means to improve performance. It is critical

to view this phase as a typical project requiring standard project management practices.

- *Phase Three*: The Program Approach is the expansion of the project phase from a limited scope project to organization-wide issues. This focuses on individual core elements rather than interrelationships and integration of elements. The emphasis is on action plans to address critical issues.
- *Phase Four*: The Systems Approach is where the pieces come together; the core elements get special attention with the goal of identifying and addressing root causes with viable solutions. Organizational resilience management is continually improved through the application of the requirements noted within the standard. This phase acknowledges the interrelationship and integration of the elements of the standard. It is understood that the process has built-in learning opportunities.
- *Phase Five*: The Management Approach provides an opportunity for the organization to show conformance with the standard as the organizational resilience management system is fully implemented with a multiyear perspective by senior management. The culture of organizational resilience is promoted to each member of the organization and everyone is advised to take ownership of risk issues.
- *Phase Six*: Holistic Management is where the organization is prepared to go beyond the standard and include external supply chain vendors to ensure a fully integrated resilience strategy. The organization emphasizes enterprise-wide relationships with a well-developed culture of resilience management in all business units.

10

Case Study: Tsogo Sun Group

RATIONALE FOR ORGANIZATIONAL RESILIENCE

To highlight the rationale for organizational resilience management, the following case study is an example of a successful implementation of the ANSI/ASIS SPC.1-2009. The case study is based on material obtained from an article in *Security Management Magazine* and from an exchange of emails with Johan Du Plooy, senior partner, Temi Group (South Africa). Through this combination of sources, this example of a real-life exercise in implementation is presented to help illustrate the challenges associated with implementing ANSI/ASIS SPC.1-2009.

In anticipation of the 2010 Federation Internationale de Football Association (FIFA) World Cup tournament in Johannesburg, South Africa, the hotel and entertainment company Tsogo Sun Group (TSG) implemented ANSI/ASIS SPC.1-2009, ASIS International's organizational resilience standard, to provide a comprehensive approach to security, crisis preparedness, and continuity management. TSG made a decision toward the end of 2009 to evaluate and strengthen, as necessary, its existing security, preparedness, and continuity efforts, and to increase their resilience in preparation of the FIFA World Cup. With the world watching such a high-profile event, TSG wanted to ensure that it was prepared for risk issues that might challenge its hotels, resorts, and casinos.

The company considered implementing the ISO28000 security in the supply chain standard along with the BS25999 business continuity standard, but concluded that this was an unnecessary duplication of effort, and that implementing two standards was too costly. After evaluating the ANSI/ASIS SPC.1-2009, they decided that this provided a more cost-effective approach by simultaneously addressing security and continuity management, as well as fulfilling all the requirements of the ISO28000 and BS25999. TSG faced an array of risks including criminal activities, disruption of supplies, potential electricity brownouts and blackouts, as well as other threats to critical services. Assuring the safety, security, and comfort of their guests was the top priority. Therefore, TSG needed a comprehensive strategy that focused on avoiding problems as a top priority, identifying potential issues, and preemptively responding to mitigate possible impacts, rapid response to events, and returning to normal as quickly as possible should an undesirable event occur. To achieve these objectives, it was clear to TSG that it needed a multidisciplinary approach. The desirable advantage of the ANSI/ASIS SPC.1-2009 Standard that Du Plooy noted was that TSG senior management liked the balance of business decision-making options with the inclusion of the various risk-centered preparedness requirements.

TSG decided not to seek third-party certification, especially given the time and cost involved. The objective of the project was to enhance security, preparedness, and continuity performance in the short timeframe available before the World Cup. A decision was made to do its own rigorous internal assessment of the implementation of the standard instead. To that end, the company selected six people to form a team that would audit the implementation. The team, which included four managers from Tsogo Sun Group and two consultants from Temi Group, completed the ISO 28000 Lead Auditor Course, the same course that a third-party certification body would require its auditors to take. To drive the process of resilience improvement, the organization used a phased approach of a maturity model coupled with a recognition program. The maturity model was based on six levels of implementation and was structured to encourage facilities to step up through the different levels almost as a competition. One of the challenges was converting a generic standard for use by the hospitality industry. An important lesson was the need to engage people in the process, because buy-in from all levels was the key to success. The phased approach taken by the company provided a manageable path for implementation (Berrong, 2010, p. 52)

Johan Du Plooy (Temi Group) was engaged as a consultant to help develop the evaluation and implementation process. According to Du Plooy, he reviewed the organization, researched how it managed its risk portfolio, and looked at the people involved with managing risk. He determined that the director of risk for the group, Dr. Gert Cruywagen, was someone who would seriously consider a new approach to the timeworn problems facing a major organization. Dr. Cruywagen's support team was very small, but it was still expected to respond to the challenges of protecting the organization against a myriad of threats. With such a "flat" organizational structure, Du Plooy realized that the project was destined to be difficult. Thus, it would be in their interest to combine all of their existing plans into a consolidated assessment effort, instead of trying to deal with each of the elements separately. The existing plans included:

- Emergency Planning
- Business Continuity Planning
- Security Risk Management
  - Risk Assessments
  - Gap Analysis
  - Action Plans
- Risk Management
  - Risk Assessments—High Level
  - Business Impact Analysis
- Occupational Health and Safety
- Disaster Management

These elements were all previously dealt with at different levels within the organization and, in some instances, were not drawn into the overall resilience plan. A combined plan was developed that allowed for easier management of the total process. Although the elements still have to be managed and measured separately at times, the overall plan allowed for a much "sleeker and streamlined" management reporting system, which was then easier to understand, implement, and audit.

TSG decided to use a six-member project team to plan and evaluate (audit) the implementation of the standard. The team consisted of two external consultants, Johan Du Plooy and Raymond van Staden (now deceased; he died saving a child from drowning in April 2010) from Temi Group, and four internal TSG managers, consisting of Colin Ackroyd, Hotel Division; and Naresh Ramdhaney, Gaming Division; and two managers from two of the premier 5-Star hotels in the group, Giel Burger and David Croft. The audit and gap analysis was conducted by the project team to ensure that the efforts of the project were aligned with the requirements of the standard. This established an understanding and verification to ensure that the implementation met the requirements of the standard. The team also analyzed the existing framework in the Gap Analysis, documenting what was in place and what was missing, which was measured against the ANSI/ASIS SPC.1-2009 Standard. ASIS International made Dr. Marc Siegel available to assist with the implementation and provide expert guidance and suggestions on the options facing TSG (Berrong, 2010, p. 52).

The decision to establish an internal auditing team with identical training to third-party auditors for the project was significant. To establish credibility of the audit process, TSG decided that the audit team would be trained on the same ISO auditing standards used by certification bodies and establish the auditing programs in conformance with the ISO auditing standards. Audit team makeup for any facility should be designed so that auditors are not auditing their own work. Du Plooy explained that the project team completed the RABQSA-SCY Security Management Systems ISO 28000 Lead Auditor Course, thereby allowing the TSG project to save an enormous amount of money by conducting audits internally, and with the same value and competency of an external auditor. TSG was able to achieve an international competency level. This decision to forego third-party certification was extremely wise. As long as the internal staff does not evaluate their own work, an internal audit is an excellent way to ensure conformance with the standard. Du Plooy also acknowledged that the use of an internal audit allowed TSG to pace the implementation in accordance with a TSG schedule that favored the company.

Du Plooy explained that because South African legislation requires proper audit capabilities using both internal and external sources, it was easier to convince senior TSG management to pursue the implementation of ANSI/ASIS SPC.1-2009. This would enhance their adherence to the different legislation as well as the requirement of good corporate governance. Dr. Gert Cruywagen served on the King Committee regarding the Risk Management component and, thus, understood how useful it would be to implement the ORM system. The use of existing legislation to gain support and approval of the project was an excellent way to reach the right level of leadership and establish a firm foundation for the justification of the project. Sometimes it is easier for people to understand the reasoning behind a project if there is an overt and well-known legislative act requiring adherence and continuous improvement. This is an example of selling the project from the very beginning and taking advantage of gaining the necessary high-level support.

After the project team completed the initial training, Du Plooy stated that they reviewed their early plans and determined that they had to make revisions and refinements to achieve the level of effectiveness in project management that they desired. A project plan was developed and presented to TSG for approval. It covered all the aspects of the anticipated route that had to be taken as well as leaving room for adaptations; it was a new area and there would certainly be changes that would have to be made. Pressure was further increased as TSG had been selected to provide accommodations for the "FIFA Family" (all the VIPs and senior officials) at some of their 5-Star venues, and it became even more critical that they ensured that a well-structured plan was in place to prevent incidents and, in the event of an emergency or disastrous event, response would be immediate and effective. According to Du Plooy, "We had horrific timelines to adhere to, the training and all the initial processes were driven very hard. Meetings normally started at 0600 (6 a.m.) and ended between 1900 (7 p.m.) and 2100 (9 p.m.) for at least four days a week over a three-month period. Afterwards, we had to catch up with refining and reviewing existing documents and processes to see if these were all still relevant."

It is an unfortunate truth in organizations that schedules are not always at the discretion of those following them. The objective was to have the basic plan implemented and the first series of standards audits completed at the selected venues at least one month before the World Cup kick-off, and this was achieved. Obviously, it is better to arrange a more reasonable and realistic timeline to avoid anyone burning out, or failure of the project because people are unable to meet schedules that are too tight. This will likely be a focus point of discussions on future projects of this nature. The TSG team deserves credit for following a tight schedule that was imposed on them and successfully completing their project.

ESTABLISHING A RECOGNITION PROGRAM

After his initial visit with the TSG and a preliminary gaps analysis, Dr. Marc Siegel suggested that, due to the short timeframe for implementation and different capabilities of the various facilities, a maturity model would help drive rapid improvements. With the aid of Maya Siegel (also trained as an auditor), they began working on the maturity model for phased implementation of the ANSI/ASIS SPC.1-2009 at the end of December 2009 and sent it to the team in January 2010. As discussed earlier, the maturity model is a tremendous tool when trying to implement the standard. The maturity model allows an organization to take advantage of an objective approach at achieving a certain level of conformance with ANSI/ASIS SPC.1-2009 within the framework of the organization. The maturity model also defines a recognition system that not only awards personnel for their performance, it also provides a structure that is critical to fostering a spirit of ongoing involvement. Ensuring that people want to continue to strive for achievement as part of the organizational resilience project is what moves a project into a program (ANSI/ASIS SPC.4, 2012, p. 25).

The project team knew the importance of involving the staff of the organization and prepared to begin the process of changing the attitudes of the workers and, thereby, begin the long process of changing the culture within the organization. Generating excitement and communicating the importance (value) of the work was a crucial element to success. Du Plooy explained the importance of this involvement and was quite clear in stating that people needed to understand that their contributions to the ORM system are perceived and recognized as valuable by senior management—with this understanding, the project picked up momentum. The project team developed different presentations according to the audience and level of the organization, so that there could be a clear understanding as to what the process involved from a strategic perspective down to an implementation level. The employees' involvement in the project resulted in a direct relationship to the employees' performance review and potential bonuses. This instilled a clear recognition of value in contributing to the ORM system and helped establish a culture throughout the organization in support of the ORM system. Gaining support is not a single-dimension approach plan for different people to view involvement in different ways. Compensation is always a good way to get someone's attention, but it is not the only means of gaining support. Public recognition is also a strong motivator for many people. TSG used both recognition and reward, which encouraged people from upper and lower ranks to feel they had a vested interest in the project's success. Some people may be interested in the challenge of improving an organization, and some may be interested in "joining" the team and accepting group goals. The important thing to remember is that everyone is different, so plan for these differences when developing the presentation and approach to gaining support.

IMPLEMENTING THE STANDARD AND FILLING THE GAPS

Du Plooy stated that Dr. Siegel returned to review the team's work and progress in February 2010. The team had already set up an auditing process for the different levels of the maturity model and also had graded the different levels to:

Level 1: Ad Hoc Approach—Coal
Level 2: Project Approach—Bronze
Level 3: Program Approach—Silver
Level 4: Systems Approach—Gold
Level 5: Management System—Platinum
Level 6: Holistic Management—Diamond

These same levels are included in the latest version of the maturity model. Pilot testing of the maturity model at the TSG lead to its refinement. The end result was the development of the ANSI/ASIS SPC.4-2012 maturity model standard. In the published standard, coal was changed to "preawareness" as the more reasonable and appropriate name. The basic idea is that Level 1 is undesirable and of very limited value, the same as coal when compared to gold or diamonds.

Due to the existing resilience levels within the company, Du Plooy and the other project team members determined that the group would start at maturity model Level 3 (Program Approach—Silver). Again, this is a perfect example of performing an analysis of the existing framework and determining that the established work product justifies starting at a higher level within the maturity model structure. Consideration should be given to the existing structures as well as which maturity level the organization may want to eventually achieve. Some organizations already have some form of structure regarding the requirements of an ORM system, but have just never thought of pulling it all together under one banner. To this end, they will be able to start at a higher level than an organization that has to start from scratch. It should be noted that once levels 3 and 4 have been completed, the actions required for levels 5 and 6 become more complex and it will take a solid business case to get management to go along with this type of implementation over a longer period. The trick is then to ensure that the successes of the initial implementation and process are continuously communicated at all levels of the organization, and to assure that organizational resilience becomes a permanent agenda item for the executive board.

According to Du Plooy, Dr. Cruywagen, Director of Risk for the Group, gave a presentation to the group management on the advantages of implementing and maintaining the maturity model. The executive board bought into the concept immediately and approved its implementation over a three-year period, the time that the project team had estimated that it would take to do a complete rollout and perform the next set of annual audits. Leadership, however, wanted to see demonstrable evidence that the project had value. The team established a pilot project to demonstrate the practical application and value of the larger project. Two 5-Star hotels, a casino resort, and a 3-Star hotel were selected for the pilot demonstration project. Presentations (briefings) were conducted for each of the unit's senior leaders explaining the project, the goals, and the value of the ANSI/ASIS SPC.1-2009. While some of the concepts were foreign to the managers, and required explanation that the team was not reinventing the wheel, in the end, each senior unit leader understood the value of the project, his or her role in the overall process, and how the new ANSI/ASIS SPC.1-2009 elements should be managed. The managers came to see that the project team was taking all the existing processes and forming a more synergistic approach with a single measurable process. Initially, managers may consider worse case scenarios when they hear about a "new" project, but perseverance and a clear strategy often result in a positive understanding.

OUTCOMES

Du Plooy explained that TSG's work during the early gap analysis effort allowed for the evaluation of existing documentation within the group to drive the various actions through policies and procedures linked to external legal requirements, internal policies and procedures, and other applicable regulations. These included, amongst other items, National Building Regulations, various standards and guidelines of the South African Bureau of Standards (SABS), regulations on fire prevention and protection systems, Occupational Health and Safety requirements, risk assessments, business impact analysis (criticality assessment), and established plans like security and business continuity plans. According to Du Plooy, TSG had recently completed the annual group-wide exercise of risk assessments, as well as updating the business continuity plans, saving the project team an enormous amount of work and time. All of the documents were reviewed to ensure they were current and relevant; nonconforming documents were either updated or discarded. Once the documentation review was completed, the project team developed an index of what would be required to form the core of the ORM system for the group. The team established an information system containing all relevant documents for an easier, more effective method for the managers to use or update. This system has proved to work very effectively for the unit managers during routine operations as well as during the audit processes.

Du Plooy stated, "As the project team completed their work on implementation, each business unit was given a preliminary audit report with nonconformancies (gaps) identified. They were normally given two weeks to rectify the nonconformancies and then a full audit was conducted. The audits, conducted using the maturity model and an auditing assessment sheet with all the requirements of the ANSI/ASIS SPC.1, used a scoring system for each item noted on the maturity model. The scoring mechanism consists of an achievable score of 2 points per item. If nothing has been done, then the score is 0 and, if there was an indication of 'work-in-progress,' then the score would be 1. Each unit had to score at least 80% to receive a certificate for a given level. The assessment sheets included a column for samples taken during the audit and they had to achieve at least 100%, otherwise they were penalized." Du Ploy further stated that "the average score has been 87% over 23 audited units. One business unit failed resulting in a management change. This shows that the TSG is very serious about the implementation. Some of the units have achieved a 98% aggregate—the competition is on! The challenge now is to keep the momentum alive and develop it even further so that they can achieve Level 5 and later 6 if they should choose to do so."

Business units received specially designed certificates as they achieved different levels of the maturity model. The group CEO, as well as the ORM system auditor, approved/signed each certificate and the respective divisional CEOs for Hotels and Gaming presided over the presentations. This senior-level involvement ensures that the respective leaders remain informed. It is an action item on their agendas and the employees recognize that their work is both valued and acknowledged by the executive. They are viewed as directly involved in the ORM process, which is an extremely important motivational tool. The business units have accepted the challenge of ORM conformance, which has fostered a "competition" between units; they have to report their respective status at their divisional meetings.

TSG continues to implement ORM through a fully accepted company concept of organizational resilience management as a requirement of doing business. Part of the continuing promotion and awareness of the project is the systematic and regular approval of the certificates along with the risk director's bimonthly status report. The status report indicates the achievements of the business units, the levels achieved by the units, and the number of certificate signed by the CEO. The various business units are striving to progressively achieve the next level of performance in the maturity model, although full standard implementation may not occur because of the additional focus on, and involvement of, external supply chain vendors.

EPILOGUE: FINAL THOUGHTS

Throughout the discussion contained within this book, we have consistently focused on the need to appreciate and embrace the necessity of the process and not just the development of a simple plan. The primary goal of this book was to provide readers with an understanding of organizational resilience and how to manage risk through the use of the ANSI/ ASIS SPC.1-2009 Standard. We have provided a clearly understandable approach to successfully addressing the various challenges and techniques necessary to plan, prepare, and implement organizational resilience management in your organization. Hopefully, you have gained that valuable insight we referenced earlier in this book, cutting through the complexities and identifying the key issues and techniques for the successful implementation of organizational resilience management. While the intent to provide practitioners with the necessary knowledge to achieve the desired goals of effective organizational resilience through cost-effective methods has been accomplished, there is a crucial piece to the puzzle that you are responsible for providing. That puzzle piece is an understanding of the complexities of your organization, and will mean the difference between success and failure. Remember, building a resilient organization is a cross-disciplinary and cross-functional endeavor; the inclusion of personnel, both internal and external to the organization, is a must.

Many people from around the world are constantly involved in developing organizational resilience into a more robust and internationally agreed upon discipline. There is continual discussion surrounding the meaning of resilience and how it applies to organizations.

The debate will continue as the very concept of eliminating silos to establish a multidisciplinary systems approach to increase the adaptive capacity and agility of organizations is a break with tradition. Organizational resilience is achieved through the contribution of a wide range of disciplines and functions working in concert to build a single business management strategy for addressing risks related to potential, undesirable, and disruptive events. Regardless of the debate, there are five important things to remember about organizational resilience:

- Organizational resilience management is a cross-disciplinary, cross-functional approach to help an organization achieve its objectives.
- Change is inherent to any organization's operations; the environment in which an organization operates is in a constant state of flux.
- To thrive and survive, organizations must be agile and adapt to internal and external changes in context.
- How an organization defines "resilience" is dependent on the business model of the organization and its objectives; thus, resilience, similar to risk management, is tailored to the organization.
- Becoming "resilient" is aspirational; there is no end-point. Change is a constant, so to maximize opportunities and minimize likelihood and consequences, organizations must be ready to be agile to changing conditions and adapt before, during, and after an event to either prevent the event from occurring or learning from the event to realign itself, or even reinvent itself, to fit its new environment. Organizational resilience is truly about an organization's capacity to adapt to a complex and changing environment.

While this may be the end of this book, it is not the culmination of the discussion concerning organizational resilience management. It is now your responsibility to join those discussions and add your voice, to consider different options, to test the effectiveness of various suggestions to achieve organizational resilience, and to further the developing of the knowledge base of organizational resilience management.

APPENDIX I

CONFORMANCE ASSESSMENT MATRIX

| | | | Findings (Conformance or Opportunity for Improvement) | | | | |
Criteria	Evidence	Documentation	Non = 0	Partial = 1	Full = 2	Opportunity for Improvement	Conclusions
4.X.Clause in standard							
"Element"							
Requirement ("shall" statement)							
Requirement ("shall" statement)							
Requirement ("shall" statement)							
4.X.Clause in standard							
"Element"							
Requirement ("shall" statement)							
Requirement ("shall" statement)							
Requirement ("shall" statement)							

CONFORMANCE IMPROVEMENT MATRIX

Element for Review	Current Status of Conformance	Relevant Stakeholders	Associated Risks	Risk Owner	Existing Risk Treatments Method	Actions Needed	Resources Needed	Time Frame	Conclusions (Priority)
Clause in Standard "Element"									
Subclause in Standard "Subelement"									
Subclause in Standard "Subelement"									
Clause in Standard "Element"									
Subclause in Standard "Subelement"									
Subclause in Standard "Subelement"									

APPENDIX 2

ANSI/ASIS SPC.1-2009 STANDARD REQUIREMENTS

Primary Requirements for Standard	Subordinate Requirement Items	Section #	Requirement Items 4.1
Know Your Organization	Define scope and boundaries for preparedness, response, continuity and recovery management program	4.1.1	• The scope of the ORM project under discussion—entire organization or a part thereof, along with developing a perspective of continual improvement. Determine what is necessary for ORM based on the mission, goals, obligations, and responsibilities of the organization.
	Identify critical objectives, operations, functions, products, and services	4.1.1	• Consider critical objectives, operations, functions, products, and services
	Preliminary determination of likely risk scenarios and consequences	4.1.1	• Determine risk scenarios based both on potential internal and external events that could adversely affect the critical operations and functions of the organization within the context of their potential impact.

Source: American National Standard. Organizational resilience: Security, preparedness, and continuity management systems—Requirements with guidance for use. 2010. ANSI/ASIS SPC.1-2009, p. 5. With permission.

Primary Requirements for Standard	Subordinate Requirement Items	Section #	Requirement Items 4.2
Policy		4.2.1	• Is appropriate to the nature and scale of potential threats, hazards, risks, and impacts (consequences) to the organization's activities, functions, products, and services (including stakeholders and the environment).
			• Includes a commitment to employee and community life safety as the first priority.
			• Includes a commitment to continual improvement.
			• Includes a commitment to enhanced organizational sustainability and resilience.
			• Includes a commitment to risk prevention, reduction, and mitigation.
			• Includes a commitment to comply with applicable legal requirements and with other requirements to which the organization subscribes.
			• Provides a framework for setting and reviewing OR management objectives and targets.
			• Is documented, implemented, and maintained.
			• Makes reference to limitations and exclusions.
			• Determines and documents the risk tolerance in relation to the scope of the management system.
			• Is communicated to all appropriate persons working for or on behalf of the organization.
			• Is available to relevant stakeholders.

236

Primary Requirements for Standard	Subordinate Requirement Items	Section #	Requirement Items 4.2
			• Includes a designated policy ownership and/or responsible point of contact.
			• Is reviewed at planned intervals and when significant changes occur.
			• Is signed by top management and a documented review of the policy relevancy is conducted annually.
	Management commitment	4.2.2	• Establishing an OR management system policy;
			• Ensuring that OR management system objectives and plans are established;
			• Establishing roles, responsibilities, and competencies for OR management;
			• Appointing one or more persons to be responsible for the OR management system with the appropriate authority and competencies to be accountable for the implementation and maintenance of the management system;
			• Communicating to the organization the importance of meeting OR management objectives and conforming to OR management system policy, its responsibilities under the law, and the need for continual improvement;
			• Providing sufficient resources to establish, implement, operate, monitor, review, maintain, and improve the OR management system;

Primary Requirements for Standard	Subordinate Requirement Items	Section #	Requirement Items 4.2
			• Deciding the criteria for accepting risks and the acceptable levels of risk;
			• Ensuring that internal OR management system audits are conducted;
			• Conducting management reviews of the OR management system; and
			• Demonstrates its commitment to continual improvement.
	Commitment to protection of critical assets and continuous improvement	4.2.2	• Identify critical assets and develop strategy to provide appropriate protection and continual improvement to protective measures.
	Commitment of resources	4.2.2	• Established management commitment to provide appropriate resources to achieve stated goals.

Source: American National Standard. Organizational resilience: Security, preparedness, and continuity management systems—Requirements with guidance for use. 2010. ANSI/ASIS SPC.1-2009, p. 6. With permission.

Primary Requirements for Standard	Subordinate Requirement Items	Section #	Requirement Items 4.3
Planning		4.3	• The organization shall define the scope consistent with protecting and preserving the integrity of the organization and its relationships with stakeholders, including interactions with key suppliers, outsourcing partners, and other stakeholders (for example, the organization's supply chain partners and suppliers, customers, stockholders, the community in which it operates, etc.).
	Risk assessment and impact analysis	4.3.1	• To systematically conduct asset identification and valuation to identify the organization's critical activities, functions, services, products, partnerships, supply chains, stakeholder relationships, and the potential impact related to a disruptive incident based on risk scenarios;
			• To identify intentional, unintentional, and naturally caused hazards and threats that have a potential for direct or indirect impact on the organization's operations, functions, and human, intangible, and physical assets; the environment; and its stakeholders;
			• To systematically analyze risk, vulnerability, criticality, and impacts (consequences);
			• To systematically analyze and prioritize risk controls and treatments and their related costs;

Primary Requirements for Standard	Subordinate Requirement Items	Section #	Requirement Items 4.3
			• To determine those risks that have a significant impact on activities, functions, services, products, stakeholder relationships, and the environment (i.e., significant risks and impacts).
		4.3.1	• Document and keep this information up to date and confidential, as is appropriate;
			• Re-evaluate risk and impacts within the context of changes within the organization or made to the organization's operating environment, procedures, functions, services, partnerships, and supply chains;
			• Establish recovery time objectives and priorities;
			• Evaluate the direct and indirect benefits and costs of options to reduce risk and enhance sustainability and resilience; and
			• Ensure that the significant risks and impacts are taken into account in establishing, implementing, and operating its OR management system.
	Legal and other requirements	4.3.2	• To identify legal, regulatory, and other requirements to which the organization subscribes related to the organization's hazards, threats, and risks that are related to its facilities, activities, functions, products, services, supply chain, the environment, and stakeholders.
			• To determine how these requirements apply to its hazards, threats, risks and their potential impacts.

Primary Requirements for Standard	Subordinate Requirement Items	Section #	Requirement Items 4.3
	Objectives and targets	4.3.3	• The objectives and targets shall be measurable qualitatively and/or quantitatively, and consistent with the OR management policy, including the commitments to:
			• Risk prevention, reduction, and mitigation;
			• Resilience enhancement;
			• Financial, operational and business continuity requirements (including continuity of the workforce);
			• Compliance with legal and other requirements; and
			• Continual improvement.
	Strategic prevention, preparedness and response programs (before, during, and after an incident)	4.3.3	• The organization shall establish and maintain one or more strategic program(s) for achieving its objectives and targets. The program(s) shall include:
			• Designation of responsibility and resources for achieving objectives and targets at relevant functions and levels of the organization;
			• Consideration of its activities, functions, regulatory or legal requirements, contractual obligations, stakeholders' needs, mutual aid agreements, and environment; and
			• The means and time frame by which they are to be achieved.
			• The organization shall establish and maintain one or more strategic program(s) for:

241

Primary Requirements for Standard	Subordinate Requirement Items	Section #	Requirement Items 4.3
			• Prevention and deterrence—Avoid, eliminate, deter, or prevent the likelihood of a disruptive incident and its consequences, including removal of human or physical assets at risk.
			• Mitigation—Minimize the impact of a disruptive incident.
			• Emergency response—The initial response to a disruptive incident involving the protection of people and property from immediate harm. An initial reaction by management may form part of the organization's first response.
			• Continuity—Processes, controls, and resources are made available to ensure that the organization continues to meet its critical operational objectives.
			• Recovery—Processes, resources, and capabilities of the organization are re-established to meet ongoing operational requirements within the time period specified in the objectives.

Source: American National Standard. Organizational resilience: Security, preparedness, and continuity management systems—Requirements with guidance for use. 2010. ANSI/ASIS SPC.1-2009, p. 7–9. With permission.

Primary Requirements for Standard	Subordinate Requirement Items	Section #	Requirement Items 4.4
Implementation and Operation		4.4	• Management shall ensure the availability of resources essential for the implementation and control of the OR management system. Resources include human resources and specialized skills, equipment, internal infrastructure, technology, information, intelligence, and financial resources. Roles, responsibilities, and authorities shall be defined, documented, and communicated in order to facilitate effective OR management.

	Structure and responsibility	4.4.1	• The organization's top management shall appoint (a) specific management representative(s) who, irrespective of other responsibilities, shall have defined roles, responsibilities, and authority for:
			
			  • Ensuring that an OR management system is established, communicated, implemented, and maintained in accordance with the requirements of this Standard; and
			
			  • Reporting on the performance of the OR management system to top management for review and as the basis for improvement.

		4.4.1	• The organization shall establish:

Primary Requirements for Standard	Subordinate Requirement Items	Section #	Requirement Items 4.4
			• An OR management team with appropriate authority to oversee incident preparedness, response, and recovery;
			• Logistical capabilities and procedures to locate, acquire, store, distribute, maintain, test, and account for services, personnel, resources, materials, and facilities produced or donated to support the OR management system;
			• Resource management objectives for response times, personnel, equipment, training, facilities, funding, insurance, liability control, expert knowledge, materials, and the time frames within which they will be needed from organization's resources and from any partner entities; and
			• Procedures for stakeholder assistance, communications, strategic alliances, and mutual aid.
		4.4.1	• The organization shall develop financial and administrative procedures to support the OR management program before, during, and after an incident. Procedures shall be:
			• Established to ensure that fiscal decisions can be expedited; and

Primary Requirements for Standard	Subordinate Requirement Items	Section #	Requirement Items 4.4
			• In accordance with established authority levels and accounting principles.
	Training, awareness, competence	4.4.2	• The organization shall ensure that any person(s) performing tasks who have the potential to prevent, cause, respond to, mitigate, or be affected by significant hazards, threats, and risks are competent (on the basis of appropriate education, training, or experience) and retain associated records.
			• The organization shall establish, implement, and maintain (a) procedure(s) to ensure persons working for it or on its behalf are aware of:
			• The significant hazards, threats, and risks, and related actual or potential impacts, associated with their work and the benefits of improved personal performance;
			• The procedures for incident prevention, deterrence, mitigation, self-protection, evacuation, response, continuity, and recovery;
			• The importance of conformity with the OR management policy and procedures and with the requirements of the OR management system;
			• Their roles and responsibilities in achieving conformity with the requirements of the OR management system;

245

Primary Requirements for Standard	Subordinate Requirement Items	Section #	Requirement Items 4.4
			• The potential consequences of departure from specified procedures; and
			• The benefits of improved personal performance.
		4.4.2	• The organization shall build, promote, and embed an OR management culture within the organization that:
			• Ensures the OR management culture becomes part of the organization's core values and organization governance; and
			• Makes stakeholders aware of the OR management policy and their role in any plans.
	Communication	4.4.3	• Documenting, recording, and communicating changes in documentation, plans, procedures, the management system, and results of evaluations and reviews;
			• Internal communication between the various levels and functions of the organization;
			• External communication with partner entities and other stakeholders;
			• Receiving, documenting, and responding to communication from external stakeholders;
			• Adapting and integrating a national or regional risk or threat advisory system or equivalent into planning and operational use;

Primary Requirements for Standard	Subordinate Requirement Items	Section #	Requirement Items 4.4
			• Alerting stakeholders potentially impacted by an actual or impending disruptive incident;
			• Assuring availability of the means of communication during a crisis situation and disruption;
			• Facilitating structured communication with emergency responders;
			• Assuring the interoperability of multiple responding organizations and personnel;
			• Recording of vital information about the incident, actions taken, and decisions made; and
			• Operations of a communications facility.
	Documentation	4.4.4	• The OR management system documentation shall include:
			• The OR management policy, objectives, and targets;
			• Description of the scope of the OR management system;
			• Description of the main elements of the OR management system and their integration with related documents;
			• Documents, including records, required by this Standard; and

Primary Requirements for Standard	Subordinate Requirement Items	Section #	Requirement Items 4.4
			• Documents, including records, determined by the organization to be necessary to ensure the effective planning, operation, and control of processes that relate to its significant risks.
	Document control	4.4.5	• The organization shall establish, implement, and maintain (a) procedure(s) to:
			• Approve documents for adequacy prior to issue;
			• Review, update and re-approve documents as necessary;
			• Ensure that changes and the current revision status of documents are identified;
			• Ensure that relevant versions of applicable documents are available at points of use;
			• Establish document retention and archival parameters;
			• Ensure that original and archival copies of documents, data, and information remain legible and readily identifiable;
			• Ensure that documents of external origin determined by the organization to be necessary for the planning and operation of the OR management system are identified and their distribution controlled;

Primary Requirements for Standard	Subordinate Requirement Items	Section #	Requirement Items 4.4
			• Identify as obsolete all out-of-date documents that the organization is required to retain; and
			• Ensure the integrity of the documents by ensuring they are tamperproof, securely backed up, accessible only to authorized personnel, and protected from damage, deterioration, or loss.
	Operational control	4.4.6	• The organization shall identify and plan those operations that are associated with the identified significant risks and consistent with its ORM policy, risk assessment, impact analysis, objectives, and targets, in order to ensure that they are carried out under specified conditions, by:
			• Establishing, implementing, and maintaining procedures related to the identified hazards, threats and risks to the activities, functions, products, and services of the organization and communicating applicable procedures and requirements to suppliers (including contractors);
			• Establishing, implementing, and maintaining (a) documented procedure(s) to control situations where their absence could lead to deviation from the ORM policy, objectives, and targets; and

249

Primary Requirements for Standard	Subordinate Requirement Items	Section #	Requirement Items 4.4
			• Stipulating the operating criteria in the documented procedures.
			• The operational control procedures shall address reliability and resiliency, the safety and health of people, and the protection of property and the environment impacted by a disruptive incident.
	Incident prevention, preparedness, and response	4.4.7	• The organization shall establish, implement, and maintain (a) procedure(s) to identify potential disruptive incidents that can have (an) impact(s) on the organization, its activities, functions, services, stakeholders, and the environment. The procedure(s) shall document how the organization will prevent, prepare for, and respond to them. The organization shall prepare for and respond to actual disruptive incidents to prevent or mitigate associated adverse consequences.
		4.4.7	• When establishing, implementing, and maintaining (a) procedure(s) to prepare for and respond to a disruptive incident expeditiously, the organization should consider each of the following actions: • Preserve life safety; • Protect assets; • Prevent further escalation of the disruptive incident; • Reduce the length of the disruption to operations;

250

Primary Requirements for Standard	Subordinate Requirement Items	Section #	Requirement Items 4.4
			• Restore critical operational continuity;
			• Recover normal operations (including evaluating improvements); and
			• Protect image and reputation (including media coverage and stakeholder relationships).
		4.4.7	• It is the responsibility of the organization to develop (an) incident prevention, preparedness and response procedure(s) that suits its particular needs. In developing its procedure(s), the organization should address its needs with regard to:
			• The nature of onsite hazards (e.g., flammable and toxic materials, storage tanks and compressed gases) and measures to be taken in the event of a disruptive incident or accidental releases;
			• The nature of local, nearby, or other external hazards with a potential impact on the organization;
			• The most likely type and scale of a disruptive incident;
			• The most appropriate method(s) for mitigation and emergency response to a disruptive incident to avoid escalation to a crisis or disaster;
			• Procedures to prevent environmental damage;

251

Primary Requirements for Standard	Subordinate Requirement Items	Section #	Requirement Items 4.4
			• Command and control procedures for and structure of predefined chain of command, (an) emergency operations center(s), and/or (an) alternate worksite(s);
			• Procedures and authority to declare an emergency situation, initiate emergency procedures, activate plans and actions, assess damage, and make financial decisions;
			• Internal and external communication plans including notification of appropriate authorities and stakeholders.
		4.4.7	• Procedures to acquire and/or provide appropriate medical care;
			• The action(s) required to minimize human casualties, and physical and environmental damage;
			• The action(s) required to secure vital information, information systems, facilities, and people;
			• Mitigation and response action(s) to be taken for different types of disruptive incident(s) or emergency situation(s);
			• The need for (a) process(es) for postevent evaluation to establish and implement corrective and preventive actions;

Primary Requirements for Standard	Subordinate Requirement Items	Section #	Requirement Items 4.4
			• Periodic testing of incident and emergency management and response procedure(s) and processes;
			• Training of incident and emergency response personnel;
			• A list of key personnel and aid agencies, including contact details (e.g., fire department, emergency medical services, law enforcement, hazardous material cleanup services);
			• Evacuation routes and assembly points including lists of personnel and contact details;
			• The potential for (a) disruptive incident or emergency situation(s) to affect or be affected by critical infrastructure (e.g., electricity, water, communications, transportation);
			• The possibility of mutual assistance to and from neighboring organizations; and
			• Procedure(s) and action(s) required to recover each critical activity within the organization's recovery time objective and the resources that it requires for recovery.

Primary Requirements for Standard	Subordinate Requirement Items	Section #	Requirement Items 4.4
		4.4.7	• The organization shall periodically review and, where necessary, revise its incident prevention, preparedness, and response procedures—in particular, after the occurrence of accidents or incidents that can escalate into an emergency, crisis, or disaster.

Source: American National Standard. Organizational resilience: Security, preparedness, and continuity management systems—Requirements with guidance for use. 2010. ANSI/ASIS SPC.1-2009, p. 8–13. With permission.

Primary Requirements for Standard	Subordinate Requirement Items	Section #	Requirement Items 4.5
Checking and Corrective Action		4.5	• The organization shall evaluate OR management plans, procedures, and capabilities through periodic assessments, testing, postincident reports, lessons learned, performance evaluations, and exercises. Significant changes in these factors should be reflected immediately in the procedures.
			• The organization shall keep records of the results of the periodic evaluations.
	Monitoring and measurement	4.5.1	• The organization shall establish, implement, and maintain performance metrics and (a) procedure(s) to monitor and measure, on a regular basis, those characteristics of its operations that have material impact on its performance (including partnership and supply chain relationships). The procedure(s) shall include the documenting of information to monitor performance, applicable operational controls, and conformity with the organization's OR management objectives and targets.
			• The organization shall evaluate and document the performance of the systems that protect its assets as well as its communications and information systems.

Primary Requirements for Standard	Subordinate Requirement Items	Section #	Requirement Items 4.5
	Evaluation of compliance	4.5.2.1	• The organization shall evaluate compliance with other requirements to which it subscribes including industry best practices. The organization may wish to combine this evaluation with the evaluation of legal compliance referred to above or to establish (a) separate procedure(s). The organization shall keep records of the results of the periodic evaluations.
	Exercise and testing	4.5.2.2	• The organization shall test and evaluate the appropriateness and efficacy of its OR management system, its programs, processes, and procedures (including partnership and supply chain relationships).
			• The organization shall validate its OR management system using exercises and testing that:
			• Are consistent with the scope of the OR management system and objectives of the organization;
			• Are based on realistic scenarios that are well planned with clearly defined aims and objectives;
			• Minimize the risk of disruption to operations and the potential to cause risk to operations and assets;

Primary Requirements for Standard	Subordinate Requirement Items	Section #	Requirement Items 4.5
			• Produce a formalized postexercise report that contains outcomes, recommendations, and arrangements to implement improvements in a timely fashion;
			• Are reviewed within the context of promoting continual improvement; and
			• Are conducted at planned intervals, and from time to time on a non-periodic basis as determined by the management of the organization as well as when significant changes occur within the organization and the environment it operates in.
	Nonconformity, corrective, and preventive action	4.5.3	• The organization shall establish, implement, and maintain (a) procedure(s) for dealing with actual and potential nonconformity(ies) and for taking corrective action and preventive action. The procedure(s) shall define requirements for:
			• Identifying and correcting nonconformity(ies) and taking action(s) to mitigate their impacts;
			• Investigating nonconformity(ies), determining their cause(s), and taking actions in order to avoid their recurrence;

Primary Requirements for Standard	Subordinate Requirement Items	Section #	Requirement Items 4.5
			• Evaluating the need for action(s) to prevent nonconformity(ies) and implementing appropriate actions designed to avoid their occurrence;
			• Recording the results of corrective action(s) and preventive action(s) taken; and
			• Reviewing the effectiveness of corrective action(s) and preventive action(s) taken.
			• Actions taken shall be appropriate to the impact of the potential problems, and conducted in an expedited fashion.
			• The organization shall identify changed risks, and identify preventive action requirements focusing attention on significantly changed risks.
			• The priority of preventive actions shall be determined based on the results of the risk assessment and impact analysis.
			• The organization shall make any necessary changes to the OR management system documentation.
	Records	4.5.4	• The organization shall establish and maintain records to demonstrate conformity to the requirements of its OR management system and of this Standard and the results achieved.

Primary Requirements for Standard	Subordinate Requirement Items	Section #	Requirement Items 4.5
			• The organization shall establish, implement, and maintain (a) procedure(s) to protect the integrity of records including access to, identification, storage, protection, retrieval, retention, and disposal of records.
			• Records shall be and remain legible, identifiable, and traceable.
	Internal audits	4.5.5	• The organization shall conduct internal ORM system audits at planned intervals, and from time to time on a nonperiodic basis (as determined by the management of the organization) to determine whether the control objectives, controls, processes, and procedures of its ORM system:
			• Conform to the requirements of this Standard and relevant legislation or regulations;
			• Conform to the organization's risk management requirements;
			• Are effectively implemented and maintained; and
			• Perform as expected.

Primary Requirements for Standard	Subordinate Requirement Items	Section #	Requirement Items 4.5
			• An audit program shall be planned, taking into consideration the status and importance of the processes and areas to be audited, as well as the results of previous audits. The audit criteria, scope, frequency, and methods shall be defined. The selection of auditors and conduct of audits shall ensure objectivity and impartiality of the audit process. Auditors shall not audit their own work.
			• The responsibilities and requirements for planning and conducting audits, and for reporting results and maintaining records, shall be defined in a documented procedure.
			• The management responsible for the area being audited shall ensure that actions are taken without undue delay to eliminate detected nonconformities and their causes. Follow-up activities shall include the verification of the actions taken and the reporting of verification results.

Source: American National Standard. Organizational resilience: Security, preparedness, and continuity management systems—Requirements with guidance for use. 2010. ANSI/ASIS SPC.1-2009, p. 14–16. With permission.

Primary Requirements for Standard	Subordinate Requirement Items	Section #	Requirement Items 4.6
Management Review		4.6.1	• Management shall review the organization's OR management system at planned intervals to ensure its continuing suitability, adequacy, and effectiveness. This review shall include assessing opportunities for improvement and the need for changes to the OR management system, including the OR management system policy and objectives. The results of the reviews shall be clearly documented and records shall be maintained.
	Review input	4.6.2	• The input to a management review shall include: • Results of ORM system audits and reviews; • Feedback from interested parties; • Techniques, products, or procedures that could be used in the organization to improve the ORM system performance and effectiveness; • Status of preventive and corrective actions; • Results of exercises and testing; • Vulnerabilities or threats not adequately addressed in the previous risk assessment; • Results from effectiveness measurements; • Follow-up actions from previous management reviews;

Primary Requirements for Standard	Subordinate Requirement Items	Section #	Requirement Items 4.6
			• Any changes that could affect the ORM system;
			• Adequacy of policy and objectives; and
			• Recommendations for improvement.
	Review output	4.6.3	• The output from the management review shall include any decisions and actions related to the following:
			• Improvement of the effectiveness of the OR management system;
			• Update of the risk assessment, impact analysis, and incident preparedness and response plans;
			• Modification of procedures and controls that effect risks, as necessary, to respond to internal or external events that may impact on the OR management system, including changes to:
			• Business and operational requirements; Risk reduction and security requirements; Operational conditions processes effecting the existing operational requirements; Regulatory or legal requirements; Contractual obligations; and Levels of risk and/or criteria for accepting risks.
			• Resource needs; and

Primary Requirements for Standard	Subordinate Requirement Items	Section #	Requirement Items 4.6
			• Improvement to how the effectiveness of controls is being measured.
	Maintenance	4.6.4	• Top management shall establish a defined and documented OR management system maintenance program to ensure that any internal or external changes that impact the organization are reviewed in relation to the OR management system. It shall identify any new critical activities that need to be included in the OR management system maintenance program.
Continual Improvement		4.6.5	• The organization shall continually improve the effectiveness of the OR management system through the use of the OR management policy, objectives, audit results, analysis of monitored events, corrective and preventive actions, and management review.

Source: American National Standard. Organizational resilience: Security, preparedness, and continuity management systems—Requirements with guidance for use. 2010. ANSI/ASIS SPC.1-2009, p. 16–17. With permission.

APPENDIX 3

ANSI/ASIS SPC.1-2009 STANDARD GUIDANCE
IMPLEMENTATION REQUIREMENTS

Primary Requirements for Standard	Subordinate Requirement Items	Section #	Implementation Guidance Section A 1
General Requirements		A.1	• The implementation of an organizational resilience (OR) management system specified by this Standard is intended to result in improved security, preparedness, response, continuity, and recovery performance. • Therefore, this Standard is based on the premise that the organization will periodically review and evaluate its OR management system to identify opportunities for improvement and their implementation.

	Define scope and boundaries for preparedness, response, continuity, and recovery management program	A.1	• This Standard requires an organization to
			  • Establish an appropriate OR management policy;
			  • Identify the hazards and threats related to the organization's past, existing, or planned activities, functions, products, and services to determine the risk, consequences, and impacts of significance;
			  • Identify applicable legal requirements and other requirements to which the organization subscribes;
			  • Identify priorities and set appropriate OR management objectives and targets;

265

Primary Requirements for Standard	Subordinate Requirement Items	Section #	Implementation Guidance Section A 1
			• Establish a structure and (a) program (s) to implement the policy and achieve objectives and meet targets;
			• Facilitate planning, control, monitoring, preventive and corrective action, and auditing and review activities to ensure both that the policy is complied with and that the OR management system remains appropriate; and
			• Be capable of adapting to changing circumstances.
	Identify critical objectives, operations, functions, products and services	A.1	• An organization with no existing OR management system should establish its current position with regard to its critical assets and potential risk scenarios by means of a review.
			• The review should cover four key areas:
			• Identification of risks, including those associated with normal operating conditions, abnormal conditions including start-up and shut-down, and emergency situations and accidents.
			• Identification of applicable legal requirements and other requirements to which the organization subscribes.
			• Examination of existing risk management practices and procedures, including those associated with procurement and contracting activities.

Primary Requirements for Standard	Subordinate Requirement Items	Section #	Implementation Guidance Section A 1
			• Evaluation of previous emergency situations and accidents.
			• The organization should define and document the scope of its OR management system.
			• Scoping is intended to clarify the boundaries of the organization to which the OR management system will apply, especially if the organization is a part of a larger organization at a given location.
			• OR management involves issues and actions before, during, and after a disruptive incident. Therefore, this Standard encompasses prevention, avoidance, deterrence, readiness, mitigation, response, continuity, and recovery.

Source: American National Standard. Organizational resilience: Security, preparedness, and continuity management systems—Requirements with guidance for use. 2010. ANSI/ASIS SPC.1-2009, p. 20–21. With permission.

267

Primary Requirements for Standard	Subordinate Requirement Items	Section #	Implementation Guidance Section A.2

Policy	Management commitment	A.2	• This policy, therefore, should reflect the commitment of top management to:
			  • Comply with applicable legal requirements and other requirements;
			  • Prevention, preparedness, and mitigation of disruptive incidents; and
			  • Continual improvement.

	Commitment to protection of critical assets and continuous improvement	A.2	• It is essential that top management of the organization sponsors, provides the necessary resources, and takes responsibility for creating, maintaining, testing, and implementing a comprehensive OR management system. This will ensure that management and staff at all levels within the organization understand that the OR management system is a critical top management priority.

Source: American National Standard. Organizational resilience: Security, preparedness, and continuity management systems—Requirements with guidance for use. 2010. ANSI/ASIS SPC.1-2009, p. 21–22. With permission.

Primary Requirements for Standard	Subordinate Requirement Items	Section #	Implementation Guidance Section A.3

Planning	Risk Assessment and impact analysis	A.3.1	• An organization should conduct a comprehensive risk assessment and impact analysis within the scope of its OR management system, taking into account the inputs and outputs (both intended and unintended) associated with:
			
			  • Its current and relevant past activities, products, and services;
			
			  • Planned or new developments, or new or modified activities, functions, products, and services;
			
			  • Relations with stakeholders;
			
			  • Interactions with the environment and community; and
			
			  • Critical infrastructure.

		A.3.1	• The risk assessment and impact analysis should:
			
			  • Give consideration to risks related to and criticality of the organization's activities, functions, products, and services and their potential for direct or indirect impact on the organization's operations, people, property, assets, compensation, image and reputation, profit, credit, and/or environment.
			
			  • Use a documented quantitative or qualitative methodology to estimate likelihood or probability of the identified potential risks and significance of their impacts if they are realized.

269

Primary Requirements for Standard	Subordinate Requirement Items	Section #	Implementation Guidance Section A.3
			• Be based on reasonable criteria by giving due consideration to all potential risks it recognizes to its operations.
			• Consider its dependencies on others and others dependencies on the organization, including critical infrastructure and supply chain dependencies and obligations.
			• Consider data and telecommunications integrity and cyber security.
			• Evaluate the consequences of legal and other obligations that govern the organization's activities.
			• Consider risks associated with stakeholders, contractors, suppliers, and other affected parties.
			• Analyze information on risks, and select those risks that may cause significant consequences and/or those risks whose consequence is hard to be determined in terms of significance.
			• Analyze and evaluate the level of resilience of each hazard or threat and each critical asset.

Primary Requirements for Standard	Subordinate Requirement Items	Section #	Implementation Guidance Section A.3
			• Evaluate risks and impacts it can control and influence. (However, in all circumstances, it is the organization that determines the degree of control and its strategies for risk acceptance, avoidance, management, minimization, tolerance transfer, and/or treatment.)
	Legal and other requirements	A.3.2	• The organization needs to identify the legal requirements that are applicable to activities and functions. These may include:
			• National and international legal requirements;
			• State/provincial/departmental legal requirements; and
			• Local governmental legal requirements.
			• Examples of other requirements to which the organization may subscribe include, if applicable:
			• Agreements with public authorities;
			• Agreements with customers;
			• Nonregulatory guidelines (e.g., Incident Command System/Unified Command);
			• Voluntary principles or codes of practice;
			• Voluntary labeling or product stewardship commitments;

Primary Requirements for Standard	Subordinate Requirement Items	Section #	Implementation Guidance Section A.3
			• Requirements of trade associations;
			• Agreements with community groups or nongovernmental organizations;
			• Public commitments of the organization or its parent organization; and/or
			• Corporate/company.
	Objectives and targets	A.3.3	• The objectives and targets should be specific and measurable wherever practicable. They should cover short- and long-term issues. Programs should define the strategic means for achieving objectives and targets.
			• The creation and use of one or more programs is important to the successful implementation of an OR management system. Each program should describe how the organization's objectives and targets will be achieved, including timescales, necessary resources, and personnel responsible for implementing the program(s).
			• The program should include, where appropriate and practical, consideration of all stages of an organization's activities and functions… .

Primary Requirements for Standard	Subordinate Requirement Items	Section #	Implementation Guidance Section A.3
		A.3.3	• Prevention, preparedness, and mitigation programs should consider removal of people and property at risk; relocation, retrofitting, and provision of protective systems or equipment; information, data, document, and cyber security; establishment of threat or hazard warning and communication procedures; and redundancy or duplication of essential personnel, critical systems, equipment, information, operations, or materials, including those from partner agencies.
			• The organization should plan for incident response and recovery, … there are three generic and interrelated management response steps that require preemptive planning and implementation in case of a disruptive incident:
			• Emergency response: The initial response to a disruptive incident usually involves the protection of people and property from immediate harm.
			• Continuity: Processes, controls, and resources are made available to ensure that the organization continues to meet its critical operational objectives.

Primary Requirements for Standard	Subordinate Requirement Items	Section #	Implementation Guidance Section A.3
			• Recovery: Processes, resources, and capabilities of the organization are re-established to meet ongoing operational requirements.

Source: American National Standard. Organizational resilience: Security, preparedness, and continuity management systems—Requirements with guidance for use. 2010. ANSI/ASIS SPC.1-2009, p. 22–26. With permission.

Primary Requirements for Standard	Subordinate Requirement Items	Section #	Implementation Guidance Section A.4
Implementation and Operation		A.4	• The successful implementation of an OR management system calls for a commitment from all persons working for the organization or on its behalf. Roles and responsibilities, therefore, should not be seen as confined to the risk management function, but also can cover other areas of an organization, such as operational management or staff functions other than risk management, security, preparedness, continuity, and response.
	Structure and responsibility	A.4.1	• … top management should establish the organization's OR management policy, and ensure that the OR management system is implemented. As part of this commitment, the top management should designate (a) specific management representative(s) with defined responsibility and authority for implementing the OR management system.
			• It is necessary that an appropriate administrative structure be put in place to effectively deal with crisis management during a disruptive incident. An organization should have a Crisis Management Team to lead incident/event response.
			• The Crisis Management Team may be supported by as many Response Teams as appropriate… .

Primary Requirements for Standard	Subordinate Requirement Items	Section #	Implementation Guidance Section A.4
			• Management also should ensure that appropriate resources are provided to ensure that the OR management system is established, implemented, and maintained.
			• Roles, responsibilities, and authorities also should be defined, documented, and communicated for coordination with external stakeholders.
	Training, awareness, competence	A.4.2	• The organization should identify the awareness, knowledge, understanding, and skills needed by any person with the responsibility and authority to perform tasks on its behalf.
			• This Standard states that:
			• The importance of conformity with the OR management policy and procedures and with the requirements of the OR management system;
			• The significant hazards, threats, and risks, and related actual or potential impacts, associated with their work and the benefits of improved personal performance;
			• Their roles and responsibilities needed to achieve conformity with the requirements of the OR management system;
			• The procedures for incident prevention, deterrence, mitigation, self-protection, evacuation, response, and recovery; and

276

Primary Requirements for Standard	Subordinate Requirement Items	Section #	Implementation Guidance Section A.4
			• The potential consequences of departure from specified procedures.
		A.4.2	• Awareness and education programs should be established for internal and external stakeholders potentially impacted by a disruptive incident.
			• Management should determine the level of experience, competence, and training necessary to ensure the capability of personnel, especially those carrying out specialized OR management functions.
			• All personnel should be trained to perform their individual responsibilities in case of a disruptive incident or crisis.
			• The Crisis Management and Response Teams should be educated about their responsibilities and duties including interactions with first responders and stakeholders.
			• It is recommended that any external resources that may be involved in a response, such as Fire, Police, Public Health, and third-party vendors, should be familiar with relevant parts of the response plans.
	Communication	A.4.3	• Internal communication is important to ensure the effective implementation of the OR management systems.
			• Arrangements should be made for communication and warnings internally and externally for normal and abnormal conditions.

Primary Requirements for Standard	Subordinate Requirement Items	Section #	Implementation Guidance Section A.4
			• Organizations should implement a procedure for receiving, documenting, and responding to relevant communications from stakeholders and interested parties.
			• The organization may wish to plan its communication taking into account the decisions made on relevant target groups, the appropriate messages and subjects, and the choice of means. Methods for external communication can include annual reports, newsletters, websites, warnings, and community meetings.
			• Effective communication is one of the most important ingredients in crisis management.
			• Preplanning for communications is critical.
			• The organization should designate a single primary spokesperson (with backups identified) who will manage/disseminate crisis communications to the media and others.
	Documentation	A.4.4	• The level of detail of the documentation should be sufficient to describe the OR management system and how its parts work together, and provide direction on where to obtain more detailed information on the operation of specific parts of the OR management system. This documentation may be integrated with documentation of other systems implemented by the organization.

Primary Requirements for Standard	Subordinate Requirement Items	Section #	Implementation Guidance Section A.4
	Document control	A.4.5	• The … primary focus of organizations should be on the effective implementation of the OR management system and on security, preparedness, response, continuity, and recovery performance and not on a complex document control system.
			• Organizations should ensure the integrity of the documents by ensuring they are tamperproof, securely backed up, accessible only to authorized personnel, and protected from damage, deterioration, or loss.
	Operational control	A.4.6	• An organization should evaluate those of its operations that are associated with its identified significant risks, and ensure that they are conducted in a way that will control or reduce the adverse impacts associated with them in order to fulfill the requirements of its OR management policy and meet its objectives and targets.
			• As this part of the OR management system provides direction on how to take the system requirements into day-to-day operations, it requires the use of (a) documented procedure(s) to control situations where the absence of documented procedures could lead to deviations from the OR management policy, objectives, and targets.

Primary Requirements for Standard	Subordinate Requirement Items	Section #	Implementation Guidance Section A.4
			• To minimize the likelihood of a disruptive incident, these procedures should include controls for the design, installation, operation, refurbishment, and modification of risk-related items of equipment, instrumentation, etc., as appropriate.
	Incident prevention, preparedness, and response	A.4.7	• It is the responsibility of each organization to develop (an) incident prevention, preparedness, and response procedure(s) that suits its own particular needs. In developing its procedure(s), the organization should include consideration of: • A potential disruptive incident should be identified, understood, and addressed and, in doing so, avoided or prevented. • Prevention can include proactive steps to coordinate with intelligence, law enforcement, and public agencies; establish information sharing agreements; physical protection of key assets; access controls; awareness and readiness training programs; warning and alarm systems; and practices to reduce the threat. • Organizational culture, operational plans, and management objectives should motivate individuals to feel personally responsible for prevention, avoidance, deterrence, and detection.

Primary Requirements for Standard	Subordinate Requirement Items	Section #	Implementation Guidance Section A.4
			• Deterrence and detection can make a disruptive act or activity more difficult to carry out against the organization or significantly limit, if not negate, its impact.
			• Physical security planning includes protection of perimeter grounds, building perimeter, internal space and content protection.
		A.4.7	• Cost-effective mitigation strategies should be employed to prevent or lessen the impact of potential crises.
			• The organization should establish procedures to recognize when specific dangers occur that necessitate the need for some level of response.
			• A potential disruptive incident, once recognized, should be immediately reported to a supervisor, a member of management, or another individual tasked with the responsibility of crisis notification and management.
			• Problem assessment (an evaluative process of decision making that will determine the nature of the issue to be addressed) and severity assessment (the process of determining the severity of the crisis and what any associated costs may be in the long run) should be made at the outset of a crisis.
			• The point at which a situation is declared to be an emergency or crisis should be clearly defined, documented, and fit very specific and controlled parameters.

281

Primary Requirements for Standard	Subordinate Requirement Items	Section #	Implementation Guidance Section A.4
			• Preparedness and response plans should be developed around a "worst case scenario," with the understanding that the response can be scaled appropriately to match the actual crisis.
		A.4.7	• People are the most important aspect of any preparedness and response plan.
			• Logistical decisions made in advance will impact the success or failure of a good preparedness and response plan.
			• Once the Crisis Management Team has been activated, the damage should be assessed and carefully documented.
			• If appropriate, existing funding and insurance policies should be examined, and additional funding and insurance coverage should be identified and obtained.
			• Transportation in a time of crisis can be a challenge.
			• Critical vendor or service provider agreements should be established as appropriate and their contact information maintained as part of the preparedness and response plan.
			• Mutual aid agreements identify resources that may be shared with or borrowed from other organizations during a crisis, as well as mutual support that may be shared with other organizations.

Primary Requirements for Standard	Subordinate Requirement Items	Section #	Implementation Guidance Section A.4
		A.4.7	• Strategic alliances identify delivery partners with which they have an interdependent relationship with other organizations to produce and supply products and services and share risk.
			• Once the extent of damage is known, the process recovery needs should be prioritized and a schedule for resumption determined and documented.
			• Once the processes to be restored have been prioritized, the resumption work can begin with processes restored according to the prioritization schedule.
			• Once the critical processes have been resumed, the resumption of the remaining processes can be addressed.
			• The organization should seek to bring the organization "back to normal." If it is not possible to return to the precrisis "normal," a "new normal" should be established.

Source: American National Standard. Organizational resilience: Security, preparedness, and continuity management systems—Requirements with guidance for use. 2010. ANSI/ASIS SPC.1-2009, p. 26–36. With permission.

Primary Requirements for Standard	Subordinate Requirement Items	Section #	Implementation Guidance Section A.5
Checking and Corrective Action	Monitoring and measurement	A.5.1	• Data collected from monitoring and measurement can be analyzed to identify patterns and obtain information.
			• Knowledge gained from this information can be used to implement corrective and preventive action.
			• Metrics should be established to measure success of the OR management system.
			• Key characteristics are those that the organization needs to consider to determine how it is managing its significant risks and impacts, achieving objectives and targets, and improving security, preparedness, response, continuity, and recovery performance.
			• When necessary to ensure valid results, measuring equipment should be calibrated or verified at specified intervals, or prior to use, against measurement standards traceable to international or national measurement standards.
	Evaluation of compliance	A.5.2.1	• The organization should be able to demonstrate that it has evaluated compliance with the legal requirements identified including applicable permits or licenses.
			• The organization should be able to demonstrate that it has evaluated compliance with the identified other requirements to which it has subscribed.
	Exercises and testing	A.5.2.2	• Testing scenarios should be designed using the events identified in the risk assessment and impact analysis.

Primary Requirements for Standard	Subordinate Requirement Items	Section #	Implementation Guidance Section A.5
			• Testing can keep response teams and employees effective in their duties, clarify their roles, and reveal weaknesses in the OR management system that should be corrected.
			• The first step in testing should be the setting of goals and expectations.
			• Lessons learned from previous tests, as well as actual incidents experienced, should be built into the testing cycle for the OR management system.
			• The responsibility for testing the OR management system should be assigned.
			• A test schedule and timeline as to how often the plan and its components will be tested should be established.
			• The scope of testing should be planned to develop over time.
			• All participants should understand their roles in the exercise, and the exercise should involve all participants.
			• After completion, the exercises and tests should be critically evaluated.
			• Design of tests should be evaluated and modified as necessary.
			• Exercise and test results should be documented.

Primary Requirements for Standard	Subordinate Requirement Items	Section #	Implementation Guidance Section A.5
	Nonconformity, corrective and preventive action	A.5.3	• Depending on the nature of the nonconformity, in establishing procedures to deal with these requirements, organizations may be able to accomplish them with a minimum of formal planning, or it may be a more complex and long-term activity. Any documentation should be appropriate to the level of action.

	Control of records	A.5.4	• Management system records can include, among others:
			  • Compliance records;
			  • Training records;
			  • Process monitoring records;
			  • Inspection, maintenance, and calibration records;
			  • Pertinent contractor and supplier records;
			  • Incident reports;
			  • Records of incident and emergency preparedness tests;
			  • Audit results;
			  • Management review results;
			  • External communications decision;
			  • Records of applicable legal requirements;
			  • Records of significant risk and impacts;
			  • Records of management systems meetings;
			  • Security, preparedness, response, continuity, and recovery performance information;
			  • Legal compliance records; and

Primary Requirements for Standard	Subordinate Requirement Items	Section #	Implementation Guidance Section A.5
			• Communications with stakeholders and interested parties.
			• Proper account should be taken of confidential information.
			• Organizations should ensure the integrity of records by rendering them tamperproof, securely backed up, accessible only to authorized personnel, and protected from damage, deterioration, or loss.
			• Legal authority within the organization should determine the appropriate period of time documents should be retained.
	Internal audits	A.5.5	• Internal audits of an OR management system can be performed by personnel from within the organization or by external persons selected by the organization, working on its behalf.

Source: American National Standard. Organizational resilience: Security, preparedness, and continuity management systems—Requirements with guidance for use. 2010. ANSI/ASIS SPC.1-2009, p. 36–38. With permission.

Primary Requirements for Standard	Subordinate Requirement Items	Section #	Implementation Guidance Section A.6
Management Review		A.6	• The management review should cover the scope of the OR management system, although not all elements of the OR management system need to be reviewed at once and the review process may take place over a period of time.
			• The OR management system should be regularly reviewed and evaluated. The following factors can trigger a review and should otherwise be examined once a review is scheduled:
			• Risk assessment and impact analysis;
			• Sector/industry trends;
			• Regulatory requirements;
			• Event experience;
			• Test and exercise results.
	Continual improvement and maintenance	A.6	• Continual improvement and OR management system maintenance should reflect changes in the risks, activities, functions, and operation of the organization that will affect the OR management system. The following are examples of procedures, systems, or processes that may affect the plan:
			• Policy changes;
			• Hazards and threat changes;
			• Changes to the organization and its business processes;
			• Changes in assumptions in risk assessment and impact analysis;
			• Personnel changes (employees and contractors);
			• Supplier and supply chain changes;

Primary Requirements for Standard	Subordinate Requirement Items	Section #	Implementation Guidance Section A.6
			• Process and technology changes;
			• Systems and application software changes;
			• Critical lessons learned from testing;
			• Issues discovered during actual implementation of the plan in a crisis;
			• Changes to external environment; and
			• Other items noted during review of the plan and identified during the risk assessment and impact analysis.

Source: American National Standard. Organizational resilience: Security, preparedness, and continuity management systems—Requirements with guidance for use. 2010. ANSI/ASIS SPC.1-2009, p. 39–40. With permission.

APPENDIX 4

**MATURITY MODEL FOR PHASED
IMPLEMENTATION OF THE ANSI/ASIS SPC.1-2009
ORGANIZATIONAL RESILIENCE STANDARD**

ANSI/ASIS SPC.1 Standard Clause	Core Element	Issues Addressed by Core Element (Establish, Implement, and Maintain)	Preawareness (Phase One)	Project Approach (Phase Two)
Generic Concepts	Key elemental theme	Description of element.	No formal organizational resilience management. Risk and resilience management actions are reactionary in nature. Not yet recognizing the importance and value of ORMS elements.	Initiates a project to address specific issue(s) by partially implementing core elements. Actions generally reactionary in nature, focusing on preidentified issue(s). Recognizes the importance of elements and the need for some preplanning. Focus is on solving an identified problem(s) to demonstrate the business value of using the *Standard*.

Program Approach (Phase Three)	Systems Approach (Phase Four)	Management System (Phase Five)	Holistic Management (Phase Six)
Establishes a division or organization-wide program to address organizational resilience issues by partially implementing core elements. Recognizes the importance of elements and the need for preplanning; however, focus is on individual elements and not their interrelationship and integration (checklist approach). May be in reaction to an incident or near miss or be driven by external concerns. Risk management applications selected for their chances of demonstrating success. Program driven by "Program Manager" who applies a program management approach.	Organizational resilience management is viewed as a matter of strategic value to the organization. Focuses on integration and interrelationships between core elements. Focuses on mission-based management of risks to minimize both likelihood and consequences of a disruptive incident. Organizational resilience management is viewed as part of a continual improvement process using PDCA model. Managing risk is seen as important at all levels and individuals in organization. Integration and feedback loops of systems approach. Organizational resilience management culture is developing and part of decision making.	The organization is conformant with the requirements of the standard. The organization establishes, documents, implements, maintains, and continually improves an ORMS in accordance with the requirements of the ORMS Standard. Examines the linkages and interactions between the ORMS elements that compose the entirety of the system for the defined scope. Manages risk using balanced strategies to adaptively, preemptively, and reactively address minimization of both likelihood and consequences of disruptive events. Organizational resilience management is demonstrably part of the routine management of projects and business processes.	The organization goes beyond conformance to the standard to fully integrate organizational resilience management into its overall risk management strategy. The organization emphasizes enterprise-wide and supply chain relationships in all aspects of its ORMS. The organization mentors other stakeholders (in its supply chain and community). The organization views its organizational resilience as an active integral part of community resilience. ORM culture is well-developed and considered an integral part of overall management and risk decision making. ORM and ORMS principles are expanded to all areas of the organization and its activities.

ANSI/ASIS SPC.1 Standard Clause	Core Element	Issues Addressed by Core Element (Establish, Implement, and Maintain)	Preawareness (Phase One)	Project Approach (Phase Two)
4.1.1 Scope of OR Management System	Understands the organization and its context. Scope of ORMS.	The internal, external, and risk management context of the organization. Scope and boundaries for development and implementation of ORMS.	No process to identify internal and external context for organizational resilience. No definition of scope.	Projects of limited scope focusing on one or a limited number of issues viewed as having significant interest. Internal, external, and risk management context limited to project scope definition.

Program Approach (Phase Three)	Systems Approach (Phase Four)	Management System (Phase Five)	Holistic Management (Phase Six)
Programs are established to address core elements based on evaluation of the internal, external, and risk management context of all or part of the organization. Scope defined based on protecting and preserving activities, functions, and services viewed as essential.	Organization defines and documents the internal, external, and risk management context. Operational objectives, assets, activities, functions, services, and products are defined. Boundaries of scope are defined and documented based on protecting and preserving activities, functions, and services, as well as relations with stakeholders. Weighting of risk management strategies is defined.	Organization defines and documents the internal, external, and risk management context. Boundaries of scope defined and documented, considering the organization's mission, goals, internal and external obligations, risk assessment, and legal responsibilities. Scope of the ORMS defined in terms of and appropriate to the size, nature, and complexity of the organization from a perspective of continual improvement.	Organization defines and documents the internal, external, and risk management context, as well as enterprise-wide risk management interactions and supply chain tiers, commitments, and relationships. Defining the organizational resilience internal, external, and risk management context related to community resilience. Boundaries of scope defined and documented.

ANSI/ASIS SPC.1 Standard Clause	Core Element	Issues Addressed by Core Element (Establish, Implement, and Maintain)	Preawareness (Phase One)	Project Approach (Phase Two)
4.2.1 Policy Statement	Setting a policy framework.	Top management policy to provide a framework for setting objectives and provide the direction and principles for action.	No defined ORM policy. Lack of top-level governance.	Policy limited to addressing identified issue(s). Driven by "Project Leader," may or may not have top management involvement beyond approval of project.

Program Approach (Phase Three)	Systems Approach (Phase Four)	Management System (Phase Five)	Holistic Management (Phase Six)
Drafted by "Program Manager" and signed by top management. Policy addresses organizational resilience management in divisions defined in scope. Communicated to relevant divisions.	Policy establishes framework for organizational resilience management by setting objectives and providing direction. Supported by top management. Communicated throughout organization.	Policy establishes framework for organizational resilience management by setting objectives and providing direction. Clear commitment to comply with applicable legal and other requirements. Supported and promoted by top management. Communicated throughout organization and to stakeholders, making them aware of content and meaning.	Policy integrated into all management structures, levels, and individual responsibilities. Clear commitment to holistic ORM. Communicated throughout organization, enterprise, and to external stakeholders (supply chain and community).

ANSI/ASIS SPC.1 Standard Clause	Core Element	Issues Addressed by Core Element (Establish, Implement, and Maintain)	Preawareness (Phase One)	Project Approach (Phase Two)
4.2.2 Management Commitment	Management mandate and commitment.	Top management commitment to meeting the requirements of organizational resilience management. Top management provision of appropriate resources and authorities for ORMS.	Management ambivalent or unreceptive. Concerned with acknowledging risk and uncertainty. No guidance from the top of organization. Ostrich effect.	Management authorization and resources provided to "Project Leader" to conduct project. Resources restricted to address limited scope. Resource allocation linked to perceived benefit. Project aims to encourage more management support and buy-in.

Program Approach (Phase Three)	Systems Approach (Phase Four)	Management System (Phase Five)	Holistic Management (Phase Six)
Top management sponsorship. Endorsement of established programs for ORM. One or more individuals appointed as Program Manager. Set prioritization and timeframes to address risks of disruptive events. Resources allocated to support program.	Top management participation. Active endorsement of ORMS by top management. Establishes an ORMS policy. One or more individuals appointed to be responsible for ORMS. Decides criteria for accepting risk, acceptable levels of risk. Sets prioritization and timeframes for managing the risks of disruptive events. Resources allocated to support ORMS.	Documents evidence of its mandate and commitment to the establishment, implementation, operation, monitoring, review, maintenance, and improvement of the ORMS. Defines and documents criteria to be used to evaluate the significance of risk, determination of appropriate risk treatments, and setting of timeframes for recovery. Sufficient resources allocated and competencies assured.	Documents evidence of its mandate and commitment to the establishment, implementation, operation, monitoring, review, maintenance, and improvement of the ORMS and its relationship to its external stakeholders (supply chain and community). Sharing best practices with external stakeholders (supply chain and community). Defines and documents criteria to be used to evaluate the significance of risk, determination of appropriate risk treatments, and setting of timeframes for managing the risks of disruptive events of organization and relevant stakeholders.

ANSI/ASIS SPC.1 Standard Clause	Core Element	Issues Addressed by Core Element (Establish, Implement, and Maintain)	Preawareness (Phase One)	Project Approach (Phase Two)
4.3.1 Risk Assessment and Impact Analysis	Risk Assessment (identification, analysis, evaluation).	Risk identification, analysis, and evaluation. Threat, vulnerability, impact, and criticality analysis (including dependencies and inter-dependencies). Evaluates the effect of uncertainty on the organization and its objectives (analyze likelihood and consequences of disruptive events).	No process. Indications of risks, problems, near misses, and warning signs identified retroactively.	No formal process. Reactive in nature with issue(s) targeted as problematic or requiring immediate attention. A gap analysis to address project issues, rather than a risk assessment examining what is needed organizationally.

Program Approach (Phase Three)	Systems Approach (Phase Four)	Management System (Phase Five)	Holistic Management (Phase Six)
Develops and implements a procedure to identify, analyze, and evaluate essential assets, risks, and impacts. Priorities based on outcomes of risk or impact analysis.	Establishes, implements, and maintains an ongoing formal risk and impact assessment process. Prioritized risks and impacts are taken into account in establishing, implementing, and operating the ORMS. Risk assessment and impact analysis recognized as providing the foundation for elements of the ORMS and for organizational decision-making.	Establishes, implements, and maintains an ongoing formal and documented risk assessment process. Prioritizes and documents risks and impacts. Periodically reviews whether ORM scope, policy, and risk assessment are still appropriate given the organizations' internal and external context. Re-evaluates risk and impacts within the context of internal and external change.	Establishes, implements, and maintains an ongoing formal and documented risk assessment process that includes external stakeholders (supply chain and community). Establishes, implements, and maintains a formal and documented communication and consultation process with external stakeholders (supply chain and community) in the risk assessment process. Establishes, implements, and maintains a formal and documented process for monitoring and reviewing the risk assessment process. Integrates risk assessment processes with external stakeholders (supply chain and community).

301

ANSI/ASIS SPC.1 Standard Clause	Core Element	Issues Addressed by Core Element (Establish, Implement, and Maintain)	Preawareness (Phase One)	Project Approach (Phase Two)
4.3.2 Legal and Other Requirements	Identifies and assesses legal, regulatory, and other requirements to which the organization subscribes.	Identification of legal and other requirements. Evaluation of internal and external requirements pertinent to the organization. Communication of relevant information on legal and other requirements to stakeholders.	No process for identifying and understanding of legal and other requirements associated with ORM.	Informal process initiated to identify legal and other requirements related to identified issue being addressed.

Program Approach (Phase Three)	Systems Approach (Phase Four)	Management System (Phase Five)	Holistic Management (Phase Six)
Legal requirements applicable to the activities, functions, and services in the scope of the program are identified.	Establishes and maintains procedures to identify legal and other requirements. Determines how the legal and other requirements apply to the organization. Communicates requirements to appropriate parties. Legal and other requirement considered in risk management process.	Establishes and maintains documented procedures to identify legal and other requirements. Determines how the legal and other requirements apply to the organization risks and obligations. Ensures that applicable legal, regulatory, and other requirements are considered in developing, implementing, and maintaining its ORMS. Documents information and keeps it up-to-date.	Establishes and maintains procedures to identify legal and other requirements relevant to the organization and appropriate stakeholders (including supply chain partners and community). Determines how the legal and other requirements apply to the organization and stakeholder risks and obligations.

ANSI/ASIS SPC.1 Standard Clause	Core Element	Issues Addressed by Core Element (Establish, Implement, and Maintain)	Preawareness (Phase One)	Project Approach (Phase Two)
4.3.3 Objectives, Targets, and Program(s)	Select and prioritize risk treatment options.	Prioritization of the issues identified as a result of the risk assessment and impact analysis. Objectives and targets (including time frames) based on the prioritization of issues within the context of an organization's ORMS policy and mission. Strategic plans for prevention, protection, preparedness, mitigation, response, continuity, and recovery. Identification of resources needed. Identification of roles, responsibilities, authorities, and their interrelationships within the organization needed for ORM. Planning the operational processes for actions effecting how the objectives and targets are achieved.	No process to define objectives and targets. No risk prioritization.	Defines targets and objectives for demonstrating project success. Develops targets, objectives, and strategic action plans to achieve immediate organizational resilience performance improvement related to identified issue(s) and to demonstrate business value. Action plans for identified issues include required resources, responsibilities, and timescales.

Program Approach (Phase Three)	Systems Approach (Phase Four)	Management System (Phase Five)	Holistic Management (Phase Six)
Organizational resilience performance objectives for program management are set based on the risk assessment and impact analysis. Strategic action plans designate actions, responsibilities, accountability, resources, and timeframes for achieving objectives and targets.	Objectives are consistent with the ORM policy and risk assessment. Documents objectives and targets to manage risks in order to avoid, prevent, protect, deter, mitigate, respond to, and recover from disruptive events. Targets are measurable and derived from the objectives. Establishes, implements, and maintains strategic programs (action plans) for prevention, protection, deterrence, mitigation, response, recovery, and continuity. Strategic plans designate actions, responsibilities, accountability, resources, and timeframes for achieving objectives and targets.	Documented objectives and targets are established to manage organizational resilience by avoiding, accepting, removing the source, changing the likelihood, changing the consequences, and sharing and/or retaining the risk. Objectives provide a basis for selecting one or more options for managing risk including asset value, opportunities for reducing likelihood and/or consequences, cost/ benefit, and tolerable levels of residual risk. Targets are documented, measurable, achievable, relevant, and time-based. Documented and maintained strategic programs (action plans) for risk treatment in order to achieve its objectives and targets. Documented risk treatment options.	Documented objectives and targets establish internal and external expectations for the organization and its stakeholders (supply chain and community) that relate to mission accomplishment, product and service delivery, and functional operations.

305

ANSI/ASIS SPC.1 Standard Clause	Core Element	Issues Addressed by Core Element (Establish, Implement, and Maintain)	Preawareness (Phase One)	Project Approach (Phase Two)
4.4.1 Resources, Roles, Responsibility, and Authority	Availability and accountability of resources essential for the implementation of the ORMS and to facilitate effective OR management.	Procedures, roles, and responsibilities to cover all normal operating conditions and disruptive events. Techniques for management of functional, tactical, and strategic teams. Provisions for adequate finance and administrative resources to support normal operating conditions and disruptive events. Arrangements for supply chain obligations, mutual aid, and community assistance. Determination of local, regional, and public authorities' roles, relationships, and interactions.	Not defined. No dedicated personnel for ORMS. Needed resources not identified.	Assigns roles and responsibilities to specific persons to address issue(s) in the limited scope. Allocates adequate resources in accordance with action plan. A "Project Leader" is designated to oversee the project. Participation based on project scope.

Program Approach (Phase Three)	Systems Approach (Phase Four)	Management System (Phase Five)	Holistic Management (Phase Six)
Identifies and defines authorities, roles, responsibilities, and appropriate resources within the organization. Identifies internal and external departments, division, business units, and partners that will play a role in addressing a disruptive event. Identifies an ORM program team and leader. Allocates adequate resources in accordance with the action plan.	Top management appoints a specific management representative responsible for the ORMS. Formal ORM responsibilities and relationships are defined and adhered to. Teams with defined roles and adequate resources are established to support ORM action plans. Establishes arrangements for stakeholder assistance, communication, strategic alliances, and mutual aid. Identifies financial and administrative procedures needed to support the ORM programs. Roles, relationships, and interactions with external resources (local, regional, and public authorities, including first responders) are defined. Adequate resources allocated in accordance with action plan.	Roles, responsibilities, and authorities are defined, documented, and communicated in order to facilitate effective ORM, consistent with the achievement of its ORM policy, objectives, targets, and programs. Documented organizational resilience (security, crisis, response, and recovery) team(s) with defined roles, appropriate authority, and adequate resources. Establishes and documents logistical capabilities and procedures to locate, acquire, store, distribute, maintain, test, and account for services, personnel, resources, materials, and facilities produced or donated to support the ORMS. Formal and documented procedures for stakeholder assistance, communications, strategic alliances, and mutual aid.	Roles, responsibilities, and authorities are defined, documented, and communicated in order to facilitate effective ORM within the organization, enterprise-wide, and within the community consistent with achieving organization and external stakeholders' (supply chain and community) objectives, targets, and programs.

307

ANSI/ASIS SPC.1 Standard Clause	Core Element	Issues Addressed by Core Element (Establish, Implement, and Maintain)	Preawareness (Phase One)	Project Approach (Phase Two)
4.4.2 Competence, Training, and Awareness	Defining and addressing competence.	Skills and competency requirements to support normal operating conditions and disruptive events. Training and education program for the organization's personnel, contractors, and other relevant stakeholders. Organizational awareness and culture to support ORM. Organizational interface protocol, identification and training requirements. Tools to enhance situational awareness.	Lack of ORM cultural awareness. Competencies and skills not identified. No training program. Little or no in-house expertise or experience. Workforce unaware of risk management needs and lacks training to adequately take ownership and control risks.	Competence, skills, and training needs identified to achieve project objectives and targets. Conducts training with some measure of competence to achieve objectives and targets. Training and awareness focus on addressing the identified issue(s) in the scope.

Program Approach (Phase Three)	Systems Approach (Phase Four)	Management System (Phase Five)	Holistic Management (Phase Six)
Determines competence requirements that are necessary for activities defined in the program scope. Develops and implements training, competence, and awareness procedures.	Identifies competencies and training needs associated with achieving the ORMS objectives, targets, and programs. Develops and implements procedures to address competence and training needs. Assesses competence against requirements.	Ensures that any person(s) performing tasks who have the potential to prevent, cause, respond to, mitigate, or be affected by significant hazards, threats, and risks are competent (on the basis of appropriate education, training, or experience). Documents and retains associated training and competence records. Ensures the OR management culture becomes part of the organization's core values and organization governance. Makes stakeholders aware of the OR management policy and their role in any plans.	Builds, promotes, and embeds an ORM culture within the organization, enterprise, supply chain and community. Shares best practices with external stakeholders (supply chain and community).

ANSI/ASIS SPC.1 Standard Clause	Core Element	Issues Addressed by Core Element (Establish, Implement, and Maintain)	Preawareness (Phase One)	Project Approach (Phase Two)
4.4.3 Communication and Warning	Identify and address internal and external communication requirements.	Procedures, arrangements, and tools for communication to support normal operating conditions and disruptive events. Exercises for plans to communicate information and warnings with stakeholders (including the media) to support normal operating conditions and disruptive events. Reliable and tested communications and a warning capability in the event of a disruption.	No procedures. Not coordinated internally or externally. Reactive in nature. Driven by demands for information.	Communication procedures address project objectives, target, and scope. Develops communication procedures for internal and external stakeholders (including authorities and media) consistent with the project scope.

Program Approach (Phase Three)	Systems Approach (Phase Four)	Management System (Phase Five)	Holistic Management (Phase Six)
Identifies what will be communicated and to whom. Determines communications and warning needs. Establishes, implements, and maintains procedures for internal and external communications and warnings. Establishes notification systems and roles in which to use them.	Identifies what will be communicated and to whom regarding the ORM policy, risks, objectives, targets, and programs. Establishes internal, external, and Net-Centric communication procedures. Identifies target audiences for communications and warnings to ensure effective two-way dialog. Determines information sharing and security needs. Ensures ongoing communications capacity in the event of a disruptive event.	Preplanning of communications for targeted audiences. Develops and documents key messages and sets communication targets, objectives, and performance indicators. Assigns and documents responsibilities and establishes timelines for communications. Establishes, documents, and maintains procedures for internal, external, and Net-Centric communications. Communication on ORM issues occurs throughout the organization and with appropriate stakeholders. Documents communication with emergency and first responders. Sets and documents communications protocols for normal and for disruptive events. Regularly exercises communications system and documents results.	Development of Net-Centric capacity for all communications with external stakeholders (supply chain and community). Determines reliability of external communications infrastructure, and to augment the system internally and externally in the event of a disruption.

ANSI/ASIS SPC.1 Standard Clause	Core Element	Issues Addressed by Core Element (Establish, Implement, and Maintain)	Preawareness (Phase One)	Project Approach (Phase Two)
4.4.4 Documentation	Identifying and addressing documentation.	Processes and procedures for management of documents which are essential to the ORMS. Procedures, processes, work plans, and forms to support the ORMS and its elements, to support normal operating conditions and disruptive events.	Informal, if any.	Develops documented procedures to support action plans. Maintains documentation to support project scope. Documentation supports elements addressed in project.
4.4.5 Control of Documents	Developing and implementing documentation control.	Processes and procedures for control of documents and records (including backup). Protection of the integrity of essential information.	No document control system other than that used in general organizational operations.	Document control with some procedures developed to help demonstrate success and business benefit. Limited backup of critical information.

Program Approach (Phase Three)	Systems Approach (Phase Four)	Management System (Phase Five)	Holistic Management (Phase Six)
Develops a document management program. Documentation supports elements addressed in program action plans.	Establishes organizational resilience management documentation system. Determines security, sensitivity, and information integrity needs and takes appropriate steps to protect information and documentation.	Documentation system is consistent with document control requirements. Prepares a formal manual documenting the structure of the ORMS.	Evaluates document and information needs of external stakeholders (supply chain and community) for sharing of documentation best practices.
Establishes processes and procedures for control of documents and records in the scope of the program.	Establishes processes and procedures for control of documents and records in the scope of the management system, including access, backup confidentiality, storage, retention, archiving, and destruction.	Formally documents processes and procedures for control of documents and records, including information security and protection and document integrity.	Implementing best practice document control with external stakeholders (supply chain and community).

ANSI/ASIS SPC.1 Standard Clause	Core Element	Issues Addressed by Core Element (Establish, Implement, and Maintain)	Preawareness (Phase One)	Project Approach (Phase Two)
4.4.6 Operational Control	Developing and implementing operational control.	Operational control measures and procedures needed to implement the ORM during normal operating conditions and disruptive events. Risk avoidance, mitigation, reduction, sharing, and treatment procedures to minimize the likelihood and consequences of a disruptive event.	Procedures and processes are undefined. Some individuals may address perceived disruptive events on an ad hoc basis.	Operational controls and procedures established to achieve objectives and targets addressed within the project scope.

Program Approach (Phase Three)	Systems Approach (Phase Four)	Management System (Phase Five)	Holistic Management (Phase Six)
Risk or impact analysis is used to determine proper operational controls within the scope of the program.	Operational controls for risk reduction are based on the risk assessment, objectives, targets, and programs. Considers ways of minimizing risk in day-to-day operations, including engineering controls, administrative controls, technical specifications, and contractual agreements. Priority is given to preemptive approaches.	Establishes, implements, maintains, and documents adaptive and preemptive procedures for those operations that are associated with the identified significant risks, consistent with its organizational resilience management policy, risk assessment, supply chain requirements, objectives, and targets. Control procedures are written and/or reviewed by persons involved in operations and communicated effectively to others including external stakeholders.	Demand signals are incorporated in capacity planning. Priority is given to adaptive approaches. Processes are in place to validate supplier responses.

315

ANSI/ASIS SPC.1 Standard Clause	Core Element	Issues Addressed by Core Element (Establish, Implement, and Maintain)	Preawareness (Phase One)	Project Approach (Phase Two)
4.4.7 Incident Prevention, Preparedness, and Response	Procedures for prevention, protection, preparedness, mitigation, response, and recovery.	Risk avoidance, mitigation, reduction, sharing, and treatment procedures to minimize the likelihood and consequences of a disruptive event. Prevention and protection techniques to minimize risk. Techniques for a response structure. Action plans for increased threat levels. Recovery strategies and plans based on risk and impact assessment and conditions of the disruptive event.	Little or no defined or documented procedures. Dependence on the reactive behavior of individuals in the organization (and hope for the best).	Defines procedures to achieve objectives and targets of issue(s) addressed within the scope of the project. Develops procedures to support action plans including measures to reduce likelihood and/ or consequences. Develops procedures based on identified issue(s)—may be predominately reactive in nature given that no formal risk assessment was conducted.

Program Approach (Phase Three)	Systems Approach (Phase Four)	Management System (Phase Five)	Holistic Management (Phase Six)
Develops and implements procedures that prevent (if possible), respond to, and recover from potential disruptive events within the program scope. Considers measures that emphasize minimizing consequences.	Develops and implements procedures linked to the risk assessment, objectives, targets, and programs, with detailed work plans describing how the organization will prevent, prepare for, respond to, and recover from disruptive events. Periodically reviews and, where necessary, revises its incident prevention, preparedness, response, and recovery procedures.	Establishes, implements, maintains, and documents procedures to avoid, prevent, protect from, mitigate, respond to, and recover from a disruptive event and continue its activities based on organizational resilience objectives developed through the risk assessment process. Ensures that any persons performing incident prevention and management measures on its behalf are competent Establishes, documents, and implements procedures for a management structure to prevent, prepare for, mitigate, and respond to a disruptive event. Establishes detailed procedures for how the organization will recover or maintain its activities to a predetermined level, based on management-approved recovery objectives.	Incident prevention, preparedness, response, and recovery are integrated with external stakeholders (supply chain and community).

ANSI/ASIS SPC.1 Standard Clause	Core Element	Issues Addressed by Core Element (Establish, Implement, and Maintain)	Preawareness (Phase One)	Project Approach (Phase Two)
4.5.1 Monitoring and Measurement	Performance evaluation.	Metrics and mechanisms by which the organization assesses its ability to achieve its objectives and targets on an ongoing basis.	No formal monitoring. No formal measurement.	Progress against specific indicators is assessed periodically with persons involved in relevant activities defined within project scope. Project indicators and metrics are established and monitored to demonstrate progress and performance improvement.
4.5.2.1 Evaluation of Compliance	Compliance evaluation.	Legal and regulatory compliance performance evaluation on an ongoing basis.	No formal procedures established beyond those already in place as part of normal operations.	Compliance evaluated and demonstrated related to the project scope.

Program Approach (Phase Three)	Systems Approach (Phase Four)	Management System (Phase Five)	Holistic Management (Phase Six)
Identifies and implements key characteristics that need monitoring and measuring within the program scope.	Establishes, implements, and maintains performance metrics and procedures to monitor and measure, on a regular basis, those characteristics of its operations that have material impact on its organizational resilience performance.	Documents procedures that monitor performance, applicable operational controls, and conformity with the ORMS objectives and targets. Documents procedures to measure the performance of the systems that protect assets, communications, and information systems.	Monitoring and measurement integrated with external stakeholders and the community.
Compliance evaluated and demonstrated related to program scope.	Establishes, implements, and maintains procedure(s) for periodically evaluating and demonstrating compliance with applicable legal and other requirements.	Documents procedures and records and reports the results of the evaluation with corrective measures and recommendations for improvement.	Integrate compliance evaluation with stakeholders and community.

319

ANSI/ASIS SPC.1 Standard Clause	Core Element	Issues Addressed by Core Element (Establish, Implement, and Maintain)	Preawareness (Phase One)	Project Approach (Phase Two)
4.5.2.2 Exercises and Testing	Assessing and validating ORMS elements.	Process to measure and evaluate appropriateness and efficacy of the ORMS: its programs, processes, and procedures to drive it. An exercise program. Continual improvement plan reviewed with and agreed to by top management to ensure appropriate action is taken.	Limited or no exercising or testing.	Exercising and testing are planned and conducted as required by project scope. Results of exercises and tests demonstrate project OR performance improvements, and business benefits.

Program Approach (Phase Three)	Systems Approach (Phase Four)	Management System (Phase Five)	Holistic Management (Phase Six)
Exercising and testing are planned and conducted as required by program scope. Results of exercises and tests demonstrate program OR performance improvements and business benefits.	Tests and exercises designed to validate appropriateness and effectiveness of action plans and procedures, as well as interrelationship of elements in ORMS – including appropriate external parties (e.g., first responders) and stakeholders.	Comprehensive documentation of exercises and tests. Produces a formalized postexercise report that contains accountable outcomes, recommendations, and arrangements to implement improvements in a timely fashion.	Integrate exercise and tests with stakeholders and community.

321

ANSI/ASIS SPC.1 Standard Clause	Core Element	Issues Addressed by Core Element (Establish, Implement, and Maintain)	Preawareness (Phase One)	Project Approach (Phase Two)
4.5.3 Nonconformity, Corrective Action, and Preventive Action	Monitor and address nonconformities.	Process to identify nonconformities and their root cause. Mechanisms for eliminating the causes of detected nonconformities both in the ORMS and the operational processes. Mechanisms for instigating action to eliminate potential causes of nonconformities in both the ORMS and the operational processes.	Minimum required by law.	Deviations from action plans, programs, objectives, and targets within the project scope are evaluated for opportunities for improvement. Adequate corrective and preventative actions taken (if necessary) to ensure the project progresses according to plan.
4.5.4 Control of Records	Developing and implementing records control.	Records to demonstrate conformity to the requirements of the ORMS and the results achieved.	Only as required by normal business practices.	Collects and retains evidence addressing project implementation and results.

Program Approach (Phase Three)	Systems Approach (Phase Four)	Management System (Phase Five)	Holistic Management (Phase Six)
Deviations from action plans, programs, objectives, and targets within the program scope are evaluated for opportunities for improvement. Establishes a corrective and preventative action process.	Establishes procedures to determine nonconformities in the ORMS, risk assessment, objectives, targets, programs, action plans, and their implementation. Evaluates actual and potential nonconformances to eliminate the causes and prevent their occurrence or recurrence.	Establishes, implements, and maintains documented procedures for dealing with actual and potential nonconformities and for taking corrective action and preventive action. Reviews effectiveness of corrective actions and takes preventative actions.	Integrate nonconformity, corrective, and preventive actions with stakeholders and community.
Collects and retains evidence addressing program implementation and results.	Collects and retains evidence addressing ORMS implementation and results.	Establishes, implements, and maintains documented procedures to collect and retain evidence addressing ORMS implementation and results.	Establishes shared record controls with stakeholders and community.

323

ANSI/ASIS SPC.1 Standard Clause	Core Element	Issues Addressed by Core Element (Establish, Implement, and Maintain)	Preawareness (Phase One)	Project Approach (Phase Two)
4.5.5 Internal Audits	Conduct management system audits.	Internal audits of system and programs. Audit reports reviewed by top management.	Not conducted for ORM.	Performance of project audited informally. Project Leader oversees development of audit procedures.

Program Approach (Phase Three)	Systems Approach (Phase Four)	Management System (Phase Five)	Holistic Management (Phase Six)
Conducts audit of program within defined scope, including all elements of the program.	Determines what needs to be audited. Plans and implements an audit program. Reports audit findings to management and acts upon them.	Establishes, implements, and maintains documented procedures for internal audits. Responsibility of audit program assigned to an individual that has knowledge and understanding of audit principles. Determines whether the control objectives, risk controls, processes, and procedures of ORMS are conducted properly and are achieving the desired results. Identifies opportunities for improvement. Ensures that actions are taken without undue delay to eliminate detected nonconformities and their causes.	Audit includes stakeholder and community interactions, as well as the supply chain.

ANSI/ASIS SPC.1 Standard Clause	Core Element	Issues Addressed by Core Element (Establish, Implement, and Maintain)	Preawareness (Phase One)	Project Approach (Phase Two)
4.6 Management Review	Top management review.	Management review of the ORMS's performance, adequacy, and effectiveness to identify opportunities for improvement. Priorities, policy, objectives, and targets to support continual improvement.	No management review of ORM	Project Leader supervisor (and other appropriate members of the management team) reviews the performance of project and reports to project sponsor.
4.6.4 Maintenance	ORM change management.	Change management provisions for improvement of ORMS programs, systems, and/ or operational processes.	No ORMS to maintain or link to change management process.	Project outcomes that improve organizational resilience performance become standard operating procedures.

Program Approach (Phase Three)	Systems Approach (Phase Four)	Management System (Phase Five)	Holistic Management (Phase Six)
Program Leader (and other appropriate members of the management team) reviews the program performance and reports to program sponsor. Uses review to demonstrate business case for ORMS and provide a basis to seek further efficiencies by linking core elements in a systems approach.	Reviews integration of ORMS elements. Reviews the suitability, adequacy, and effectiveness of the ORMS. Top management reviews the policies, objectives, evaluation of program implementation, audit results and changes resulting from preventive and corrective actions	Top management participates in documented reviews of the ORMS at planned intervals to ensure its continuing suitability, adequacy, and effectiveness. Assesses opportunities for improvement and the need for changes to ORMS, including the ORMS policy and objectives, and targets and risk criteria.	Integrates review with overall risk management and fiscal review processes. Review includes evaluation of suitability, adequacy, and effectiveness with regard to stakeholders, community, and supply chain. Top management promotes OR with external stakeholders (supply chain and community).
Program and action plans outcomes that improve organizational resilience performance become standard operating procedures.	Any internal or external changes (including outputs from exercises, audits, and reviews) that impact the organization are reviewed in relation to the ORMS.	Establish documented change management procedures for ORMS tied to other change management programs.	Integrate change management for ORMS with external stakeholders (supply chain and community).

ANSI/ASIS SPC.1 Standard Clause	Core Element	Issues Addressed by Core Element (Establish, Implement, and Maintain)	Preawareness (Phase One)	Project Approach (Phase Two)
4.6.5 Continual Improvement	Evaluate and implement opportunities for improvement.	Continual improvement process for the ORMS, risk management, and organizational resilience performance.	No ORMS to link to continual improvement process.	Opportunities for improvement identified for use in other projects.

Program Approach (Phase Three)	Systems Approach (Phase Four)	Management System (Phase Five)	Holistic Management (Phase Six)
Implement procedures for continuous improvement of program.	Continually improves the effectiveness of ORMS through the use of the organizational resilience management policy, objectives, audit results, analysis of monitored events, corrective and preventive actions, and management review.	Continual improvement is a part of the organization's culture, demonstrated at all levels.	Integrate continual improvement of ORMS with external stakeholders (supply chain and community).

Source: American National Standard. Maturity model for the phased implementation of the organizational resilience management system. 2012. ANSI/ASIS SPC.4-2012, pp. 9–24. With permission.

APPENDIX 5

CRITICALITY ASSESSMENT BLANK TEMPLATES

Criticality Assesment Survey
This Criticality Assessment (CA) survey is designed to identify the critical business processes required for a business unit to operate. Through completion of this survey you will be able to determine the financial impact to your operation; the important processes that are related to reputation, legal/regulatory compliance, and other qualitative considers; the necessary infrastructure dependencies; recovery time objectives; and the resumption prioritization, from the business unit's perspective, during an unacceptable business interruption. The critical decision of determining which processes to recover and in which order, if at all, is a management decision derived through analysis of the aforementioned information.
Section 1—Project Cover Sheet
Business Unit Surveyed:
Survey Respondent:
Business Unit Manager:

CA Survey/"Process Assessment & Impact Analysis" Section 2—Processes, Recovery Time Objectives (RTOs), and Business Resumption Sequence					
Refer to Appendix A.5 for detailed steps and sample responses.					
Complete columns A through F as they pertain to your business unit based on the following denitions:					
A "Primary Business Activity" is a fundamental high-level activity (or family of related activities) that are critical to the continuity of business, regulatory compliance, business/process controls and reporting requirements, adherence to applicable Company policies, and the overall survival of the company. A Primary Business Process is made up of one or several subset activities.					
"Functional Processes" are supporting processes that, along with other supporting processes, contribute to the execution and completion of a company Core Business Process.					
Recovery Time Objective (RTO) is the business unit's expectation for recovering from a business interruption and resuming a specific business process/function. RTOs are subject to justication, management approval, and proper funding of the associated recovery solution.					
Primary Business Activity	**Functional Processes**	**Critical RTO**	**Desired RTO Range**	**Preferred Business Resumption Sequence (Specify 1,2,3>>)**	**Routine Work Location**
		24 hrs	24 to 48 hours		
		72 hrs	48 to 72 hours		
		N\A	0 to 2 hours		

CA Survey/"Process Assessment & Impact Analysis"
Section 3—Financial Impacts on Unit Operation

Refer to Appendix A.5 for detailed steps and sample responses.

Primary Business Activity (autofilled from Section 2)	Functional Processes (autofilled from Section 2)	Financial impact estimate for each identified process in your business operation of the Criticality Assessment Survey. Provide worst-case estimates for the busiest day of the week/month/year.				Financial Impact Risk Score / Financial Loss Range 5 $1,000,000 > / 4 $500,000 to 999,999 / 3 $100,000 to 499,999 / 2 $25,001 to 99,999 / 1 < $25,000	Financial Impact Risk Score (automatically computed)	Describe how financial estimates were reached (production volume, requirements, expenses/revenues, calculations, etc.).
		Daily Incurred Costs/ Expenses ($)	Daily Lost Revenues ($)	Daily Regulatory Penalties ($)	Row Total (auto-calculated)			
		0	0	0	0			
		0	0	0	0			
		0	0	0	0			
		0	0	0	0			
		0	0	0	0			

CA Survey/"Process Assessment & Impact Analysis"
Section 4—Nonfinancial Impacts
Estimate the extent of "nonfinancial" impacts based on the choices below.

This will provide a quantitative understanding for operational issues not realizing a financial impact.

Primary Business Activity (autofilled from Section 2)	Functional Processes (autofilled from Section 2)	Functional Operations Risk Score (autofilled from Section 2)	Risk Impact Score (Non-financial Impact) Impact Score Ranges 4 to 5 = High Impact 3 = Moderate Impact 1 to 2 = Minimal Impact	Reputation Risk Score (Non-financial Impact)	Total CA Impact Score (sum of 3 preceding scores)	Business Critically Rating (Defined by CA Score) Criticality Score 11 to 15 = Critical 6 to 10 = Important 3 to 5 = Deferrable	Describe how the "nonfinancial" impacts were determined—justify answer
		1	1	1	3	Deferrable	
		1	1	1	3	Deferrable	
		1	1	1	3	Deferrable	

CA Survey/"Process Assessment & Impact Analysis" Section 5—IT Applications Required						
For each process, indicate the IT Application required.						
Primary Business Activity (autofilled from Section 2)	Functional Processes (autofilled from Section 2)	Appli- cation 1	Appli- cation 2	Appli- cation 3	Appli- cation 4	Appli- cation 5

CA Survey/"Process Assessment & Impact Analysis" Section 6—Other Critical Applications, Shared Drives, etc.			
Examples: MS-Word, MS-Excel, MS-PowerPoint, Visio, etc..			
Examples: Z:\Shared\Security\Projects\Reports; Be specific as to the path, folder name(s), file names, etc.			
Primary Business Activity (autofilled from Section 2)	Functional Processes (autofilled from Section 2)	Applications, Shared Drives, etc. (list in order of importance)	Comments

335

CRITICALITY ASSESSMENT INSTRUCTIONS

The Criticality Assessment/Business Impact Analysis spreadsheets presented in this book are the work product of Mark Kern, John Nones, and Steve Guss. Kern, Nones, and Guss are business continuity professionals that developed the associated spreadsheets to function as a simple, but effective method to collect information relevant to a business operation. The spreadsheets were modified in various ways for use in this book by the authors. Any changes by the authors have not diminished the value of the spreadsheets as practical examples of a simple assessment tool.

The following instructions shall explain the proper approach to completing the Criticality Assessment (CA) Survey. This survey consists of six spreadsheets that require the business unit leader or coordinator to complete and return to the designated business continuity or emergency preparedness manager. Each part of the survey is documented so that the user shall have the necessary understanding to complete the form. As discussed earlier, the CA is a process to identify the processes and resources associated with a business function. The CA is used to assist in determining which processes and associated resources are critical to the continuation of the business activity. Through the use of the CA, an organization shall have an opportunity to protect and recover critical processes, functions and resources from unacceptable business interruptions. The CA report is only as valuable as the effort expended to accurately completing the survey and information collected therein.

These instructions assume that you are familiar with your business processes and the associated resources necessary to operate or perform the processes and activities of the business unit. Completion of this survey is through an assigned business leader or predetermined designee. The survey form shall have predetermined information on the cover page as appropriate. It is normal to have business unit members who are thoroughly familiar with business processes and their importance to participate in this survey process—the value of the completed form is in direct relation to the information entered into the form fields. Each business unit has been assigned a sponsor(s) responsible for providing the necessary resources and validation support steps necessary to complete and approve the survey.

CA Section 1

Project Cover

Section 1 contains predetermined (assigned) information about your business unit. The fields in this section have been completed through discussions with the project sponsors and business unit manager. Please verify the information for accuracy:

- Business Unit Surveyed
- Survey Respondent
- Business Unit Manager

It may be necessary to include more information on the cover sheet in accordance with the demands of your organization in order to properly store and retrieve the survey after completion. Remember, this survey is an example and may be altered according to the needs of your organization.

Please correct any inaccurate or missing information to ensure a properly completed survey. Once complete, please continue to Section 2—Processes, Recovery Time Objectives, and Business Resumption Sequence.

CA Section 2: Processes, Recovery Time Objectives, and Business Resumption Sequence

Section 2 contains crucial information in the CA because it establishes the processes, allows for the identification of resources, and associates quantitative values to processes, thereby documenting the criticality of a process. This survey is centered on the business processes identified in this section; the accuracy of the information is extremely important. Many of the answers that are provided will automatically carry through to other sections via linked cell/sheet commands.

This section requires that you determine the Recovery Time Objective (RTO) and identify the preferred "business resumption sequence" for the processes/functions. These measurements allow the risk managers/stakeholders to more fully understand the business continuity and recovery priorities. It is important to understand which processes need to be reestablished and in which order to ensure the proper recovery of those functions. The identified functions are those that are considered most critical to the survival of the business unit. Regular work areas or locations are established so that Facilities Management and Information Technology may evaluate the contingency plans with respect to space planning needs, telecommunications, electrical power, and other facility/technology considerations.

A "Primary Business Activity" is a high-level activity (or a grouping of activities) that is critical to the continuity of business or associated support priorities for the business (regulatory conformance, management requirement for reporting or support for another business unit, etc.). A Core Business Process is made up of one or several subset activities.

"Functional Processes" are supporting processes that, along with other supporting processes, contribute to the execution and completion of a Core Business Process. While your business unit may have outsourced certain processes/functions, it is still necessary to document these processes because they provide value to other processes/functions within the organization. It is important to ensure that all Functional Processes are identified for a business unit and attached to a primary business activity.

Identify and enter the name of the primary business activity and functional process for a given row on the spreadsheet. Select the appropriate recovery time objective for each activity. (Your organization shall have to determine the RTO categories. For example, 0–2 hours, 24–48 hours, 48–72 hours, etc. are possible timeframes that may work for your organization. It is very possible that these times will not work. Make your own ranges based on the needs of your organization.) It may be necessary to increase the number of rows to accommodate more activities and functions for your survey. It is easy to insert more rows into the spreadsheet via Excel commands.

(It is helpful to standardize the choices open to the participants when completing the survey. You may wish to consider having drop down boxes for cells, such as the RTO. Each cell under the RTO column should have a drop down box with choices based on the time ranges associated with the needs of your organization.)

The "Preferred Business Resumption Sequence" column requires a prioritization listing, 1, 2, 3, etc., to indicate the order of process restoration; 1 is the first process that will be recovered for that business unit.

CA Section 3: Financial Impacts

This section is one of the most important, but also one of the most difficult because it addresses the potential financial impacts on the business unit during a disruption to the business operation.

It is necessary to clearly explain the method used to determine the estimated financial impact. It will make the review process of this form easier. It is best to focus on a single business day when determining an estimate; exceptions should be thoroughly explained. There is information that will carry over from Section 2. Do not alter this information in this section. (See below for examples of Excel commands to allow for this carryover.)

Cell A6 on the Financial Impact sheet has = 'Sect 2. Processes RTOs & Seq'!A9 as the command to have the text entered on the Section 2 sheet, cell A9 carry over to the A6 cell with "Building Security" listed; this is an auto populated entry. The other cells for activities and functions use the same command.

The determination of the financial impact score is based on the value calculated in the raw total cell. Here are the possible ranges, but again, these must be reviewed and determined for your organization.

$1,000,000 >
$500,000 to 999,999
$100,000 to 499,999
$25,001 to 99,999
< $25,000
= IF(F6<25000,1,IF(F6<100000,2,IF(F6<500000,3,IF(F6<1000000,4,5))))

The above range is indicated in this command, which appears in cell G6 ($3,240) on the example CA. The Finance Department will be able to assist in developing this section of the form.

CA Section 4: Nonfinancial Impacts

The "nonfinancial" impacts for the established processes/functions are identified and quantified through the use of various spreadsheet commands and simple formulae. These impacts are potential outcomes from an unacceptable business interruption.

(The spreadsheet command to autopopulate the financial risk score from Section 3 is: = 'Sect 3. Financial Impacts'!G6

The criticality rating is determined through the use of the following command: = IF(F7<5,"Deferrable",IF(F7<10,"Important",IF(F7< = 15,"Critical")))

This sheet page is fairly simple and self-explanatory.)

CA Section 5: IT Applications Required

The IT Applications required for the identified business processes/functions must be specified so that the necessary IT resources are provided for recovery. The sheet has the same carryover commands for the processes and functions. The person completing this form must enter the application information. This section allows you to identify and allows IT to verify the application requirements for subsequent review by the staff managing the IT Disaster Recovery efforts.

CA Section 6: Other Applications, Shared Drives, Critical Files/Databases Required

Section 6 provides for the documentation of the specific application details, to include path information, for those IT applications related to processes and functions.

REFERENCES

American National Standard. 2010. *Organizational resilience: Security, preparedness, and continuity management systems—Requirements with guidance for use.* Alexandria, VA: ASIS International, ANSI/ASIS SPC.01-2009.

American National Standard. 2012. *Maturity model for the phased implementation of the organizational resilience management system.* Alexandria, VA: ASIS International, ANSI/ASIS SPC.4-2012.

Berrong, S. 2010. Hotel makes room for resilience. *Security Management* July: 50–53.

Crosby, P. 1979. *Quality is free.* New York: McGraw-Hill.

Guidelines for auditing management systems. 2011. ISO 19011:2011(E). Geneva, Switzerland: International Organization for Standardization.

Risk management—Principles and guidelines. 2009. ISO 31000:2009(E). Geneva, Switzerland: International Organization for Standardization.

FURTHER READING

American National Standard. 2008. *A guide to the project management body of knowledge,* 4th ed. Newtown Square, PA: Project Management Institute, ANSI/PMI 99-001-2008.

American National Standard. 2010. *Business continuity management systems: Requirements with guidance for use.* London: ASIS International and British Standards Institution (BSI), ANSI/ASIS/BSI BCM.01-2010.

Bull, R. C. 2010. *Moving from project management to project leadership: A practical guide to leading groups.* Boca Raton, FL: CRC Press.

Devlin, E. S. 2007. *Crisis management planning and execution.* Boca Raton, FL: Auerbach Publications.

Doughty, K. (ed.) 2001. *Business continuity planning: Protecting your organization's life,* Best Practices Series. Boca Raton, FL: Auerbach Publications.

Kahan, J. H., A. C. Allen, and J. K. George. 2009. An operational framework for resilience. *Journal of Homeland Security and Emergency Management* 6 (1): 1–48.

Kern, M., J. Nones, and S. Guss. 2000. Business Impact Analysis Spreadsheet and Instructions. Internal work document. Philadelphia, PA.

Koller, G. 2005. *Risk assessment and decision making in business and industry: A practical guide.* Boca Raton, FL: CRC Press.

Leflar, J., and S. Stahl. 2009. Implementing organizational resiliency at universities and colleges. Paper presented at the Annual Conference for ASIS International, Anaheim, CA, September 21–24.

Lewis, G. 2006. *Organizational crisis management: The human factor.* Boca Raton, FL: Auerbach Publications.

McCreight, R. 2010. Resilience as a goal and standard in emergency management. *Journal of Homeland Security and Emergency Management* 7 (1): 1–7.

Peltier, T. 2001. *Information security risk analysis*. Boca Raton, FL: CRC Press.

Siegel, M. 2010. How mature are you? Using the ANSI/ASIS organizational resilience standard to improve resilience and preparedness: Building resilience using a maturity model. Paper presented at the Annual Conference for ASIS International, Dallas, TX, October 12–15.

Siegel, M. 2012. Conducting a risk assessment—The foundation for successful risk management. Paper presented at the Third ASIS International Middle East Security Conference and Exhibition, Dubai, February 19—21.

Stephenson, A., E. Seville, J. Vargo, and D. Roger. 2010. Benchmark resilience: A study of the resilience of organisations in the Auckland Region. *Resilient Organisations Research Report 2010/03b*: 1–49. Online at: http://www.resorgs.org.nz

INDEX